OUT OF DOOR SPORTS

IN SCOTLAND.

"KING OF THE CORRIE."

OUT OF DOOR SPORTS

IN

SCOTLAND:

Their Economy and Surroundings.

DEER STALKING, GROUSE SHOOTING, SALMON ANGLING,
GOLFING, CURLING, &c.

*WITH NOTES ON THE NATURAL AND SPORTING HISTORY OF THE
ANIMALS OF THE CHASE,
AND ESTIMATES OF THEIR ECONOMIC VALUE.*

BY

"ELLANGOWAN."

"I will tell you what our sport shall be."—SHAKESPEARE.

LONDON:
W. H. ALLEN & CO., 13 WATERLOO PLACE,
PALL MALL, S.W.

1889.

LONDON:
PRINTED BY WILLIAM CLOWES AND SONS, LIMITED,
STAMFORD STREET AND CHARING CROSS.

PREFACE.

THE following pages have not been penned with any idea of teaching people "how to sport;" that is a task which the Author has thought it would be somewhat presumptuous for him to undertake, seeing that it has already been more than once successfully accomplished. Sufficient work, however, has been left for another hand in the chronicling of the facts and figures incident to the deer-stalking, grouse-shooting, and salmon-fishing of the period, which during late years have so largely attracted the attention of economists and political agitators.

The Author claims to have brought together much information of an interesting kind, hitherto found chiefly in newspapers or other periodicals in cases where it is in print, and to have collected from those who know most about it, and from attentive personal observation, much that has never yet come under the cognisance of a printer. He has also endeavoured so to arrange the matter collected as to avoid repetition, which, however, has proved a somewhat difficult task.

It may, their Author thinks, be claimed for the following chapters that they are at least illustrative and, in most instances, informing, no similar collection of facts and figures pertaining to sport and the economic value of the animals of the chase having, so far as he is aware, ever been attempted. Painstaking labour has been devoted to the gathering and setting forth of what all in search of sport on the hills and in the glens of "dear old Scotland" would doubtless like to know.

The truthfulness of the details given in the succeeding pages of the natural history of deer, grouse, and other birds and beasts of sport may be relied upon so far as they go; it is not pretended, however, that they are scientific, nor do they need to be so, the object of the Author being to tell what he knows himself, and to retail the knowledge he has collected from other people in a way that may be easily understood.

Much of what is related by the writer may be best described as being "reminiscent"; when he who holds the pen is a sexagenarian, that is unavoidable.

July, 1889.

CONTENTS.

———•◇•———

INTRODUCTION.

PAGES

Scotland's most famous Out of door Sports—The rise of Sport
—What Sir Walter Scott did for Scotland "sixty years
since"—Shooting rents at the beginning—How Grouse-
shooting began—Facilities of travel open up the ground
—Other Sports in Scotland—The Turf—Growing taste
for Horse-racing, Football, and other pastimes . . 1–10

CHAPTER I.—SCOTLAND'S DEER AND GROUSE GROUNDS.

Acreage of Deer Forests and Grouse Moors—List of the chief
Forests—Note of the area they occupy—The Counties:
extent of their sporting ground—Number of Stags that
may be killed 11–20

CHAPTER II.—DEER.

Natural history of the Deer—Habits of the animal—In-
breeding: propriety of "crossing": what has been done
—Roe-deer as Venison—About the horns of Deer—Age
of these animals—Traditions and Stories—Stock of Deer
in the forests 21–36

CHAPTER III.—STALKING.

"No royal road to Deer-stalking"—Deer-driving—Sport
defined—The labour incident to a Stalk—Practical hints
by practical men—Two descriptions of Deer-stalking:
the toils and humours of the work . . . 37–53

CHAPTER IV.—COURSING: HARES.

PAGES

Coursing in Midlothian fifty years ago—Dog-breeding—
'North Briton'—Anecdotes of Scottish sporting—Natural
history of the Hare—Growing scarcity of Hares . 54–66

CHAPTER V.—RABBITS FOR SPORT AND FOOD.

Fertility of the Rabbit—Tables of natural increase—Island
Rabbits—Political Economy of the Rabbit supply . 67–73

CHAPTER VI.—THE GROUSE FAMILY.

Natural history of the Red Grouse—Enemies of the Birds—
Which sex is the more numerous?—Caithness Grouse the
best—Capercailzie: Story of its rehabilitation in Scotland
—Extent to which it has bred—The Blackcock becoming
scarce—The Ptarmigan 74–87

CHAPTER VII.—NATURAL ECONOMY OF A GROUSE MOOR.

Mortality on Grouse Moors—How a Moor becomes re-
plenished—Facts and figures—Breeding and feeding
power of a given area—Economic considerations—Grouse
disease—Changing the Blood—The Food of Grouse—
Arithmetic of Grouse-shooting 88–103

CHAPTER VIII.—THE POLITICAL ECONOMY OF SPORT.

Parliamentary Attacks on Sport—Money expended on Deer
Forests—Deer or Sheep?—Deliverances of Lord Napier's
Committee—Would it pay to convert Deer Forests into
Sheep Runs?—What Sport has done for the Highlands—
The "Dog in the Manger" Spirit . . . 104–114

CHAPTER IX.—ON THE HEATHER.

Signs of the Twelfth—*En route* to Glen Hoolichan—Opening of the Season—Work on the Heather—The Round of
Life on a Grouse Moor—What "Christopher North" said
to his Young Friends. 115–127

CHAPTER X.—L. S. D.

PAGES

Reliable information as to cost of Moors—Pot Shooters—
Miscellaneous Expenditure—Rents of Moors and Forests
—Expenditure on Fishing—Shooting-lodge economies—
Scotch Breakfasts—Shooting Luncheons—Dinner Bill of
Fare 128–141

CHAPTER XI.—PHEASANTS AND PARTRIDGES.

The Pheasant in Scotland—Hatching Machines—Breeding
Birds for the Gun—Pheasant supply—Numbers bred—
The Partridge in Scotland—Scarcity of the Bird now as
compared with former years 142–153

CHAPTER XII.—OTHER BIRDS OF SPORT.

Miscellaneous Birds of Sport—Woodcock in Edinburgh—
Snipe — Moorhen — Pigeons — Anecdote — The Crows —
Rook-shooting—Solan Geese—Birds of St. Kilda—Gulls
—Wild Duck shooting—Mallard—Plovers' Eggs . 154–174

CHAPTER XIII.—POACHING.

Prices received by Poachers—Mode of Business—Jamie
Skinners, a waif—Anecdote of a poaching Coachman—
Poaching not a moral offence!—Sketches of Poachers—
Grouse-poaching—Salmon-poachers—Fish Tam—Salmon
Job—Poaching on Tweed—A Story about Hare-stealing
175–198

CHAPTER XIV.—GAMEKEEPERS.

General trustworthiness of Keepers—An Interview with
one of them—The Keeper's Round of Work—Perquisites
and Wages—The Gamekeeper's Wife—Dishonest Keepers
—The Question of " Tips " 199–209

CHAPTER XV.—THE GAME SUPPLY.

Scarcity of Facts and Figures—Legal Sale of Game—Grouse
Commerce—The price of Grouse—Figures of the National

PAGES

Game Bag—Weight of Game—Value of Game—Foreign
Birds—Scottish Venison—Hares and Rabbits . 210–225

CHAPTER XVI.—GAME IN LARDER, KITCHEN, AND
DINING-ROOM.

The Pheasant—About high Game—Grouse Soup—Hare Soup
—Other Soups—Rabbit Cookery—What Soyer advises—
Woodcock—Wood Pigeon—Partridges—Soyer's Grouse
Salad 226–245

CHAPTER XVII.—SALMONIA.

How to Catch a Salmon—Natural History of that Fish—
The Par Controversy — Shaw's Experiments — Salmon
Growth—Stormontfield—Cost of Salmon-angling—Com-
merce in Salmon—Statistics of the River Tay—Tweed
and its Salmon—Fishing Legislation—River-pollution—
Salmon Disease 246–279

CHAPTER XVIII.—TROUTIANA.

Writing Anglers—Popularity of Trout-fishing—Loch Leven
—Resorts of Anglers—Loch Awe—The Great Lake Trout
—Scottish "Fisheries"—Howietoun—The Solway Fishery
—Prices of Trout Ova 280–299

CHAPTER XIX.—TROUT AND SPORT IN THE BORDERS.

Gipsies and Fishers—Younger and Scrope—" My ain flees "
— Thomas Tod Stoddart — The Ettrick Shepherd —
St. Mary's Loch—The Purdies—Burning the Water—
The Abbotsford Hunt—Abbotsford Festivities—Border
Sports 300–320

CHAPTER XX.—VERMIN OF THE MOORS AND MANORS.

Badger-baiting — Otters and Otter-hunting—Wild Cats —
Diary of a Stoat—The Rat—The Balance of Nature—
Owls and Hen Harriers—The Crow Family . . 321–338

CHAPTER XXI.—THE FOX : FOX-HUNTING.

PAGES

Natural History of the Fox—Characteristics of that Animal
    described — Fox-hunting in Midlothian — Ramsay of
    Barnton—Jamie Jack's Smiddy 339–348

CHAPTER XXII.—GOLF.

A Boom in Golf—History of the Game—Honourable Com-
    pany of Golfers—Club Dinners—Social Habits of Players
    —St. Andrews—Mr. Chambers' Description of the Game
    —Golfing Characters—Caddies—Note on Shinty . 349–364

CHAPTER XXIII.—CURLING.

Jubilee Celebration of the Royal Caledonian Curling Club—
    Love of Curling—Diagram of a Rink—Description of the
    Game—History of the Sanquhar Club—Poetry of the
    Game 365–379

CHAPTER XXIV.—PATRONS AND PARASITES OF SPORT.

Eglinton Tournament—Sporting gentleman—" Money Bob "
    —The Squire — " Mr. Peters " — Cuddy Wully — The
    Omits 380–389

OUT-DOOR SPORTS IN SCOTLAND.

INTRODUCTION.

NOTHING in the social history of Scotland is more remarkable than the developments which have taken
place in its Sports and Pastimes. At one time Curling
and Shinty were the two out-of-doors games in which
all who pleased to do so might take part. An occasional bout at Quoits also afforded recreation in rural
districts. At holiday seasons, "Shootings" for prizes,
chiefly in kind, such as cheeses and various articles of
clothing, were entered upon with great zest, whilst
Angling has for a long period formed a favourite
pastime of the Scottish people. The modern sports
of Cricket and Football, as also Pedestrianism and
Cycling, have during the last ten or twelve years
attained a degree of popularity which was not anticipated when they were introduced.

But the out-of-doors sports for which Scotland is
to-day most famous are Deer-stalking, Grouse-shooting,
and Salmon-fishing. These, as will presently be shown,
prove the means of circulating, in the remote districts
of a country which otherwise would be poor, thousands
of pounds, much to the benefit of those interested. The
shootings and fishings of Scotland have from first to
last added largely to the material prosperity of the
country, the total sporting rental of which, all told,

B

is not probably less to-day than half a million sterling. When this prosperity began, warnings were given out by the wise that it would not, could not last ; but, happily, it has gone on increasing, grouse-moor and deer-forest rental gradually growing higher and higher, whilst expenditure of all kinds keeps rising in accordance with the luxurious tendency of the time.

It has been well said that Sir Walter Scott *made* Scotland, in the sense of picturing to far-off peoples its attractions of lake and stream, and its " beauties of mountain and glen." The author of ' Waverley ' and ' Rob Roy ' so painted the picturesque features of his native land as to attract crowds of visitors from even distant parts of the globe; since the day the ' Lady of the Lake ' was published, tourists and travellers have come upon the scene, distributing their gold with an open hand. No sooner had the poem been issued than the authorities of the Inland Revenue Department began to note a steady increase in the amount of the Post-horse Duty then demanded in Scotland.

Before Scott, Scotland, in a sense, was unknown. Going back a hundred years ago we might ask what was then the value of a hundred acres of moorland, and if we were to say they had no value, it would be an answer that could scarcely be gainsaid : a few Highland sheep sought their scanty supply of food upon the moors, but although trout were plentiful in the streams and salmon leapt in many of the lakes, while moorfowl were abundant on the heather, none, other than those who dwelt beside them, knew the fact; at that time they were of no commercial value. A hundred years ago the ' Lady of the Lake ' had not been written, nor had

'Waverley' or 'Rob Roy' made their appearance. Nor
was it till the vivid pen of the "Wizard of the North"
had sent a revelation of its scenic beauties throughout
the world that "the land of the mountain and the
flood" became so famous as to cause its salmon to be
coveted and its moorfowl to become of value to "the
southrons." At first, let us say fifty years since,
"shootings" were cheap enough; it came as a revelation to many "heather lairds," as they have been called,
who had all their lives, perhaps, been struggling in
their endeavours to feed a few sheep and cultivate a
few patches of arable ground, that there were people
ready to take a lease of their lands for the sake of the
moorfowl upon them, and to rent their streams for the
privilege of catching the trout and salmon they contained. The small rents then offered were more thank-
fully accepted than the bigger sums of to-day : fifty
pounds fifty years ago was "money," and for such a
sum the right of sporting over an area of two or three
thousand acres, and of fishing a mile or two of good
water, was to be obtained. As time wore on, however,
rents began to rise, and when first steamboats, and
then railway carriages, brought their annual thousands
to the land of Scott and Burns, moors for which the
proprietors had hitherto been well pleased to obtain
fifty or sixty pounds speedily became of double and
treble that value, whilst prolific stretches of heather,
on which had been erected comfortable dwelling-places,
were soon thought cheap at "hunners," as Saunders, in
'Rob Roy,' calls hundreds. Gentlemen happily now
receive in some instances thousands for moors or
forests that their fathers were very glad to let for a
tenth part of the sum.

Sir Walter Scott intended at one time to write a chronological account of Scottish out-of-door sports, but from some cause he never began the task, although from his pen such a chronicle would have proved interesting, and it is therefore much to be regretted that it was not written. When Sir Walter touches upon pastime of any kind in his poems or novels, he shows that he feels what he writes about; and, as all the world knows, he wrote of Scotland and its people as no man ever wrote before and as no man has written since, and by doing so Sir Walter enriched his country and improved the position of his countrymen. Sir Walter unhappily did not live to witness the many benefits that have accrued to Scotland by means of his works, nor in his lifetime could he have formed the idea that Scottish moorfowl would ever become birds of such value as they are to-day. Various stories were at one time in circulation as to how the prosperity of the Highlands of Scotland began, but most of the tales told were imaginative, the following no doubt among the others :—" A Highland laird and his lady of an ambitious turn of mind, anxious to see their daughters well married, used to exchange houses for a few weeks with an Edinburgh Writer to the Signet, who was passionately fond of sport and rural pursuits. The Highland gentleman and his wife and daughters thus enjoyed for a time the delights and gaieties of the Scottish capital, whilst the lawyer indulged to his heart's content in the sports of the Highlands, salmon-catching or grouse-shooting from dawn of day till sunset. Both families were delighted with the exchange, and the pleasures of his Highland holiday, and his prowess with rod and gun, were recited by the lawyer to troops of friends and clients, who, becoming in time smitten with like enthusiasm, soon began to look around for like opportunity."

Facts and figures of a reliable kind pertaining to the progress of shooting and fishing in Scotland are difficult to procure: two of the greatest and best-known Scottish sportsmen lived to see all that took place from the dawn of grouse-shooting onward to the period of their death; but only one of those gentlemen, Mr. Colquhoun, has left any note of the changes that occurred; the other, Mr. Horatio Ross, had he pleased to do so, might have penned an informing record of the changes incidental to his day.

The Earl of Malmesbury, in his interesting 'Memoirs of an Ex-Minister,' mentions that it was in the year 1833 that "the Highlands became the rage," and that deer-forests began to be made. At that time rents, compared with the sums paid to-day, were almost nominal. His lordship states that he was offered the moors, forests, and fishings of the Island of Harris for the bagatelle, as it would be thought now, of £25 a year; in other words, he could have secured a right of sport over an area of 40,000 acres, which to-day commands a rental of £2000 per annum. Upon the occasion of the death of Mr. Butter of Faskally a few years since, a little peep was obtained at the cost of shootings half a century ago. In a memoir of that gentleman, it was stated that two moors on his estate, which now let for £800 per annum, had, fifty years since, been tenanted at the rate of £8; and the tenant thought himself a very ill-used man indeed when his rent was raised. At the period indicated, the total game or sporting rental of Scotland and its isles was probably not £25,000 per annum; to-day, as has been already said, it cannot be under half-a-million.

In the first list of shootings to be let in Scotland, issued from Inverness in 1836, there were only eight entries. The rents asked were almost nominal; in the year named, the shootings of Glen Urquhart and Glen Moriston, now so valuable, only produced a hundred pounds each. Monalia was one of the first shootings to be let, the rent being fixed at the sum of £30, of which a sixth part was returned by way of "luck-penny." A long list might be compiled of moors and forests now bringing hundreds to their owners that fifty years ago were gladly let at sums ranging from five to forty pounds per annum, and if some of the old Highland lairds could rise from the dead and be told of the rents paid to-day for areas of heather now in use, they would undoubtedly think them fabulous.

The facilities incident to modern travel proved a chief factor in opening up the Highlands of Scotland to tourists and sportsmen. Had it not been for the aid afforded by steamboats and railway carriages, Scotland might not to-day have been so prosperous. Improved means of locomotion has done much for the country. Modern travelling is not only rapid—it is cheap. Sixty years since a man could not come from London to Inverness at less cost than about twenty guineas, now-a-days the journey to the "capital of the Highlands" can be comfortably made for a fourth, or even a fifth, of the sum; but it was not till after the Battle of Waterloo had been fought that any mail coach ran farther north in Scotland than Aberdeen!

At one time, in the beginning of the present century, fishing for trout and salmon—that is to say, angling

—had no commercial value in Scotland, and even net-fishing stations on Tweed and Tay were let for a few pounds only that now yield hundreds per annum. Trout-fishing, it may be said, was everywhere free to all who pleased to fish, and at the time indicated no man in the country had probably thought that a day would come when a trout stream would bring a money rent. The water rental of Scotland for nets and rods, in loch and stream, cannot, at the present time, be less than a hundred thousand pounds per annum, which sixty years since would have been thought a wonderful sum to be derived from such a source. But Scotland is the "land of the mountain and the flood," and the flood has helped to make the country prosperous. At the present time, too, it is in the nature of a great fact, as will be shown on another page, that hundreds of thousands of trout are annually reared for behoof of anglers who reside in or visit Scotland in quest of sport upon its waters.

Fox-hunting and coursing the hare are among the oldest of what may be termed the modern sports of Scotland, and these are now carried on with even greater zest than they were half a century ago. " The Royal Caledonian Hunt " is still an institution in the " Land of Cakes," in which to-day we have a dozen packs of foxhounds and harriers at work in the proper seasons.

Horse-racing has long been an admired branch of sport, and the recent opening of a new racecourse in the grounds of Hamilton Palace, near Glasgow, has given quite a fillip to the "sport of kings" in "dear old Scotland," as Mr. Gladstone calls the country. One of our racing trophies, "The Paisley Bells," has been in existence for nearly three hundred years; it is held by the winners from year to year, each of whom adhibits to the trophy a silver label with the names of owner and horse, as well as the year of victory. Some fine struggles have been witnessed on the courses of Ayr and Edinburgh (at Musselburgh). The names of several gentlemen who have been associated with the sport of horse-racing in Scotland may be here recalled. The turf career of the Earl of Glasgow has been often referred to. The Earl was a kindly but very eccentric man, who strove hard to render racing everywhere a pure sport. Sir David Baird, Sir James Boswell, and "Robertson of Lady Kirk," are names still remembered in Scotland as belonging to good sportsmen, as also the names of Lord John Scott, Mr. Hope Johnstone, "Sharpe of Hoddam," and "Ramsay of Barnton" who was both a racing and a hunting man of great renown. But before all these may be mentioned the Earl of Eglinton, whose name has a sweet savour in connection with the turf. Mr. Merry of Belladrum, Mr. Stirling Crawford and Lord Rosebery, and the present Dukes of Hamilton and Montrose, came later on the scene, but their names are familiar to sportsmen of the period, as also are those of Messrs. Jardine and Houldsworth. Among the men who promoted the pastimes of deer-stalking and grouse-shooting, Colquhoun of Luss and Horatio Ross stand out as chieftains, and to their names might be added others of only a lesser degree of renown.

Nothing in Scotland in connection with its play-grounds is more remarkable than the growth of football, now one of the leading recreations of the country. There are more than a hundred first-class clubs of football players in Scotland, and in such centres of the game as Glasgow splendid " gates " are obtained on the occasion of particular matches being played. It was stated lately by a local journalist that the success of the great Exhibition recently held in Glasgow was due most of all to its football matches; on the days and evenings on which matches were arranged to take place, the recreation-ground rapidly became populous, while the picture galleries and courts of exhibition were deserted. Notwithstanding their habitual reserve and reticence, Scottish people have warmed to all the sports and pastimes of the period, which have become a constant and increasing feature of Scottish out-door life.

Scottish ladies, too, in contrast to the reserve of their grandmothers, have taken kindly to many of the out-door pastimes. I recollect, when at school, some most respectable ladies being hissed and groaned at because they ventured on the ice to skate. In those days few ladies were seen in the hunting field, and it has been related of a Scottish landowner that he was strongly advised by his mother not to marry a lady who had gained his affections because she went to " the hunting." Now, ladies not only go a-hunting, but they go a-fishing as well—indeed, it is difficult to tell where they will stop; some of them even go grouse-shooting and deer-stalking, and there are many ladies who can handle their golf clubs and their bows and arrows with skill and dexterity.

In Scotland to-day there is sport of a kind for all degrees of people : for the masses there is football in particular; for the classes there are deer-stalking and salmon-fishing, as well as grouse-shooting, and, with

the intermediate bodies of people, curling and greyhound coursing never go out of favour; golfing may be
called a middle-class game, although largely shared in
by many of the professional aristocracy of the day.
That sport of every kind is progressing in Scotland by
leaps and bounds, is daily placed in evidence by the
space devoted to it in Scottish newspapers, thousands
of which are every morning sold because of their containing programmes of the day's racing. The evening
papers, too, those published in Edinburgh and Glasgow
especially, are disposed of every night in tens of
thousands, more particularly in the height of the football and cricket seasons, when results of the day's
doings are anxiously looked for and perused. Who,
half a century ago, would have ventured to predict that
in the course of one Saturday afternoon and evening of
the present year nearly a quarter of a million evening
newspapers would be sold in " Godly Glasgow " because
of a football match? Every night the results of the
day's horse-racing are also eagerly sought after : large
numbers of persons impatiently await the news relating
to starting prices and the names of the running steeds.
Quantities of London and other sporting journals are
also greedily bought both in Edinburgh and Glasgow,
and, indeed, throughout all parts of Scotland. I can
remember a time when only two copies of *Bell's Life*
were publicly known to reach Edinburgh, and *Bell* was
then the only journal entirely devoted to sport in the
kingdom.

CHAPTER I.

SCOTLAND'S DEER AND GROUSE GROUNDS.

OF the nineteen and a half million acres of land and water which comprise the area of Scotland, not more than five millions (taking the round figures) are at present used for all kinds of crops, leaving fourteen and a half million acres as a domain for the animals of sport. Of this vast area of moor, mountain, and loch, much is inaccessible even to the keenest sportsmen, some of it being still the home of the eagle, whilst nearly the whole expanse is yet arrayed in that dress in which it was originally clothed by the bounty of Nature; much of it, indeed, has never yet been trod by the foot of man.

A mere enumeration of acreage can, of course, prove no real guide to the deer and grouse grounds of Caledonia, or to the waters which contain its salmon and trout. It has been ascertained that about two million acres of the "wild land" of Scotland is taken up by what are called "deer forests," but these "forests" are only very partially wooded, for, as sportsmen well know, the browsing grounds of the "high-antler'd deer" must be clear of trees. It is in the Highland counties the chief forests are situated; in these the acreage of cultivable land bears but small proportion to the total area. The counties which furnish the best sport and possess the largest areas of deer ground, are those of Argyll, Inverness, Ross, and Sutherland.* There are forests in some of the other

* The following list of the chief deer forests in Scotland is made up from an official report issued a few years ago, but as some alterations in ownership or extent may have taken place since it was issued, it is only reprinted here as being illustrative. As will be seen, the largest holder appears to be the Duke of Sutherland with 147,010 acres, in addition to which the Duchess of Sutherland is the owner of 34,730 acres in the conjoined counties of Ross and Cromarty. His Grace the Duke of Richmond's forests cover 59,750 acres of the county of Banff. Sir George M'Pherson Grant is proprietor of 61,090 acres in Inverness-shire. The united forests of Her Majesty the Queen extend over an area of 22,070 acres.

Forest.	Proprietor.	County.	Acreage.
Mar	Earl of Fife	Aberdeen .	80,100
Blackmount .	Earl of Breadalbane . .	Argyll . .	70,330
Reay	Duke of Sutherland . .	Sutherland .	64,600
Glenstrathfarrar, &c. . . .	Lord Lovat	Inverness .	51,290
Auchnashellach, &c. . . .	Lord Wimborne . . .	Ross and Cromarty	49,580
Kinlochewe . .	Sir Kenneth M'Kenzie .	Ross and Cromarty	42,750
Amhuirmsnidh .	Sir E. H. Scott's Trustees	Inverness .	40,100
Glenavon . .	Duke of Richmond . .	Banff . .	37,150
Langwell . .	Duke of Portland . .	Caithness .	36,030
Ben Arim, &c. .	Duke of Sutherland . .	Sutherland .	35,840
Athole . . .	Duke of Athole . . .	Perth . .	35,540
Glencanisp . .	Duke of Sutherland . .	Sutherland .	34,490
Glenquoich . .	E. Elliot's Trustees . .	Inverness .	34,400
Ceanacroc . .	J. M. Grant's Trustees .	Inverness .	32,760
Glenfeshie . .	Sir George M'P. Grant and The Mackintosh	Inverness .	31,830
Craskie, &c. . .	The Chisholm . . .	Inverness and Ross .	30,810
Applecross, &c. .	Lord Middleton . . .	Ross and Cromarty	30,420

In addition to these there are 18 forests each containing an area exceeding 20,000 but below 30,000 acres.

Scottish counties, as will presently be stated, but the four just enumerated are burdened, as it may be said, with an uncultivated area of over seven and a half million acres. It will not probably be any exaggeration to say that, in addition to the two million acres of land devoted to the deer—and in part also to grouse—an area of even greater extent is occupied by the various birds of sport, seeing that there are grouse, blackcocks, pheasants, and partridges in almost every county of Scotland. But although moors and lochs, and hills and dales, abound everywhere, it is undoubtedly in the Scottish Highlands that sportsmen of the period find their quarry in the greatest abundance, whether they seek to slay the monarch of the glen, or to capture the monarch of the brook.

As the picturesque aspects of the Scottish Highlands have been voluminously described by more than a hundred pens, it is not necessary to say anything in these pages about the mountains and moors, except in so far as they afford breeding and feeding ground to the creatures of sport; but as regards individual counties, it is proper that a few words should here be said about them, taking first of all the largest county in Scotland, Inverness, which may be described as the deer district *par excellence,* in the same way as Perthshire is looked upon as being the representative grouse-producing county of the kingdom : it is ninety miles in length, and fifty miles wide, and as one of our most representative deer-slayers and salmon-killers has asked, " Where else in the wide world can there be found such a theatre of sport ? " Fish, fur, and feather abound throughout the county, and there are probably over two hundred miles of running water in which salmon and trout find

a liquid home, whilst some of the forests are of vast
extent; there are stretches of heather, too, which in the
proper season are populous with the bird of sport;
moors on which big bags have before now been made.
In the county of Inverness men with plethoric purses
will find an outlet for their sporting vigour; forests
are there with rentals running into thousands to tempt
the millionaires, whilst snug little "shootings" are not
wanting at rents even under a hundred pounds for the
season.

Those in search of such places must look up "the
guides," which afford copious details of shootings to
let.   As the vulgar phrase goes, it positively "makes
one's mouth water" to read of these places: "The house
is a palace," says one advertisement; "it contains two
drawing-rooms, a morning-room, thirteen bed-rooms
and dressing-rooms, large dining-room, fine entrance-
hall, and excellent accommodation for servants, as also
a ten-stalled stable, coach-house, and extensive gardens
with well-stocked green and fruit houses."   As to
game, a surfeit is offered : sixty stags, half as many
hinds, two hundred and eighty brace of grouse, with
pheasants, partridges, blackcocks, greyhens, and other
wild fowl galore ; while sea-fishing and salmon and
trout are, as we may say, thrown into the bargain ! Not
Paradise surely could offer greater attractions to sportsmen.   What has been mentioned, however, is but a
sample of the sporting wealth which may be found in
the heart of the Highlands.   There are forests which
yield their hundred stags.   What wonderful work the
killing of these demand !—hours of hard labour, nights
of passing anxiety, well rewarded as the days flee past
by the downfall at last of some antlered hero of the

scene, that for years it may have been the ambition of many stalkers to kill.

Among the forests of Argyllshire is that of Blackmount, which covers an area of over 70,000 acres, and is good for " a kill " of about a hundred stags. It was tenanted for several years by the late Earl of Dudley, who kept up " a fine old hospitality " and entertained troops of friends during the season. His Grace the Duke of Argyll is not, as is frequently stated, owner of half the county, his holding does not quite cover 170,000 acres, whilst the Marquis of Breadalbane, who.is proprietor of Blackmount, possesses an area of land and water that is more extensive by 30,000 acres. There are other landowners in Argyllshire whose estates may range from eighty-five thousand to twelve or fifteen thousand acres. Game of every kind is found in the county, in which there are over one hundred and forty sporting estates or shootings that can be occupied at sums varying from £4000 to £20 per annum. Deer are abundant and afford excellent sport, and there is angling for all classes. In Loch Awe is to be found the " fighting ferox," or Great Lake trout, which many fishermen come from far distances to capture. An account of this fish is given in another place.

Ross-shire, with which is conjoined the county of Cromarty, is a land of sport; in it are to be found some of the finest sporting grounds of Scotland. Several of the forests command a high rent: Auchnashellach figures at £4500; Kinlochluichart and Aultderg are let for a sum of £3300; Strathconon brings to its proprietor an annual income of £2500; other forests of the county and of the Island of Lewis figure at rentals ranging from £800 to £1600. The sums named are only stated as being illustrative, and must not, however, be taken as stereotyped, as they change from year to year. Good bags of grouse are made in some seasons in these counties, and they are wealthy besides in miscellaneous birds and beasts, such as woodcocks, snipe, wild duck, as also roebucks, hares, and rabbits ; whilst sea and river angling may be indulged in by those who are fond of these delightful pastimes.   The feeding for the deer in some of the forests is good—so good that it tends to attract animals from distant, but less abundant feeding grounds.   Park Forest, by Stornoway (Island of Lewis), is likely to become in time, when the crofters cease from troubling, a perfect paradise for sportsmen ; it is estimated that in early seasons a thousand brace of grouse will be at the command of the owner or lessee. Probably the whole of the ground has not yet, as has been proposed, cleared of sheep or cattle ; but if so there will be 80,000 acres over which sportsmen may seek their prey, and within a few years' time there may be a hundred stags to slay.   The grouse obtained are fine birds.

In the county of Sutherland the chief landowners may be counted on the fingers.   Over a million acres of this shire are the property of "the Duke," who has endeavoured to lessen the sporting area of his county by strenuous efforts at land reclamation, which, it is to be regretted, have not proved successful, or at all events have not paid in the breeches-pocket sense of the question.   The Duke has the reputation of being a good landlord, who has tried numerous experiments for the benefit of his tenantry, and it is reported that he is at present endeavouring to ascertain whether it will pay better to feed cattle or let his land for deer forests.

His Grace being an eminently methodical man, we shall
expect to be speedily told the result, in the exact
figures of profit and loss, but we may anticipate from
what is already known that cattle-raising will be found
to be less profitable than the raising of stags to be
killed at the rate of fifty guineas each. Lochs and
rivers abound in this county ; ten thousand sea and
river trout are known to have been killed in a season
in " the thousand waters of the Earl's high domain."
Sutherland has not become a common arena for anglers,
but those who know the county like it, and speak with
approbation of the " good fishing " which can be got by
all who choose to take the trouble to look for it. Sixty
considerable shootings are situated in the county, for
which tolerably good rents are exacted, and speaking
roundly they are well worth the money usually charged
for them ; bags on good heather range from sixty to
a hundred brace of grouse, but birds of many kinds are
plentiful, including blackgame, ptarmigan, and snipe.

Having glanced at the capabilities of four of the
chief sporting counties, Perthshire may next be briefly
reviewed. As has been indicated, it possesses the
reputation of being the best district of all Scotland so
far as sport is concerned, more especially grouse-
shooting ; in Perthshire the sportsman can foot it over
a million and a quarter acres of " brown heath and
shaggy wood." There are throughout the county four
hundred sporting estates, and adopting round figures,
the game rental of the county, including its fisheries,
should be about a hundred thousand pounds per annum.

The shire of Perth exceeds in area that of Sutherland, covering as it does 1,656,082 acres, of which
not so much as one-third are available for cultivation.

C

Although a big slice of the land is in the hands of three owners, there is a fairly numerous proprietary, the three largest land-holders being the Marquis of Breadalbane (234,166 acres), Duke of Athole (201,604 acres), and Sir Robert Menzies (98,284 acres). About one hundred and forty others could be enumerated, ranging in extent from 76,000 to 700 acres. The shire of Perth is in extent the fourth largest in Scotland. Throughout the county game is plentiful, including partridges and pheasants, and 100,000 acres are devoted to deer. The stag affords plenty of exciting sport, the capercailzie is flourishing since its rehabilitation, and brown and mountain hares are killed in abundance, whilst from the Tay and other streams the silver salmon adds to the luxuries of the commissariat. The residential seats are numerous, commodious, and situated in picturesque places. The climate of the county is somewhat diversified; it is in some parts of southern mildness, but partakes in other places of northern severity.

The fine oat and turnip growing county of Aberdeen, with its 614,000 acres of cultivable area, has also a reputation for its deer-stalking, grouse-shooting, and salmon-fishing. Dee and Don, the chief streams of the county, run each a course of eighty miles. These rivers are famed for their fish, and for their size were at one time reputed to be the most productive of the Scottish salmon streams. The chief landowners are, or were, the Earl of Fife with more than 124,000 acres, Colonel Farquharson of Invercauld and the Marquis of Huntly follow with 87,000 and 80,000 respectively. The Queen, it is well known, has her Highland home in this county; her united estates now cover over 40,000 acres of ground, including that of Ballochbuie, purchased, and that of Abergeldie, held on a long lease. The estate of Balmoral consisted originally, if I am not in error, of 10,000 acres.

Aberdeenshire is studded with two hundred and fifty sporting estates of various dimensions, ranging in rental from the forest of Invercauld at £4500 per annum, to small but productive areas of heather at rents ranging from £80 to double that sum. Shootings known to fame command, of course, much larger rents ; one of these has been described in an advertisement as yielding some such bag as the following : " 1400 grouse, 120 blackgame, 460 pheasants, 1000 partridges, 200 snipe, 100 plovers, 100 ducks, 100 woodcocks, 80 roe-deer, besides hares and rabbits in quantity, and, though last not least, 250 salmon and grilse." Since the Queen took up her residence at Balmoral, that district of the county has become a fashionable place of residence, crowds of tourists finding their way to Deeside to gaze on the " royal residence." Aberdeenshire has long been famed for its cattle ; it supplies London and other parts of England with the finest of beef.

In the neighbouring counties of Kincardine and Forfar there are many fine stretches of heather, and both contain a fair supply of grouse and other birds. In the latter county there are also two or three deer forests of magnitude, one of which commands a rent of £3500 per annum. There are also in Forfarshire a considerable number of what may be called " small shootings," such as are let under £50 per annum. In the northern counties of Banff, Caithness, and Elgin, excellent sport can in most seasons be obtained, game of many kinds being plentiful ; Caithness grouse (as also Caithness geese) are said to be the finest in Scotland; in that county the Duke of Portland can stalk deer or shoot grouse and other birds and beasts on an area of wild land which comprises 50,000 acres.

There are more than a hundred deer forests in Scotland, the rental of the whole being, in a good season when all are let, close upon one hundred and fifty thousand pounds, which is equal to an average of 1s. 6d. per acre. The gross sums at which individual forests are let no doubt seem large, but the extent of the area embraced requires to be considered; in several instances the return to the owner is only one shilling per imperial acre, whilst the land, had it been situated in an agricultural county, would have let at pounds for the shillings obtained for it as deer-forest ground. In the deer-forest counties it has been computed that 4377 stags will, or, at any rate, might annually be killed; and at the estimated price of fifty guineas each the sum total would amount to two hundred and thirty thousand pounds, but the estimate of fifty guineas per stag, it must be borne in mind, embraces other items of expenditure than rent. It has been computed, indeed, that a sum nearly equal to the rent will annually be expended by some tenants of Scottish deer forests.

CHAPTER II.

DEER.

" IN my opinion, sir, deer are animals that take a lot of studying ; the more you know about them, the more you want to know ; and it's only gentlemen who are constantly coming to the corries that learn very much about their habits of life, and how to stalk them."

So said a friendly old forester whom I one day interviewed at some length on the subject of Deer-growth. He answered all my questions offhand, and evidently possessed abundant knowledge of the natural history of these animals.

It would take up too much space to place all my interrogatories and his answers before the reader. I asked him, among other questions, if he thought the numbers of these animals were diminishing because of the desire of men to secure fine heads.

" Certainly not," he replied. " On the contrary, they are increasing, at all events in this county " (Inverness) ; " all stags have not fine heads, you know, sir; but they breed all the same."

My next question was, " At what age do you say, from your own knowledge, that the males and females first come together ? "

" I really do not believe anybody can tell. There is no rule, and some animals come to their time a good deal sooner than others. I know personally of a hind calving at three years, but in many other cases hinds have been four, and even five, years old before having a first calf."

" And is one calf each time the rule ? " I asked.

" My father has seen doublets dropped more than once, and on a particular occasion three at one time ; but the rule, I think, all over the country is one at a time. My father's story of triplets was laughed at, but it was quite true for all that. I have never seen more than one young one dropped myself."

" And what," I continued, " is the period of gestation ? "

" Well, sir, in the case of red-deer it usually runs to full thirty-four weeks. We have often been able to count, although it is rare to see them cohabiting. We never interfere, but just leave them to old mother nature, who is a clever doctor when she gets her own way. We call the young ones *calves*. They are tender animals when just dropped, but grow rapidly, and may be considered out of leading-strings at six months."

" And how do they get on till they can be trusted to look about on their own account ? "

" Well, sir, when her time comes, the hind, of course, is among the soft high heather, where the calf is hidden quite out of sight. She leaves it there about all day, and comes back at night to feed and fondle it ; but she is never far away, keeping watch in case of an attack by a fox or wild-cat."

" Does the little thing lie at rest all the time, then ? "

" You see, before leaving, the mother makes it lie down by pressing with her nose ; once down, it will peacefully lie all the day with its nose to its tail, and

never look up unless some one comes suddenly upon
it. It is liable, of course, to suffer from attacks by
wild animals; and in such case, at the first sound of
alarm the mother will bound to the spot and fight
vigorously for the life of her little one."

Mr. Crerar, of Blair Athole, gave it as an experience
of his that, " if you find a young fawn that has never
followed its dam, and take it up and rub its back, and
put your fingers in its mouth, it will follow you home
for several miles; but if it has once followed its dam
for ever so small a space before you found it, it will
never follow a human being. When once caught,
fawns or calves are easily made tame, and there were
generally a few brought up every year by the dairymaid
at Blair. I speak of hinds only; stags generally turn
vicious and unmanageable."

While in Inverness-shire making inquiries into the
natural history of the deer and grouse, I obtained many
interesting particulars of the habits of these animals of
sport, particularly as regards the grouse—(that information will be found embodied in another place). I am
always glad to pick up, for digestion and after use, such
little crumbs of knowledge as can be had at what may
be called " first hand." Speaking personally, I rarely
obtain half the information I require from books;
and judging other people by myself, I fancy that everybody wants to know as much as I do. Merely to tell
us " the deer is a wild animal very common in some
countries, and that it is hunted as a means of affording
sport," is simply no information at all, especially to
those who hope one day to undergo their " baptism of
blood " in some deer forest of Scotland.

In the words of the ninth edition of the ' Encyclopædia Britannica' (completed in 1889), "the deer family comprise eight genera and fifty-two species, distributed all over the great regions of the earth except the *Ethiopian,* and living under the most diverse climatic conditions." Although occasional chronicles of deer-stalking have been published, few of the writers tell us much about the natural history of the animal. The most interesting work on the subject, so far as I am versed in the bibliography of the sport, was written many years since by Scrope, who acquired his experience of deer and deer-stalking in the forests of Athole while the guest of the duke and the pupil of John Crerar, to whom he was greatly indebted for his knowledge of the natural history of the deer.* Crerar was for a long period in the service of the noble family of Athole, and in addition to being an unsurpassed sportsman in his day and generation, was a composer of excellent dance music. The Crerars were for three or four generations identified with the sports of Scotland, and I often wonder none of them ever put pen to paper on their own behalf.

Such accounts of the deer as are to be found in old encyclopædias and dictionaries are exceedingly bald, and of little use to inquirers. "Deer, a wild beast of the forest," is, for instance, all the definition given in one work of the kind; but it is better to be thus put off than to have palmed upon us the so-called "information" of some other books, which, in reality, is of no value whatever, as those who wish to know may ascertain by examining it for themselves.

As all experienced foresters and stalkers know, deer,

---

* The book has recently been reprinted.

especially red-deer and roebuck, are endowed with positively wonderful powers of sight, smell and hearing. A stag can scent a man a long way off, and will, when he does so, most probably at once take alarm and run for his life. The sense of smell possessed by these animals is wonderful; wind carries the scent to them unbroken, and whenever they have got, as it is called, "the wind" of man, they move off to a place of safety. When a herd is disturbed, the deer at once betake themselves to a distance; and it is generally a considerable time before they again settle down to rest or feed in quietness. The red-deer is excessively shy, and easily frightened. The melancholy note of a flying plover, the crowing of a cock-grouse, or the running past it of a mountain hare, sometimes cause him to gallop in a state of alarm for a mile or two before he pauses to see what has happened; and consequently, it is generally the policy of the devoted deer-stalker to discourage the rearing of grouse or hares in his deer forest.

According to Scrope, "He is always most timid when he does not see his adversary, for then he suspects an ambush. If, on the contrary, he has him in full view, he is as cool and circumspect as possible: he then watches him most acutely, endeavours to discover his intention, and takes the best possible method to defeat it. In this case he is never in a hurry or confused, but repeatedly stops and watches his disturber's motions; and when at length he does take his measure, it is a most decisive one; a whole herd will sometimes force their way at the very point where the drivers are the most numerous, and where there are no rifles; so that I have seen the hill men fling their sticks at them while they have raced away without a gun being fired."

Much has been said and written during the last twenty years of the desirability of " crossing," for the sake of imbuing herds with " new blood." In fact, this is a matter that has been keenly discussed, and good results have already been achieved by crossing in four or five Scottish forests. It was the Duke of Sutherland, I believe, who first of all took active steps in the matter, a good many years since. Red deer from Windsor were brought to the Duke's estates, the animals being the gift of Her Majesty the Queen. Other owners of deer forests in Scotland followed the Duke's example, the Duke of Portland in particular sending deer from his estate at Welbeck Abbey to his place in the county of Caithness, to the manifest improvement of the native-born animals. In Ross-shire, on the estate of Applecross, similar plans have been followed with similar advantages, and it is to be hoped that still more good will be done in this direction. In such forests as new blood has been introduced, deer generally have improved ; in some of them the difference, as noted by the keen eye of the foresters, is quite marked, both as regards the weight of the animal and the quality of the venison. Thirty years ago it was a general opinion in some districts that deer were " going back," and season by season losing in weight, and that island breeds were in active process of decay from in-breeding.

With regard to the best modes of securing the required infusion of new blood, numerous suggestions have been offered. It is thought that hinds should be transported at an early date to English deer pastures, and be afterwards brought back to drop their calves in the forests from which they were taken. Another plan which has been proposed is to take away very young stags from Scotland, feed them for a couple of years in England, and then bring them back—to be placed, however, in a different forest from that they originally inhabited. A practical man in the North twelve years ago gave it as his opinion that simple ways are always the best ways in the end. " Bring us yearlings or two-year-olds," he said, " male and female, but especially the latter, from your finest English herds of red-deer, and let them mix at once with the native-bred animals ; they will soon make themselves at home, and breed through-ither, to the great advantage of the whole stock." In good time, no doubt, different plans will be tried, and in the end some practical issue will be the result. It is well to know, at all events, that a considerable degree of improvement has already taken place, some heavy stags having of late years been killed ; and it is pleasing to offer praise to gentlemen who have done good practical work rather than enter into such hare-brained projects as the acclimatization of the chamois on Scottish mountains, or the introduction of the buffalo.

Should the bringing to the deer forests of the North of a score or two of English stags be carried out, as has in some quarters been proposed, the result in the course of a few years should be an increase of weight all round of probably two stones. The average weight in forests to which fresh blood was brought has been increased and is increasing. In one deer preserve the increase in the weight of full-grown stags within the last twenty years has been quite startling ; whilst the flavour of their flesh has also improved, and has become much less harsh than it used to be, so that in time Scottish venison may have that market value which would render it greatly more valuable than it is at the present time. The foregoing plans have each their partisans, as others will that may yet come in vogue. His Grace the Duke of Portland is said to have found the first mode to be serviceable in his forest of Berriedale, where some of the finest deer in Scotland are now stalked. What has been done at one place can be done elsewhere, and we may all live in the hope of knowing in a few years hence that stags in Scottish forests have largely increased in weight and staying power.

Some curious particulars have now and again been printed with regard to deer of all kinds. One writer asserted recently in the columns of a Society paper that roebuck were never found in "deer forests," but he did not say where else they were to be found. Presumably it was meant that the roe did not herd with red-deer, which is well enough known, because they prefer to find out feeding grounds of their own, about the edges of plantations, and they remain in such neighbourhoods as long as they can find food. In winter they will dare to frequent the scenes of civilization, driven to them by hunger. But as regards the latter phase of life, the same has to be said of red deer. Hunger in some severe winters has driven them from their corries to the fields of the farmers in search of food. These deer congregate in herds, each herd, as some forester or gillie will tell you, having its king in the person of a fine old stag of great experience. Herds are composed of families, the young ones keeping always under the protection of the mother hind, as long

as she is in life to protect them. Many generations of
these animals may, it is averred, be represented in one
herd ; and each particular family keep to their own
side of a forest, which, it is superfluous to say, is usually
large enough to afford breeding and feeding room to
half-a-dozen herds, each comprising a hundred or two
distinct animals of all ages. Fierce fights take place
in what is called the "rutting season," stags not infrequently being killed while doing battle with each
other.*

Roe deer afford better venison than the red deer of
the stalker. This animal differs considerably from the
other in its habits, which are more nomadic than those
of the red deer proper, as they do not form into herds,
but rather live in families as father, mother, and
children. The rutting season of roe deer is in the
beginning of October, but there are no "scenes" incidental to their breeding season, the buck being faithful

---

* "Rutting" begins at the end of September or early in October,
and that is a wild and picturesque period in the history of these
animals, as they fight at times with an energy terrible to witness.
The noise of harts bellowing all over the forest can be heard, and
when, as often happens, one of them is attended by three or four
hinds, a second, and sometimes a third hart, may rush forward to
claim the females, when there will immediately commence a fierce
battle between the harts, which will not terminate sometimes till
one (or perhaps two) of the combatants is killed. The most active
of the lot speedily brings the fight to a close by goring his opponent
with his horns; the conquering hart receives, of course, as in the
days of chivalry, the favours of the females. The rutting season
tells with terrible effect on the health of the animals, some of which
do not for many weeks recover from their excitement, whilst one
or two may die. At such a time a good sportsman avoids killing
the animals; if he did so, it would be labour thrown away, the flesh
of a deer in the rutting season being rank and unfit for food.

to one doe; and the result is always, or at any rate
usually, twins. These animals are exceedingly graceful,
and the buck and doe, as a rule, are always found
together; a larger number, I notice, are now being
brought to market, which may be taken as being
significant of increasing sport. As to fallow deer, the
finest in all Scotland are (or at any rate were, to be
found) at the Earl of Aberdeen's, Haddo House, animals
ready to be used as venison being plentiful. There are
other small herds of deer in Scotland; and on one or
two of the islands of Loch Lomond the Duke of
Montrose and the Laird of Luss both used to breed a
few of these animals for table use. In some of the
English deer parks, "crossing" is, I believe, now
being successfully resorted to, in order to improve the
" venison."

A curious and often discussed matter in connection
with the natural history of our Scottish deer may be
adverted to. It is that, although they shed their horns
at stated intervals (annually), these are never found in
quantity answering to the number which must be shed.
Horns are a perquisite granted to the keepers, and,
being valuable, are eagerly searched for, but rarely
obtained. There are foresters who maintain that, after
the horns are shed, they are eaten by the animal that
sheds them, in order to provide materials for a new
growth! A forester in a Sutherlandshire forest was
one day rewarded for his trouble of watching by seeing
a hart in the very act of shedding his horns. "Whilst
the deer was browsing, one of his antlers was seen to
incline leisurely to one side, and immediately thereafter
fell to the ground. The animal tossed his head as if in
surprise, and then began to shake it somewhat violently,

when the remaining antler fell to the earth. Relieved from the weight, the stag expressed his sense of relief by bounding high from the ground, as if in a sportive mood, and then tossing his denuded head, dashed off rapidly," not waiting to eat the horns! It is the hind, it is said, that really eats the antlers; and one was found one day dying, being choked by a portion of the horn that had stuck in her throat. On this matter a new idea has recently been propounded—it is, that the horns are eaten by field mice!

No pain is thought to be experienced by the animal shedding its horns; a little blood flows, but that very soon stops, and the new shoot is speedily seen. The infant horns are covered with a sort of thick skin, called "velvet," which, by the aid of a little manœuvring on the part of the animal, is speedily worn off. The horns of deer grow with marvellous rapidity; the antlers generally begin to appear at the end of spring, and in ten weeks are full grown. With twelve points the animal is known as a royal stag.

"If not killed by the bullet of a deer-stalker, what age do you think a deer will reach, bar accident?" is a question I have often asked of foresters and ghillies; and the answer has always been pretty much to the same effect: "Oh, they last a long time; they live till they are very, very old."

That, indeed, is a general belief entertained by all who are connected with stalking. They feel certain every deer will see out three generations of men, "if it live long enough," that is, if it be not wilfully or accidentally killed in the interim—an opinion in all probability founded on old Gaelic sayings with which

every Highlander is familiar, and which in English
read as follows :—

> " Thrice the age of a dog is that of a horse ;
> Thrice the age of a horse is that of a man ;
> Thrice the age of a man is that of a deer ;
> Thrice the age of a deer is that of an eagle ;
> Thrice the age of an eagle is that of an oak tree."

No one can live long in a forest without hearing
something about the longevity of deer. Stories about
aged harts of celebrity are everywhere on hand, ready to
be repeated at the cost of a dram, or maybe two drams,
if the tale-teller prove loquacious. There are persons
of credit and good intelligence who retail such legends,
and it is only fair to say that in some instances they
are able to adduce strong evidence in favour of their
being true. Talking with a Highland piper at one
of the bagpipe competitions held in Edinburgh in the
course of the " thirties," he told me (he was a gillie at
home) that there was a hart in his forest which had been
marked ninety years previously, when it was calved.

Scrope tells that a fine stag killed by Glengarry in
the year 1826 was found to contain on its left ear the
mark of Ewen-Mac Jan Og, a forester, who had been in
his grave for a period of one hundred and fifty years,
and who about thirty years before his death had
marked every calf he could lay hold of. The animal
killed by Glengarry, on that evidence was thought to
be one hundred and eighty years old. The head was
preserved, and the horns have a very wide spread.
Unless some one had forged the old forester's mark on
the ears of younger animals it was considered by the
Chief mentioned that the evidence obtained from

half-a-dozen foresters and gillies was reliable, and that the stag had in all probability attained the great age which has been named.

Many curious traditions are afloat in all parts of the Highlands of aged harts which have been known to generation after generation of the same family. Ewen M'Gillivray, who about half a century ago acted as porter at a popular auctioneer's rooms in Edinburgh, used to tell stories of the days of his young life in Ross-shire, of a "muckle hart" that was never seen in the district except for two days once in every twelve years. His grandfather had seen it five times as boy and man; and his father, after his grandfather's death, had seen it on three occasions. The beast had marks upon it by which it was easily recognised, and came at last to be looked upon with such a feeling of superstition that no one would take any part in stalking it. Throughout the Scottish Highlands there are tales of traditionary deer that have been stalked at intervals during seven or eight years. One of these is described by Mr. St. John as "the Muckle Hart of Benmore," which, after six days' pursuit, was at length brought down, falling a prey to the prowess of the author.

. . . The writer has several stories of similar purport in his mind's eye, but they need not be given here. This feature of deer biography, however, is not a little remarkable; but, as Sir Walter Scott said once on the occasion of the bagpipers' competition at Edinburgh, "It would be a pity to disturb those grand old traditional beliefs of our gallant Highland men. For my own part, I am greatly annoyed when some terrible matter-of-fact fellow comes in to prove that all such legends are a pack of nonsense, and so let down

devoted gillies and their poetic mothers to the level of
our prosaic lowland labourers and millwrights."

This rather brief essay on the natural history of
Scottish deer may be supplemented by an extract from
a poem by no less a personage than the late Lord
Beaconsfield.   The lines are paraphrased from the production of a celebrated Gaelic poet :—

> " And, lo! along the forest glade
>   From out yon ancient pine woods' shade—
>   Proud in their ruddy robes of state,
>   The new-born boon of spring,
>   With antlered head and eye elate
>   And feet that scarcely fling
>   A shadow on the downy grass,
>   That breathes its fragrance as they pass,—
>   Troop forth the regal deer :
>   Each stately hart, each slender hind,
>   Stares and snuffs the desert wind ;
>   While by their side confiding roves
>   The spring-born offspring of their loves—
>   The delicate and playful fawn,
>   Dappled like the rosy dawn,
>   And sportive in its fear !
>   The mountain is thy mother,
>   Thou wild secluded race ;
>   Thou hast no sire, or brother
>   That watches with a face
>   Of half such fondness in thy life
>   Of blended solitude and strife
>   As yon high majestic form
>   That feeds thee on its grassy breast."

Attempts have been more than once made to take
a census of the red - deer breeding and feeding in
particular corries.   The first person who is known to
have tried his skill at this work was the Mr. Scrope

already mentioned; and at a later date Mr. Bass tried to ascertain as accurately as possible the number of deer in his own forest. Mr. Horatio Ross had also before his death collected some illustrative facts and figures, which have not, however, been published. Any statement which can be made on the subject must, therefore, of necessity be in the nature of a " good guess," and be taken as simply illustrative. There are at present, or at any rate there were when the Parliamentary inquiry was held into the condition of the crofters, 110 deer forests, occupying an area of 1,975,209 imperial acres. Scrope thinks that while living with the Duke of Athole he saw all the deer in the vast forest of Athole which belonged to his Grace, and which was then of the extent of 51,708 imperial acres, and he estimated the number as being between five and six thousand of both kinds and both sexes, but other persons gave a larger figure by a thousand. In the year 1766 the herd of deer in the forests of Athole did not number above one hundred animals.

The number of stags which the deer forests of Scotland annually yield to the gun has been set down as close upon 4500, and it has been computed that even after that number has been shot many more of all ages are left to afford future sport. Although a large percentage of the hinds are annually massacred—thousands, it has been said—a large breeding stock always remains, particularly in the counties of Ross and Inverness, in which the majority (78) of the deer forests are situated. In these two counties " the kill " of deer in favourable seasons is seldom under 3000, in addition to the hinds which are shot. The yield of stags for the gun varies considerably in different forests; in some the number on 10,000

acres will be a dozen; the same area elsewhere may
yield a score. Economists who have studied the question say that for each stag that is slain 20 deer of all
ages, from the calves of the year to the venerable harts
of many seasons, will be left in the forests, which in
some years, when 4500 is the number killed, would
indicate a total stock of 90,000; but if the Athole
forest calculation, say of 5000 deer to every 50,000
acres, may be regarded as being at all near the mark,
then the stock on 2,000,000 of acres ought to be 200,000
animals of all ages, but for such a number there is
really not food.

CHAPTER III.

STALKING.

As was well said once upon a time by a famous
Scotsman, "there is no royal road to deer-stalking."
That is so, and, as that gentleman would continue,
"deer-driving is not deer-stalking—driving is fitting
sport for feather-bed sportsmen only; it is quite pitiful
to think that it has now become a fashion for deer to be
forced up to the gun, just as partridges or pheasants
are driven upon those assembled to shoot them. These
modes may seem good sport to some—they certainly
mean certain death to the poor animal; such sport
only serves to remind one of the little nursery story of
'The boys and the frogs.'" Another gentleman belonging to the old school recently gave equally emphatic
utterance to his opinions in a letter to a friend, from
which the following is an extract: "I am thankful to
be home once more, my visit having terminated a few
days ago. Politeness of course kept my mouth shut,
but assuredly I swore considerably in private places at
what was going on. No insult to me could of course
be intended, but for all that I felt insulted. You will
naturally ask, why? Let me tell you. Just imagine
half a score of men hiding about two ruined huts till a
battalion of some thirty beaters, guided by the foresters
of the estate, had driven up a lot of deer to the mouths

of their guns. I would much rather bring down only
one stag during a whole season, so that I killed it fair
and square, than shoot half a dozen a day in the barn-
door style. The essence of sport, in my humble opinion,
is that the hunted animal should get some little chance
of saving its life, which it does not obtain when it is
driven to the gun."

To kill deer or other animals thus forced upon one's
gun is certainly not sport of that good old-fashioned
sort beloved of Horatio Ross and sportsmen of his
kind. "Sport" has, during late years, been a good
deal sneered at, especially by certain members of
Parliament, and not, it must be candidly admitted,
without cause. One of the first laws of sport is to give
the hunted animal—I am not now speaking of vermin
—a chance for its life. Beasts or birds of sport should
have "law" given to them, but now it is largely for the
mere sake of killing that men equip themselves. In
the case of herds of deer driven to guns in waiting, a
large percentage of the animals is certain to be killed;
well, that kind of shooting is not "sport" as old-
fashioned sportsmen used to interpret the word, which
in fact requires a new interpretation. In the debates
on the Hares and Rabbits Bill which took place in the
House of Commons, some plain speaking was evoked
about what an outspoken member designated as "the
modern craze for killing a thing just for the sake of
killing it."

The keen desire to make big bags and show a great
record has much to do with the arrangements of
modern sportsmen, many of whom seem to shrink from
the fatigue of such pastimes as grouse-shooting and
deer-stalking. As to what is sport and what is not

sport opinions will always differ, but if hard and con-
tinuous work be admitted as a factor in the definition,
stalking will carry the day. Rabbit-shooting, for
instance, in some of its phases, is not *sport* in the
manly sense of the word. Who could think it sport,
shooting among a thousand rabbits, where one could
not miss if one tried, and where one, to save time, had
three men to load for one; nor is it *sport* in a sense,
although it is a time-honoured pastime, for thirty or
forty hounds to chase one poor little fox, with sixty or
seventy men in attendance. It is, however, use and
wont so to hunt the fox, which is vermin, and it is the
way our fathers and grandfathers used to kill the same
animal, "a custom of the country," so to put it, and
the ride with the hounds, it has to be said, is exhilarating in a high degree, but many like better to see a
single-handed encounter, even with animals to which
some persons would give no "law." * What, then, ·is
sport? will naturally be asked. Well, it is sport, and
the best of sport, for one man to kill a twenty-pound
salmon, although it is not considered sport for a man
to take a haul of twenty of these fish in a net : such an

---

* "The hunt is a most valuable institution, it affords the opportunity of frequent reunion for country gentlemen, magistrates, the
clergy, and for such of the tenant farmers as choose to take advantage of 'the meet.' County topics are discussed, politics and
poachers are criticised, good wishes exchanged, and new introductions
effected. As a mere sport, fox-hunting is 'not in it' with deer-
stalking, partridge-shooting, or grouse-killing; but it is an old-
established fashion to chase the fox with hounds, and for men to be
there to see 'the kill.' So be it. As a social custom 1 am an
advocate of the sport and like it myself, although if given a choice,
I would prefer to hunt the otter or stalk the red-deer."—*From the
Note-book of the late Colonel Mannering.*

act comes under the category of a commercial function,
although there is excitement even in that sort of fishing.
Sport should never be allowed to degenerate into a
" matter of business," but should be pursued as personal
recreation.   It is a feature of grouse-shooting (as now
carried on) that it cannot be made to *pay*.   The same
rule applies to deer-stalking and salmon-fishing.

It is, perhaps, because there is no royal road to deer-
stalking that many sportsmen have praised it so highly,
looking upon it as the very poetry of sport, and who,
in pursuit of the wild red-deer, display an enthusiasm
that no labour, trouble or disappointment can damp.
Men will tramp long miles of uneven ground, crawl
in damp moss, climb rugged rocks, wade breast high
through foaming streams and placid lochs, or tear along
with determined face for miles in the rough furze or
underbush, and, after enduring six or seven hours of
such hard pedestrian work, may yet be disappointed in
their search, never see the horns of a stag, and return
home, shooting by the way a few mountain hares to
hide their chagrin.   Other men, however, find deer-
stalking hard work poorly rewarded, even when they
succeed in grassing their quarry, and the monarch of
the mountain side lies dead before them.   A business
man, hailing from an English manufacturing centre,
became quite indignant over troubles and toils encountered while engaged in stalking.   " I shall not try
this sort of thing again, it is far harder work than what
is allotted to any of my people at the mills, and as for
the cost, it is something awful.   I am losing flesh
rapidly, but with all my efforts I have not yet killed
anything larger than grouse, and these are plentiful
enough."

Wonderful execution is every season done in the deer forests by men who delight in the work. The fatigue sometimes undergone by deer-stalkers, the distances which they traverse, and the corporeal powers which they exercise with such patience and determination, cannot be easily described. Some lucky men obtain an easy stalk, whilst others may toil after the deer for a long day and then have no story of victory to relate. It took Mr. Fox-Maule, better known as Lord Dalhousie, over forty hours to stalk "Grandfather," a well-known stag of his district, which, speaking figuratively, had for six or seven years looked with scorn on all who tried to shoot him: the late Lord John Russell, while at Balmoral, attending on Her Majesty, is said to have signalised his *début* as a deer-stalker, while on a visit to Sir Alexander Duff, at Corrie Mulzie, by shooting a well-known but "very old-fashioned" hart, which had for years defied the prowess of several deer-stalkers.

As has been stated in the preface to this book, it makes no pretence to teach sportsmen how to sport; probably many who take the trouble to read it will be better able to teach the author, but some of his experiences may afford hints to beginners. "Crack sportsmen," writing for men like themselves, often neglect to put forward many little matters of information that novices would gladly know. No finer animals for good sport exist than red-deer and roebuck, and sportsmen delight in killing them, the doing so being a capital test of skill and endurance. Deer-stalking is undoubtedly hard work, but is worth engaging in, for a fellow who can bring down a stag or two on our Highland hills is a fellow who should be able to make his way.

The time to get the sport at its very best—I allude
to stag-shooting—is about the middle of September.
Young stalkers have much to learn before they can
pass muster as masters in the art. If they have such
a chance, they should, so to put the case, take private
lessons in the work. I would recommend any fellow
who has not yet been baptized to avoid a "drive," and
to practise stalking with a couple of foresters and a
friend or two. As to "dress and deportment," these
are matters that should be studied as the work goes
forward from day to day. Old clothes are good enough
to stalk in, but the garments should, if that can be
arranged, suit "the tone of the locality" where the
work is to go on. Highland scenery is exceedingly
changeable, some spots are sombre enough, others are
bright. Novices may rest assured of good coaching
when the time comes for them to put in a first appearance at a stalk. Foresters and ghillies will be quick
to evince an interest in the green hand; their best
advice will be at his command as it had been at the
disposal of his predecessors when making their *début*
in the forests; a supply of "palm oil," an article now
well known in the Scottish Highlands, will bring out
the hidden secrets of the most experienced professional
deer-stalker. The following scraps of information,
which cost at first hand a couple of sovereigns and the
larger portion of perhaps a dozen flasks of whisky, are
heartily placed at the service of the reader; but I
cannot say positively that the instructions obtained
are original; at all events they will often have done
duty.

" Well, sir, first of all you will have to find your
deer, and to do that needs a lot of practice ; in fact, to

discover them easy is a sort of gift, as they are ill to
see even with a powerful glass—they are so like the
ground on which they are at rest. Whether you stalk
on the open hill-side or in the scrub, you must take
precautions to note the wind—observe and study the
wind. It is not easy for men who don't know their
habits to believe the long distance at which these
animals will smell you, so that young stalkers, too
eager for 'the fray,' often lose their opportunities by
crossing the breeze to avoid taking a long roundabout,
although in the end that is always best."

"Look you," said an experienced hand, "for any sake
keep mind o' the deer's nose, it has full command o'
the air. You can outwit the beastie wi' colour, you
may get quite near him on some occasions, but take
care no' to cross his nose; if you should do that, he
will smell you in an instant, and before you can look
about you almost he will be a mile away. He knows
that the smell of a man forbodes his doom."

"That's all true, sir, as true as death," said another
old hand, "the sum total o' deer-stalking is to get
within shootin' distance o' the deer; a' the rest is easy
enough, if you can only keep cool in the head and quiet
in the hand."

Many similar "stage directions," as they may be
called, might be cited, but enough is better than a feast.
To get to the deer, to *steal* up to him, till near enough
to fire, requires qualities of endurance and nerve which
are not the gift of all. To get within range of deer
without being either seen or "smelt," is a qualification
of the stalker that cannot be underrated, and to achieve
this desirable end no labour is thought hard. " The
rifle plays a subordinate part ; it is not of much purpose

to shoot well if the hunter knows not where to look
for, or has not learned how to approach, his prey ; when
engaged in doing so he must possess a keen eye, much
promptitude and vigilance, as well as a thorough knowledge of the habits of the animal."

Many good stories of deer-stalking adventures have
been written by men well versed in the sport, some of
them indeed being brilliant chronicles. The writer of
this work has one or two such narratives in his possession that possess the merit of being descriptive of the
actual work accomplished ; two of these may be presented here as affording contrastive pictures of the
sport ; they represent pretty fairly what may be called
the prose and poetry of deer-stalking.

" Although almost unable to hold a pen, in consequence of my hand being in a rather paralytic condition,
I hasten to tell you that I have taken part in a 'stalk,'
and been present at the killing of no less than three
stags, one of which fell to my gun ! Pray don't be
angry with me, but to tell you the truth, I was not
from the beginning at all enamoured of the business,
which I found vastly fatiguing—plenty of hard work
and not a great deal to show for it, besides a suit of
good clothes spoiled in the bargain ; but as you know,
the gods have not made me poetical, and I can never
find either sermons in stones or books in the running
brooks ; I leave that sort of thing to our friend Belchamber, from whom you will doubtless hear, with a
brilliant chronicle of our stalk, which he says he will in
all time coming look upon as the event of his life best
worth remembering. So be it. I shall remember it
also—for the deuced hard work it entailed. I must

have walked or crawled some twenty miles, I think, over hill and dale. Happily I started on that best of all foundations, a capital breakfast. Attend and envy me : *item* first, a steak of broiled salmon ; *item* second, a helping from a pie composed of jellied sheep's head nicely seasoned and palatable ; *item* third, a savoury omelet piping hot ; *item* fourth, half of a rizzard haddock ; add to these home-baked bread in the form of scones and oatcakes, as well as honey, marmalade at discretion, plenty of cream and real good coffee, and you will give me credit for having breakfasted. There was a dram after, but that is never counted, although the whisky is well disguised in several tablespoonfuls of heather honey. We started for the seat of war about seven o'clock, mounted on hardy ponies, and in about an hour we had arrived at the beginning of our stalk, which we inaugurated by tossing off ' nips ' of whisky all round. Our commander-in-chief was Hughie Mill-roy, who, as you know, is the laird's chief forester, and has been on the estate since he was born. He is a most despotic character when on duty, and kept us in plenty of work, but I shall not bore you with too many details, and may at once express the opinion that the game is not worth the candle, any way you like to take it : a clean stag of twenty stones would not bring in Glasgow, or any other large city, twopence a pound weight as " butcher's meat." Well, we went on and on in a long tail, up one side of a hill and down another, in search of our quarry, crossing quagmires, and wading across various watercourses, not at the time, as it happened, a difficult task, as the summer had been a somewhat dry one. At length, on climbing the rocky spur of one of the Hoolichan hills,

a glimpse of deer was obtained; at all events Hughie
spied a horn projecting over a rock. 'Down, all down!'
became then the order, and down we squatted accordingly, till Hughie had taken stock of the surroundings;
yes, there were deer at hand, but too near to be of
immediate use, and a detour was at once undertaken
in order that we might come upon them at the right
distance for a fair shot. We now skirted the 'hips
of Hoolichan,' as the place is designated; two semi-
circles, that require more than half an hour's work.
Assured that the animals were feeding at the other
side, all were in good spirits, except your humble servant,
who was rapidly getting into a state of temper at the
sort of work he had been called upon to perform, for
which, I need not tell you, he felt himself unsuited.
To make a long story short, we got at length to the
right place, but the deer either saw or heard us, or
rather, as Hughie said, they had 'snuffed us,' and went
off at a gallop. Very provoking! We all went on again,
creeping from crag to crag to another vista, looking up
which we again saw the enemy. Then we had to crawl
to a small thicket of birch trees. Here misfortune
again overtook us. I could not resist laughing loud at
Belchamber's breeches; he had been sitting in a mossy
place, and they were really a sight to be seen. My
cackling set the deer off again, to the disgust of the
party. Hughie looked as if he could kill me, but was
a little mollified by an apology and the offer of my
flask. At length, after another short spell of mixed
walking and creeping, we came within gun-shot of the
animals, one of which, by a wonderful stroke of luck,
fell to your correspondent's gun. Hughie was delighted,
and, putting a knife in the animal, sprinkled me with

its blood—that little civility, I may as well tell you, cost me a sovereign. In time we got back to dinner, and as I had the appetite of an ogre I enjoyed it exceedingly. We sat down to table at 7.50; grouse soup, salmon, braised turkey poult, roasted blackcock, excellent champagne and Chambertin, and a good dessert. *Au revoir!*"

The following jubilant and somewhat poetic description is from another correspondent who took part in the same stalk:

"I have at length been made free of the forest; have killed my first stag, and been baptized with blood! It was glorious work, and seems now as if I had dreamt it rather than taken part in the business as one of the actors therein. Do not, pray, deem me verbose in narrating to you so interesting an event; I know you are full of sympathy, and everything that occurred was full of importance, to me at least. On the Sunday afternoon we held a council of war and determined on a stalk for the benefit of the novices next morning. To speak the truth, I became not a little excited over the projected expedition, and was astir very early and enjoyed a good plunge in the Maiden's Pool. I could not eat much at breakfast time, and after a pick or two was off and away with one of the gillies who was going on with the dogs in a spring waggon, and we were speedily a mile ahead of the main cavalcade, which we waited for at the spring of Blamathrapple, where the business of the day was planned to commence.

"As I jogged along with Roderick on the waggon, in the bliss of solitude, I felt somewhat depressed as I looked at the mist which played on the hill-tops and

ever and anon was forming itself into fantastic shapes.
In these pictures of nature I saw a noble deer being
pulled down by three gigantic hounds; then giant
horses with pigmy riders ran a Derby race along the
mountain-sides, followed by troops of cavalry in
marching order; marine animals of huge proportions
floated past on the vaporous background; anon the sun
would disperse the watery gloom, and one solitary
sublime-looking rocky peak—a Teneriffe of the Highlands—hidden just a moment ago from the view by an
impenetrable veil, burst on my sight, revealed by the
magic of nature.   Another moment or two passed, and
then a breath of wind dispersed the whole phantas-
magoria of the scene for ever.   The heather-bells were
encased in crystalline dew globes, and the cries of some
wild birds gave life to the scene as we trotted along by
the side of a brawling Highland streamlet.   ' Halt ! '
said the Doctor, as we arrived at a little clump of
birches at the Silver Well.   ' We cannot take the ponies
through the pass, and may as well send them home at
once.   Come up, Angus, about six to Craig Derig, and
bring two other ponies with you ; I fancy we shall
want them,' said the cunning son of Esculapius.

" The wind unfortunately was with us, which vexed
Hughie considerably, causing him to take a long roundabout, over a mile, walking, or rather scrambling, on
the brow of a rugged hill, studded every here and there
with projecting rocks, fast and loose, in great plenty,
not to speak of almost impassable ruts in the side of
the mountain caused by the rains and snows of winter
swelling the little rills that then trickle down its sides
into an occasional torrent.   I felt no fatigue, however,
but rather a sense of jubilation ; I was determined to

make my mark as a stalker, and besides I enjoyed the
sublime solitude of the moors and mountains around
me, as well as the intoxicating atmosphere, and beheld
a series of views that would have made the fortune of
any painter who could have successfully transferred
them to canvas : in the foreground a brawling stream
overhung with the wild greenery of nature, and in the
immediate distance receding into far perspective a
series of sun-tinted mountain-tops, while behind lay
miles of moor-ground and desolate stretches of grouse-
bearing heather.

" The labour of deer-stalking demands great muscular
exertion and power of prolonged endurance, as well as
a cool head and a firm hand, but I find I can stand it
very well. At one place we required to cross a stream
of some breadth, with water up to our waists. I took
off boots and breeches and got over. At another place
we had to creep for three-quarters of a mile along the
channel of a mossy rivulet, the bed of which was more
damp than dry ; and after leaving the bed of the stream,
we came in sight of a big stag standing on a mass of
rock, a ' King of the Corrie gazing proudly around ; '
but seeing us he fled at once, and we had to round
what one of the gillies called ' the big hip of Houlichan,'
that is one end of a long range of hills, which being
achieved, Hughie once more, by the aid of his master's
Dollond, saw deer. The information put us in such
excellent spirits that, as of one accord, we halted in
order to look our satisfaction in each other's faces.
The Doctor was beaming, and at once ordered a liba-
tion, and so the mainbrace was spliced ; Hughie, for
his good news, being rewarded with a very full quaich
of the real Glen Houlichan blend.

E

" Being again cautioned we started, taking our way
in the very rough bed of a streamlet, as that afforded
us a short cut to the point we were making for. We
had absolutely to crawl, so as to avoid being seen
through the cut. It was unpleasant but necessary,
and was not prolonged, for we speedily found better
walking ground, where we left the stream at the end
of a crag, and here Hughie got his glass on half-a-dozen
deer, four of them fine stags, three being at once
singled out as worthy of our guns. An unfortunate
burst of hearty but unseasonable laughter on the
part of young Belchamber sent the animals off at a
gallop to the other side of the crag, thus undoing our
spell of hard work. It was really mortifying, and I
believe, had I understood the Gaelic language, I would
have become acquainted with some strange oaths which
fell thick and fast from the head forester, who was red
with rage and jumping sky high. Our mortification
having been drowned in a ' wee drappie,'—a ' wee
drappie,' as the Doctor says, is a balm for many of the
ills that are attendant on sport—well, ' Turn again,
Whittington,' became the order of the day. By this
time it was about one o'clock, and back again we came,
hoping to find the same deer on a spot of heather we
had passed an hour before. Great caution required
now to be observed, and our work was very slow. We
trod our way through a slit in the crag, and, winding
up another of the innumerable waterways, we were
able unobserved to creep behind some projecting
masses of rock. Another hour was thus taken up, and,
that we might get into good humour and have time to
steady our nerves, the Doctor gave the word for
luncheon ; and, although it was a slight affair that did

not occupy many minutes, we were glad of the bite
and the rest afforded us. A council of war being then
held, Hughie was deputed to mount and take an
observation, which he did with the agility of a boy.
With a celerity wonderful for a man of sixty-three
summers, he worked his way up the stones, and,
crawling to a point of vantage, we soon knew by his
way of working one of his arms that he had ' found.'
' But they canna be got at very weel frae here,' said
Hughie to Doctor Bulwer, when he rejoined us, ' we
maun gang roond to yon ither crag before we can have
them at oor mercy.' ' So be it,' whispered the Doctor,
for none dared to speak above his breath. Another
toilsome half-hour was expended in reaching the base
of our new operations, and after a welcome " nip "
the order of battle was arranged. During our palavers
and reconnoitrings the dogs had become impatient,
looking as if they smelt blood. It was arranged that
Allister Beg and the Doctor, with two dogs, should go
half a mile round to be at the open ground in case any
one failed to bring down his prey. Belchamber was
deputed to fire first, I was to have the second stag, Sir
John the third ; but at the supreme moment Sir John
and I changed places. It took nearly an hour to get
to a favourable spot. All this time, as you may
suppose, I was not a little excited, being kept in a
constant fever of expectation. No one spoke a word,
not even a whisper was permitted by the tyrant in
command—Hughie, who played the part to perfection,
speaking in most impressive dumb show and working
his arms like a semaphore. At length he got us
arranged to his mind, allowing us to rest quietly for
seven or eight minutes in order to compose ourselves,

E 2

during which I noticed he was the recipient of a nip from the Doctor's bottle.

"At length came the grand finale; we were all at attention, and from the position occupied I had perfect command of the stag which Hughie had assigned to my gun. Giving us a warning look, full of meaning, as much as to say, 'Now, then, be ready to do or die,' Hughie lifted a loose stone of considerable size and hurled it down the slope, and it rattled over the boulders with sufficient noise to startle the deer, which in a moment were flying from us. Crack! crack! went the guns, and I saw one fall dead, while another came to his knees. The stag allotted to me was only slightly wounded, and had made off, but ere I could reach the foot of the slope I noticed that he had been turned by the dogs. The Doctor, who had come by a short cut from the place where he had been stationed, kindly handed me his gun, and in the course of a second or two the animal lay dead, just as he was about to leap over a burn. The remaining stag fell to a second shot, but being rather excited I failed to notice who killed it. All's well that ends well, and I can tell you that after my exertions I quite enjoyed the liberal jug of whisky and water which the Doctor prescribed. I need not describe our triumphant march home; Hughie was jubilant at having successfully engineered the stalking which ended in the death of three such heavy stags.

"P.S.—I had almost forgotten to mention that as soon as Hughie had put his knife in the animal, in order to 'gralloch' it, as disembowelling is called, he made the sign of the cross in the gore of the deer on my forehead, and so I obtained my baptism of blood.

It is a ceremony, I believe, that is never omitted when the green hand kills his first hart. I felt distinguished, it being somewhat of a feat to kill a stag at the first trial."

The foregoing narratives outline the work of the stalker pretty well. It shows that chasing the deer is a sport—it has been called "the pastime of princes"— that requires pluck, patience, and endurance. From daybreak to sundown has often been spent in trying to circumvent the monarch of the mountain; but often, after a hard day's work, the noble hart has got the better of his pursuers, and found his way to a place of safety. The red-deer is at all seasons difficult of access : a suspicious and wary animal. The stag must be watched from afar with a powerful telescope, the anxious stalker and his gillies requiring to be circumspect in all their movements. As an intelligent forester told the writer : " You creep on your stomach like a serpent; you crouch as you go like a collier at work; while, to make sure of your prey, you may have to walk a couple of miles, even though you are just about within range. You must force your way through the morass, and, if necessary, go a few hundred yards up to your middle in water—that is all in the way of business, sir, when you go deer-stalking. A slight rustle, or the displacing of a stone on the mountain-side, as you laboriously creep or climb to overlook your quarry, and your chance is gone ; the deer being perhaps a mile away before you can realise the fact that you have disturbed him."

These words contain an epitome of the work of deer-stalking.

CHAPTER IV.

COURSING: HARES.

MY recollections of coursing events and of coursing men and dogs are not, perhaps, of great value, although they extend from the days of " Ramsay of Barnton " to the present time, but during these later years I have not seen so much of the sport. In Midlothian, during the palmy days of Barnton, coursing was always in vogue and much enjoyed in its season—from about the middle of September to the end of February one could hardly proceed a mile on a country road without seeing a couple of greyhounds being led from place to place by a trusty keeper's assistant or some smart farm lad. Around Edinburgh—or, as I may say, throughout the three Lothians (Linlithgow, Edinburgh and Haddington shires)—there were, in those days, some (locally) famous breeds of these dogs in private hands. As a matter of fact there were at the time indicated no public trainers, so far as I knew. In the neighbourhood of Davidson's Mains (then called Mutton Hole), three miles from Edinburgh, there lived two or three men who had usually a couple or more of such dogs for sale.

On one occasion a sensation was caused in " Jemmy Jack's Smiddy "—a favourite meeting-place during the " thirties " for the sporting characters of the parish of

Cramond—at the price obtained by a person who bred
a few greyhounds. For a couple which he sold to
Mr. Liddell, the Barnton keeper, who purchased them
for an English gentleman, a friend of his master,
thirteen pounds were asked and paid, which at the
time, and by the class of people breeding them, was
considered " a big, big price." The breeder in this
instance, a " labouring man," as he was called, had a
good strain of blood to breed from, and the two in
question—they were both bitches—had done wonders
in a couple of trials on a farm to the west of Corster-
phine Hill. Whether the price was a big one or not,
on its merits, I am unable to say, but to the breeder of
the dogs it would be, indeed was, at the time, a sort of
godsend ; a sum of thirteen pounds being in those days
" money " to a man who could only earn about ten
shillings a week all the year round. " What will Tam
Shedd do with the siller ? " was, I well remember, a
question which agitated the village. It was answered
in time by the sensible purchase of a cow in calf to a
noted Ayrshire bull of the neighbourhood, which calf
(female) its owner sold within a few months for sixty
shillings, which was thought at the time a most profitable deal. " Tam " was afterwards called " Tammas "
by his neighbours as a proof of their rising respect for
him. He died an elder of the Kirk, and for some years
before his death was well known as " Mr." Shedd, the
potato merchant. This, however, is a digression ; but
I think the little story not devoid of interest, although
in all probability there are those who will be inclined
to set it down as a chronicle of the small-beer sort.
Be that as it may, the sale in question, and one or two
that followed it, gave a distinct impetus to greyhound

breeding in several counties of Scotland. Mr. Wilson, so well known as a coursing critic under the *nom de plume* of "North Briton," told me in Edinburgh a few years since, that he remembered the sale referred to, and was of opinion that it gave an impetus to breeding, especially throughout the Lothians.

It would serve no purpose to give details of coursing, as one run is so like another, but no Scottish sport comes in for more attention among a certain class than coursing. Besides being an open pastime at which many can look on, it is a sport that has existed in Scotland for a very long period. Near Glasgow, in Lanarkshire, there is a farm which is said to have been gained by the running of a greyhound; the laird of the land coveted the dog, and the price asked for it was the ground which the animal could cover on being slipped to a hare.

"Country-side coursing matches" have always been popular in Scotland, and in far-away places neighbours for miles around go to look on, harvest being over and care banished for a time. On such occasions laird and tenant meet on terms of perfect equality, the best man being the man who for the time has the best dog; and, when a greyhound of one locality is matched against a greyhound of another locality, the interest rises to what may be called white heat. The sport, however, has this great disadvantage, namely, that men can do no more than look on, while the dogs do the work. There are those who call coursing a cruel sport, but there are people who are never satisfied. "Hares apparently were created to be coursed," said Dr. Gregory, "and, when killed, to be made into soup." On a fine day in October there is no more exhilarating exercise of its

kind than that required to keep up with the judge and
his slipper; it is positively pleasant to see the aged
ones of the district fighting the battles of their youth
over again, putting on a spurt in the excitement of the
moment, and clearing hedges and ditches, drains and
dikes, in their enthusiasm that they would shrink from
encountering were "the steam" not up. It is wonderful
to note the excitement which prevails at a coursing
meeting, how keenly the desperate dodges of poor puss
are watched, how the turns of the despairing little
animal evoke alternate bursts of sympathy and regret,
and how relieved many of the spectators seem to feel
when the final wrench and kill denote that all is over.

Many amusing and interesting anecdotes connected
with Scottish coursing meets might be easily collected.
A good laugh was once enjoyed by the members of a
Midlothian club. Each of the committee-men used to
offer a contribution to the dinner, which was usually
arranged to take place on the occasion of a meet. One
day the cook of the club received seven *gigots* of black-
faced mutton and seven bottles of claret. Every one of
the donors had unfortunately selected a similar joint
of meat as his contribution, at which it may be readily
surmised there was much merriment. Such a *contretemps* did not, however, occur very often; indeed, as a
rule, there was much variety. The Duke of Buccleuch
usually sent a fine haunch of park-fed venison, Major
Hamilton Douglas a haggis, Mr. W. Sharpe a pair of
ducks, Lord Melville a cut of pork, Mr. Wauchope a
perigord pie, and Sir Graham Montgomery a *gigot* of
black-faced mutton. At the coursing meetings held on
the different farms of a country-side, creature comforts
are liberally provided: whisky and ale, bread and

cheese, and a cold round of corned beef, with perhaps a
sheep-head pie, being set out on the dining-table of
the farmers, of which homely fare all are welcome to
partake. Then, early in the afternoon, the day being
short, there is "high tea" for the farmers' wives and
daughters, and a dram for all before they depart in gig
or waggonette to their respective homes, much pleased
with a day's sport that has given a little variety to
their monotonous round of life.

From deer-stalking to hunting the hare and snaring
the rabbit looks a far descent, but none of the animals
devoted to sport during the last twenty years have
attracted more attention than hares and rabbits, which
many farmers anathematise, whilst landlords protest in
reply. Economists, too, political and social, have
lectured about the poor little rodents and their hundred-
and-one evil deeds, till everybody ought to be familiar
with the subject; moreover, the legislature has aided
the farmers, while the newspapers carefully chronicle
all that is said and done. Some farmers move heaven
and earth to get into a good farm, and then the moment
they obtain possession begin to grumble about the
excess of game. As all farmers know, there must be a
greater or lesser stock of hares and rabbits on land,
and if *that* is to be made a grievance, they should
abstain from renting it. No person is forced to take a
farm against his will. Good landlords are never slow
to recognise out-of-the-way or abnormal degrees of
damage to crops, by awarding liberal compensation to
their tenants. No doubt, on many farms hares and
rabbits were at one time over-preserved; but farmers
did not suffer from that circumstance, because such
farms were marked, and their rents were less in con-

sequence. Under the Ground Game Act there is now, of course, less to grumble about.

The natural history of the hare affords room for a vast amount of inquiry and investigation. The writer has taken a great deal of pains and expended much of his time with the view of being able to compile a correct biographical sketch of that animal. Opinions vary greatly as to the reproductive power of the hare, and always have done so. Forty or fifty years ago it was the general belief that the hare only bred once a year, giving birth as a rule to two young ones, and that no hare under the age of twelve months was capable of repeating the story of its birth. Now we know better. Hares generally breed three or four times in the course of a year, producing two, three, four, and occasionally, but rarely, five young ones at a litter ; and cases have been known of the young ones breeding within the year of their birth. More than once a *leveret* has been found quick with young.

In a ' Dictionary of Sport,' once in great request, some interesting particulars of the hare are given : it is described as " a beast of venery, or the forest, peculiarly so termed in the second year of her age ; in the first she is called a leveret, and in the third a great hare. By old foresters the hare is called the king of all beasts of venery. There are four sorts of hares ; some live in the mountains, some in the fields, some in the marshes, and some everywhere, without any certain place of abode. The mountain hares are the swiftest ; the field hares are not so nimble ; and those of the marshes are the slowest ; but the wandering hares are the most dangerous to follow, for they are so cunning in the ways and mazes of the field." No account of the breeding power of the hare is contained in the Dictionary referred to, nor is the age at which it becomes reproductive stated, but it mentions that the animal lives seven years.

An account of the hare is contained in the new edition of the ' Encyclopædia Britannica,' but all that is said about its powers of reproduction is comprised in the following extract :—

" Hares all possess long ears, and in most species the hind-legs are much longer than those in front. They are without exception timid, defenceless animals, although during the breeding season two males have been known to fight together for possession of the female till one was killed ; while all the species are protectively coloured. They occur in all the great zoological regions of the world, but are especially characteristic of the northern and temperate areas of both hemispheres. . . . The hare is a night-feeding animal, remaining during the day on its ' form,' as the slight depression is called which it makes in the open field, usually among grass. . . . Hares are remarkably prolific. They *pair* when scarcely a year old, and the female brings forth several broods in the year, each consisting of from two to five leverets. They have their sight at birth, and after being suckled for a month they are able to look after themselves."

In ' Chambers's Encyclopædia ' we find the following :—

" Being evidently designed to seek safety from enemies by fleetness, the hare, however well supplied with food, never becomes fat. It ordinarily lies quiet in its form during the day, and goes in quest of food in the evening and morning. When through game preserving it is abundant, it does no little damage to crops. It is a prolific animal, although not nearly so much so as the rabbit. The female produces from two to five at a birth. The young are covered with hair and with the eyes open. The common hare (brown hare) is not found in Ireland. The Irish hare has been described as a distinct species."

Harking back to one whose writings used to be frequently referred to, Thomas Pennant, we find him thus speaking of the hare :—

" The hare never pairs, but in the rutting season, which begins in February, the male discovers and pursues the female, by the sagacity of its nose. The female goes with young one month ; brings usually two young at a time, sometimes three, and very rarely four. Sir Thomas Brown, in his treatise of Vulgar Errors, asserts the doctrine of superfœtation, *i.e.*, a conception upon conception, or an innovation on the first fruit before the second is excluded, and he brings this animal as an instance, asserting from his own observation that after the first cast there remain successive conceptions, and other younglings very immature, and far from the term of their exclusion ; but, as the hare breeds very frequently in the year, there is no necessity of having recourse to this accident to account for their number. . . . Being a weak and defenceless animal, it is endowed, in a very distinguished degree, with that very preserving passion, fear; this makes it perpetually attentive to every alarm, and keeps it always lean. To enable it to receive the most distant notice of danger, it is provided with very long ears, which (like the tube made use of by the deaf) convey to it the remotest sounds. Its eyes are very large and

prominent, adapted to receive the rays of light on all
sides. To assist it to escape its pursuers by a speedy
flight, the hind-legs are found to be remarkably long,
and furnished with strong muscles; their length gives
the hare singular advantages over its enemies in
ascending steep places ; and so sensible is the animal
of this, as always to make to the rising ground when
started. The various stratagems and doubles it uses,
when hunted, are so well known to every sportsman as
not to deserve mention, except to awaken their attention to those faculties nature has endued it with,
which serve at the same time to increase their amusement, as well as to prevent the animal's destruction."

In answer to communications having for their object
the desire to obtain trustworthy information as to the
breeding of hares, and which were sent to gamekeepers
and other persons likely to be well informed on the
subject, a few interesting notes were forwarded to me,
of which the following lines are a summary :—

From the English Midlands.—Hares, as I dare say
you are already aware, do not breed so prolifically as
rabbits. A healthy female hare will not probably yield
more than three litters in the season, the first of which
may be two, the second time three, and on the third
occasion there may even be five ; four is a usual
number, however. Another correspondent writes somewhat dogmatically : "Year-olds never litter oftener
than once ; they usually have two, but have been
known to drop three. Older animals have generally
two litters in the course of a season—one late in March,
or early in April ; another about the middle of August.
I only write what I know." A third opinion is as
follows : " Breeding depends greatly on place and

weather. A fine strong hare in the south of England, where breeding begins early, will have ten, or even twelve, young ones in the year, or season, running from the middle of March to the end of September. Two, three, four, and five have all been known in a litter." One of my correspondents reminds me of an old experi-- ment made to ascertain the breeding power of the hare. A couple, being enclosed early in the season in a large and well-stocked garden in a salubrious part of the country, were left undisturbed till late in autumn, when it was found that they had so increased as to number fifty-six, along with the parental pair.

Scottish opinions.—" I think," writes a very intelli- gent keeper, " the female hare breeds four times in the year, and in fine warm seasons even more than four times. Upon two occasions I have seen litters of five, and a friend of mine in Wales once saw a litter of seven. A very great deal depends on the weather ; in genial seasons all nature is up and blooming at an early date." The following " memorandum " speaks for itself. The writer, it will be noted, is cautious. He says : " I have talked the matter over with a few friends, but not one would commit himself to a distinct verdict. The general opinion is that the breeding power of very young hares does not go beyond the production of five or six young ones in the year ; older ones become more and more prolific, and may deliver as many as four litters in the course of a season, of perhaps fifteen or sixteen in all. In very early seasons young of the first litter will breed and produce one or two. Exceptional cases abound, but the hare nowadays is so quickly dealt with, chiefly by the poaching fraternity, that it does not live long enough to afford much oppor-

tunity for observation. I regret not to be able to give
a more definite answer to your questions." A dealer
with whom I have had occasional business relations
has given me some additional information. " Keep in
mind," he says, " that hares do not *pair*, and that one
' Jack' is sufficient for the service of numerous females ;
the male discovers his opportunity by the *seasoning* of
the female, and acts accordingly. The female carries
for about thirty-five days, and then finds relief. The
littering places of the hare are exceedingly primitive ;
a place in a plantation or at the sheltered side of a
hedge suffices for puss's procreant cradle. The female
suckles her young for about a month or five weeks,
after which they look after themselves. Many leverets
fall an easy prey to their enemies, which are numerous,
and increase in the same ratio as their prey."

The hare has been often made the hero of many little
anecdotes and narratives, and the subject, as one may
say, of much folk lore. Most of the more curious
stories regarding the natural history of the animal have
proved to be mere vulgar errors, unworthy of belief ; as
one instance, the old idea of the double and treble
conception of the female hare, representing the animal
as a kind of machine for the reproduction of its kind
by superfœtation, teaching the idea that after the first
cast there still remained the fruits of successive conceptions, has been proved to be erroneous. Another
story of hare life was at one time firmly believed in,
and is given in an old account of the hare, which says :
" They have certain little bladders in their belly, filled
with matter out of which both sexes suck a certain
humour, and anoint their bodies all over with it, by
which they are defended against rain." Here is an old

wrinkle from the same source : " As for such hares as are bred in warrens, the warreners have a crafty device to fatten them, which has been found by experience to be effectual; and that is by putting wax into their ears to make them deaf, and then turning them into the place where they are to be fed, where being freed from the fear of hounds and for want of hearing, they grow fat before others of their kind."

Unfortunately for the commissariat, hares are yearly becoming scarcer in Scotland. There is not a lowland parish in the country in which the brown hare is at the present time so abundant as it was ten, or even seven, years ago ; in Highland districts also white hares are being killed in a greater ratio than their breeding powers will warrant. In East Lothian and also in Berwickshire, where these animals were once quite numerous, so much so, that almost no heed was paid to their preservation, it is now complained that the animal is likely to become extinct in the course of a very few years. A Glasgow poulterer, who used at one period to receive large consignments of hares from many estates in Lanarkshire, Renfrewshire, and Stirlingshire, does not at present get a fourth of the number. In the counties of Fife and Forfar the scarcity is becoming even more pronounced ; and a similar tale has to be told of Kincardine and Aberdeen shires. The hare, as has been shown, is, in a comparative sense, a slow breeder, not having been endowed with the fertility of the rabbit. It is almost impossible, in the face of the persecution to which it is at present subjected, that it can long hold its place among the animals of the chase. A bill is before Parliament for the protection of this animal by means of allowing it a close time during its

F

breeding season, but it seems to hang fire. At the
present time the hare is often killed even when it is
quick with young. A series of inquiries has elicited
the information that this spring [1889] fewer breeding
hares have been seen than is usual, and that leverets
are "anything but plentiful."

CHAPTER V.

RABBITS FOR SPORT AND FOOD.

As is generally known, rabbits are wonderfully fertile. Were they suffered to breed without interruption, they would speedily be numbered by tens of millions. As is shown in another part of this work, an enormous supply is annually brought to market, the contribution to the national commissariat from this source being a factor of importance in the national food supply. As an economist of some note recently wrote : "Were it not for the supply of these rodents, the price of butchers' meat would probably become prohibitive to at least a third part of the population." From every Scottish county a supply of rabbits is now obtained during nearly every month of the year ; there being no close time for these animals, they are constantly being killed, sometimes it has to be confessed when they are most unfit for food, as a glance at the supplies in the poultry shops will show. Less happily has of late been heard of the damage done to farmers' crops by rabbits, and farmers themselves admit that the case against them was much exaggerated.

The natural history of this food-yielding animal has often formed a theme of discussion, and there has long been much diversity of opinion on the features of its breeding power. In Pennant's ' British Zoology,' it is stated, " Rabbits breed seven times a year, and bring eight young ones each time ; on a supposition this happens regularly during four years, their numbers will amount to 1,274,840." Dr. Daniels says these rodents begin to breed at six months, will bear seven times annually, and bring five young ones each time. Were this " to happen regularly during the space of four years, and that three of the five young at each *kindle* are females, the increase will be 478,062." It is the popular opinion that rabbits breed for a period of from six to eight months in each year, according to the openness of the season, having a litter of from three to seven each time ; and, as they have five litters and sometimes six, one female may produce as many as forty young ones, nearly all of which in the course of about twelve months will have begun to breed. In a state of nature the rabbit is known to be monogamous, and the sexes pretty equally divided.

One of my gamekeeper friends who, day by day, notes many matters of natural history that come under his observation, and writes down his observations, tells me that he has seen females barely three months old ready and eager for the buck, and has known, although he believes it is rare, of three generations in one year ! Such stories—indeed, all stories illustrative of the natural history of wild animals—must be received with caution, but I have every reason to place confidence in the above statement. Eighty years have elapsed since Pennant promulgated his figures of rabbit breeding, and they have done duty ever since, being frequently " requisitioned " by writers of sketches of natural history, but it is not difficult to arrive at something like correct figures if a calculation be ventured upon within the lines of present knowledge.

It is only in very fine seasons, when the preceding winter has been what is termed very open, and the spring time more than usually warm and mild, that rabbits breed six times, and the first two or three litters do not as a rule number more than four individuals. Taking it for granted that circumstances of all kinds will be favourable, a pair of healthy young rabbits, of a litter of the preceding August, will multiply and replenish in the following ratio: namely, five broods of four each time, making twenty in all. Three at least of these litters will become reproductive in the same season, and will yield, in all probability, ten animals, whilst probably three pairs of the second series of litters will also have become reproductive to the extent of a pair each, giving a stock of, say, thirty-eight rabbits, including the parental pair, which provides us with nineteen pairs of breeders for the second year's work. But, to facilitate calculation, let us conclude that we have twenty couple on hand. These may be expected to breed as in the previous season, five times, but the older members of the family will have become more productive than they proved in the previous year, not dropping less certainly than five each time, so that every couple will fall to be credited with twenty-five young ones.

To make matters plain, it may be as well to tabulate the results in a simple way, so that the progress made in breeding during the second year may be shown at a glance :—

Number from 20 pairs as estimated . .	500
Number littered in June from March brood of 30 pairs	90
Produce of same 30 pairs in August . .	90
„ „ „ October . .	120
September, litters from 45 pairs born in June	135

Leaving as stock at the end of the second season a supply of .   . } 935 rabbits,

adding to that number the 20 pairs brought forward, gives a grand total of 975 individual rabbits, or, let us say, as our figures have been throughout modestly stated, 480 pairs.

Barring all incidents conducing to mortality, which in the case of wild animals is invariably going on at a high rate, the increase in rabbit production from our original pair begins in the third season to bulk very large. The produce of the breeding stock of 480 pairs, calculating that an average of five will be littered each time, and that as usual there will be five litters from the 480 pairs in the course of the season, should in the course of the third season result in the following fashion :—

Produce of 480 pairs on five occasions at the rate of five each time . . . }	12,000
Add in June from March brood of 6000 pairs, at the rate of three per pair . }	18,000
August produce from March brood . .	18,000
Littered in October from March and August broods . . . . . }	36,000
September, from litters dropped in June .	24,000
Add original stock of 480 pairs . .	960

Making a total at the end of the year of .   .   .   .   . } 108,960
individual rabbits.

These figures are not given in other than an illustrative sense, and must be taken with a more than
ordinary allowance of salt. It would serve no purpose
of utility to extend the calculation farther; but, admit-
ting that 54,000 pairs were left to breed from in the
fourth season, the produce of such a number on
their five occasions of littering, at the rate of five per
litter, would of course be the production of 1,350,000
single rabbits, and, adding the produce of the pairs
littered in March, June and August (second and third
generations), the grand total would prove enormous, as
curious readers may calculate for themselves.

Fifty years ago there was a warren on Cramond Island
in the Firth of Forth, opposite Dalmeny, the estate
of Lord Rosebery. It was a small affair, comparatively
speaking, the surface not being very many acres; but
small as it was, and cheap as were rabbits at that
period, the business was extensive enough to afford
support to a family. In those days rabbits as food
were not expensive, but for many years their skins
were of considerable value and realised in some
seasons almost as much as the flesh of the animal.
At the period in question skins were more in demand
than the flesh of the rabbits, which could not be
utilised in consequence of the very slow modes of
conveyance incidental to the time. Despite the provisions of the Ground Game Act, rabbits are really as
plentiful as they were ten or twelve years ago, when
they were so hotly denounced by a body of political
agitators, who posed as friends of the farmer. The
coney has often been set up on the political chess-
board. Much was advanced in the course of the discussions which ensued on the Ground Game Act, about

the destructiveness of rabbits, and the public were led
to believe that, with the killing of these " vermin,"
would come the days of cheap mutton ; yet here we
are, and mutton is as dear as ever, and so are rabbits !

" Three rabbits eat as much in a season as a
sheep ! " Such was the tale told by the Parliamentary
friends of the farmer, " and it stands to reason," said
these gentlemen, " that for every three pair of rabbits
you kill off you will be able to feed a couple of sheep
more than you now do." That was all very fine
theoretically, but in point of fact just so much nonsense ; and, if all the rabbits and hares in the country
were killed off to-morrow, I question very much if two
thousand sheep additional would be fed. If the breeding
figures that have been indicated in a previous page
could be ensured to go on productively for a period of
eight or ten years, the country would then be overrun
with rabbits. To exterminate such an animal looks to
be impossible ; but all must bear in mind that the
aforesaid calculations are hypothetical : they ignore
those dangers to which wild animals are subjected, and
which keep their numbers down. The seasons, too,
form an important factor in their breeding power ; in
cold, ungenial, and backward years, their food is scarce,
and it may be accepted as an article of faith that
plentifulness of food is a wonder-working element in the
rabbit's power of productiveness. It must, however, be
admitted that the rabbit will not be so easy of extermination as the hare ; it will thrive and multiply its kind
in places where no other animal of value to man could
live and breed, to any advantage.

I shall not say anything about this breedy creature
as a factor in Scottish sport ; there are many who are

glad enough to lend a hand in killing the rabbit. " Ferretting " is not bad fun, and under certain circumstances it is not quite so easy to shoot a coney as some folks think ; but in places which are crowded with these " vermin," as many designate them, the killing of them is a good deal in the nature of poulterers' work. As the late Mr. St. John once said, " the rabbit is not so much an animal of sport, as a moving target at which our boys may be trained to shoot."

With respect to island rabbits, I may be permitted to say a word or two, having had frequent opportunities of studying and—eating them. The breed on Cramond Island, just referred to, was excellent, their flesh was delicious, and their skins met with a ready sale. As a rule, however, island-bred rabbits are lean, and consequently poor in flavour, resulting from two circumstances, one of these being the fact of there being generally too many rabbits for the area of ground, the other being degeneracy from in-breeding. I recently read that on one of the islands of the Hebrides the stock had so degenerated from this cause, that it was thought best to destroy the whole lot and institute an altogether new breed, which was done with signal success. Care should be taken to procure an infusion of new blood to keep up the health of rabbits as well as other animals—grouse and pheasants included.

CHAPTER VI.

The Grouse Family.

I.

The bird of sport, *par excellence*, is the red grouse (*Lagopus scoticus*); and, of the four species of grouse which are found in the British Isles, it is of most importance, as being the bird that has attracted sportsmen to the Scottish moors, and rendered these vast stretches of heathery waste profitable to those who own them. The head of the family is the Capercailzie (*Tetrao uro gallus*), which shall of course be noticed: a few words must also be said about the black game (*Tetrao tetrix*) and the ptarmigan (*Lagopus albus*). The red grouse always breeds true, and its geographical range is well known, ranging from Derbyshire to Shetland, where it has lately been introduced, and it is found in most of the Scottish islands. These birds breed in every county in Scotland, and also in some parts of Ireland and Wales, but they do not naturally occur beyond the limits of the United Kingdom. Opinions differ a little on some points of the natural history of this bird (the red grouse), but the following details may be relied upon, having been compiled from personal knowledge, or obtained as the fruits of anxious inquiry from persons able to impart information founded on long years of observation.

Grouse begin to come together about the middle of March, a little earlier or a little later, according as the season is mild or rigorous. During a warm spring-time, all the birds and beasts of the fields and the forests awake, as it were, to a new life and to the duties of recuperation, a full fortnight earlier than when the spring proves to be late. On a Galloway moor, a nest containing five eggs has been seen very early in April! but as a rule the end of that month passes before many nests are seen, and in some seasons the close of that month is reached before shepherds are able to report the heather as likely to be populous. Opinions differ as to the average number of eggs deposited by the hen ; many widely different figures have been named as an average, but it may, without exaggeration, be put at *eight*. Nests are occasionally heard of containing nine, eleven, thirteen, and even sixteen eggs, although there are far more with from six to seven, but that as many as a dozen eggs have been again and again seen in a nest is well in evidence, and I feel sure the bird cannot comfortably cover more. The great question, however, that grouse-moor economists have to face is not so much the number of eggs produced as the number of birds which are hatched, and the percentage of these that become food for powder. Grouse have a hundred enemies lying in wait to do mischief—to destroy the nests, suck the eggs, or kill the tender brood ; nor are the parents spared, when the enemy is their superior in strength and cunning. Walk the heather in June and July with an observant eye, and note the damage which has been done during the breeding season by foes, both quadruped and biped. See yonder carrion crows, how deftly they sweep down on spots of heather populous

with nests and young ones ! And what a delicious titbit
for stoat and weasel do the day-old " cheepers " afford !

Many a gallant battle is fought by the male grouse
on behalf of his mate and her eggs, as he does not
hesitate to defend them from the greedy crow, nor is
he afraid even of the blood-sucking weasel. These
enemies, each and all of them, keep up day by day a
never-ceasing warfare, the impelling power, of course,
being " the sacred rage "—hunger ! I am sure I am
well within the mark in estimating that thirty per cent.
of eggs and young pay tribute to their ever-devouring
hosts of enemies in the breeding season. There are, it
appears, birds and beasts quite as well able to appreciate
a suck at the backbone of a grouse as the epicure of the
genus homo. The weasel, in particular, has a most pronounced taste for young and tender birds, and in the
course of a season a score of weasels will eat many
hundred birds. But, whenever danger threatens, the
cock-grouse is up in arms, ready to do all he can for
the protection of madame and her chicks. Before
twenty-four hours have elapsed, the nest in which the
young ones have been hatched seems to be no longer
necessary for rearing purposes, and is consequently
forsaken ; the parents and their family take to a nomadic life, travelling with about a rapidity which is
wonderful, considering the tender age of the brood. It
is also a curious circumstance that one or two birds of
almost every nest come to maturity at an earlier date
than their brothers and sisters—the percentage that
displays this precocity of growth being about two out
of every seven ; and it is a saying of the shepherds that
" these are the cock's own birds."

Both parents are attentive to their young ones, and

tend and nurse them with assiduity and care; but the birds which are specially looked after by the male "come on," it is thought, the quickest. The father of the brood, however, seldom takes in hand to pay attention to more than three members of his family, no matter how numerous may be the total number hatched. The cock-grouse is a brave parent; and, in addition to being courageous, he is cunning as well; in times of danger he frequently outwits his enemies by his superior resources. He is often able, when his brood is threatened, to find a safe hiding-place for them, or is skilful in devising modes of escape from sudden danger; many a time a bold cock-grouse has valiantly fought and conquered a carrion crow in search of prey. Those who have studied the habits of this bird— and in doing so some of the hill shepherds play an intelligent part, having so many opportunities for observation—tell us that the young ones commence a nomadic life in about twenty-four hours after being hatched, and never again return to their infantile cradle. It is a remarkable circumstance that these little ones soon become able to bear the fatigue of travel. It is known, for instance, that two tender birds, which were well identified by deformed legs, had travelled nearly seven miles in the course of two days and two nights. I call the very little ones "runners"; in a few weeks they may become "cheepers," but as a rule they do not fly so quickly as some sportsmen think. The parent grouse are most attentive, and watch their young ones very assiduously. The "father grouse" is, I think, the better parent of the two; he acts also as superintendent of madame and the rest of the family, being in the truest sense "cock of the walk," giving the daily marching orders and heading the little army, the mother acting as whipper-in.

It would be interesting if we could know for certain that the cock-nursed chicks become from the first the best and strongest birds of the covey. There is another feature of grouse life about which I have never been able to obtain reliable information. Some years since, in writing on the subject in Baily's excellent *Magazine of Sports and Pastimes,* I asked the question, " whether or not the male or the female bird is the most numerous ? " and appealed to readers of the magazine to aid me by giving me their opinions and information, but I was not favoured with many communications on the subject. To my own personal inquiries replies were made in the following fashion :—

" Oh, the cocks undoubtedly predominate," said one person who was consulted on the subject; " The hens," replied another gentleman, "are as two to one " ; whilst, as if to confound confusion, an old shepherd, who has lived on moors all his life, says that the sexes are as nearly as possible equal, which, however, is not my own opinion. As showing how such matters escape observation, I may mention that a very intelligent dealer, who puts four or five thousand birds through his hands in the course of a season, "never gave a thought to the subject." One other point in grouse life has always interested me : If both parents are killed while the brood is of tender age, do the young ones die ? I rather think not. There is, at all events, not wanting evidence that mere " cheepers " have been pulled through *by the aid of the two or three larger birds trained by the cock already alluded to,* which appear in some degree to supply the place of the parents. Of course, if the little ones are quite able to seek their own food, they are more likely to thrive "right away," and grouse soon become capital feeders, but they are dainty withal, and prefer the tender buds of the sprouting heather to grosser sorts of food; the birds of a district speedily find out a stretch of heather which, having been fired early in the previous year, contains a rare show of buds. That grouse will migrate from the heather to the corn-fields, and greedily feed on the grain, we know. A pot-shooter, who had rented a bit of heather, made it into a gold-mine by purchasing from a farmer a score of sheaves of corn and setting them up on a part of his moor. Grouse came at once from distant shootings to feast upon the oats, and were easily shot in the act of feeding; the person referred to sent to his poultryman by this plan about five brace of birds for other sportsmen's two, and so paid his rent and put money in his purse.

The red grouse found in the county of Caithness are considered by good judges to be the finest produced in Scotland, and the birds of different localities have different qualities, some being remarkable for plumage, others for flavour, as in the case of those of Caithness-shire. They cook to perfection, and "come early to the spit"; two of the birds of that county, it has been said, are equal in weight to three of the grouse of many counties of Scotland; again, Scottish birds are thought to be superior in flavour to those of England and Ireland, as the palate of an epicure is quick to determine. As between a heather-fed bird and one fed on the corn-stooks there need be no hesitation in declaring the bird of the heather to be the finer of the two. As food the flesh of the red grouse is much esteemed. The grouse is a bird of solitude : as man intrudes on its wild domains it recedes from him, and the fair inference would be that with a lessening venue the supply would fall off, yet the contrary is the fact! Let the heather be desolated by disease, let particular moors be shot over till they are exhausted, " the cry is, Still they come ! " To-day, on the moors of Northern Scotland, it is believed there is a larger stock of breeding birds than there probably ever was in any previous year. It has become a saying in regard to grouse, that " the more that are shot the more there are to shoot," and they seem to be five times as numerous as they were fifty years ago, despite the lessening of the area they breed upon.

Seeing that fifty years ago there was a greater expanse of heather than there is now, the increased abundance of game is not a little remarkable, though the apparent increase may partly be accounted for by modern methods of suppressing moorland " vermin." Formerly, hawks, carrion crows, stoats, and other grouse-foes roamed the moors comparatively unmolested, committing great havoc. Nowadays, gun and trap are used to destroy those creatures, and secure a larger head of game to the sportsman. That being so, grouse are sent in larger quantities to market in order to be sold, much to the benefit of the general public.

II.

Coming to the capercailzie, some sportsmen are afraid that the re-introduction of the " cock of the woods" may prove hurtful to established sporting interests ; one gentleman, whose word is entitled to attention, is of opinion that they drive away other game and spoil the trees; but that is probably an overdrawn picture, as the capercailzie occupies its own ground; its home being in the pine plantations, it cannot, therefore, in the woods and forests do any harm to grouse, partridge, or pheasant. It will likely be found ere long that the usefulness of the bird in eating up grub and other vermin which infest the trees will far more than counterbalance the evil it can commit.

A member of the grouse family—which, it is thought, may suffer from the introduction of the capercailzie—is the blackcock (*tetrao tetrix*), which, along with its mate, the *greyhen*, affords tolerable sport. That bird, which is of beautiful plumage, is much larger than the common moor grouse, but still not quite so large as the capercailzie, which in many instances reaches the size of a small turkey. Blackgame, it is said, are not nearly so numerous in Scotland as they were wont to be, the clearings now being effected in many counties being greatly inimical to their increase.

Restored to its old-time place of abode, the cock of the woods may be heard crowing to-day in many of the Northern pine-tree plantations. The capercailzie has multiplied astonishingly in Scotland during the last twenty-five years, so that its rehabilitation may be, I think, taken for granted. As many sportsmen know, the bird was at home in Caledonia a long time ago, and is said to have disappeared with the Stuart race of kings in the days of " bonnie Prince Charlie."

In re-introducing the bird, the first attempt was made at Mar Lodge about sixty years ago, but the experiment being tried on an inadequate scale the result was a fiasco, only a single cock and hen having been obtained,

G

the hen dying, however, before it could reach Scotland. Another pair were procured, which reached Scotland in safety, and began to lay in January or February, 1829 ; in all two dozen eggs were produced, only eight of which, however, were saved for hatching, the rest having unfortunately been destroyed. Only one of the eggs produced a chicken, which died almost as it came to life. Although in time several eggs became productive, the Braemar experiment ultimately ended in failure, none of the young ones having lived for any time.

It is to the late Sir Thomas Fowell Buxton that the credit of the bird's restoration is largely due. That gentleman having been for some time the guest of Lord Breadalbane at Taymouth Castle, became desirous of making some return to his lordship for the hospitality he had so much enjoyed in the North, and with that view had placed himself in communication with Mr. Lloyd, the author of the 'Game Birds and Wild Fowl of Sweden,' who had been endeavouring to find some nobleman or gentleman possessing an estate in Scotland willing and able to try the experiment of restoring the capercailzie to that country. In the year 1836 Sir Thomas gave instructions to Mr. Lloyd to procure the requisite number of birds in order to their acclimatisation in the woods of Perthshire.

To aid in selecting and bringing the birds safely to Taymouth, Sir Thomas sent his head-keeper to Sweden on two different occasions, so that particulars of the importation of the birds are not difficult to obtain, a very full account of the keeper's journey in his own words having been published. Two batches of birds were brought from Sweden, and reached their future home at Taymouth in safety : the first flock of twenty-nine birds included thirteen cocks and sixteen hens ; these were followed by another batch of sixteen hens in the year following (1838), making forty-five in all, two or three of which, however, did not reach Perthshire, having been sent to Norfolk.

The restoration of the capercailzie was now assured. By the year 1839 it was calculated that a stock of between sixty and seventy young ones had been successfully reared, and in the course of a few years the flock had become largely augmented. Great pains were taken in the beginning to ensure the hatching of their eggs, many of which had been placed under greyhens (the greyhen is the mate of the blackcock). Some of the imported birds were introduced to their new homes in the following manner : they were carried out at night in closed baskets, and placed in plantations near the house, and early on the following morning, the covers of the baskets being removed, the birds were at liberty to wander about at their leisure, and become accustomed to their new dwelling-place.

Calculating that twenty-five of the hens would each lay ten eggs, and that eight of these each produced a fowl, we have thus 200 in addition to the parent birds ; the mortality under such circumstances being, however, always considerable, ten per cent. must be allowed under that head—which leaves at the credit of the account 180 young capercailzie. Repeating the same figures for the second year, the flock of young ones totals up to 360 birds, of which 300, including the original breeders, would be capable of breeding ; let us imagine 200 of this lot to be laying hens, and it will at once be apparent that the power of reproduction would be largely increased, taking it at the modest figure given above. In 1862-3 it was computed that the total number of capercailzie in the district of Taymouth would not be less than 2000. The birds may now be said to be native to all parts of Scotland; they have, by this time, spread themselves over a very wide district, and capercailzie are occasionally announced as being shot in most unexpected places, both in the north and south. A great deal of trouble was taken a few years ago by Mr. Harvie Brown, the well-known ornithologist, to find out to what places in Scotland the capercailzie had extended its range;* it was then found, as was natural enough in the circumstances, that the fine county of Perth, the best county for varied sport in all Scotland, was well stocked with these birds, and that the adjoining county of Forfar also contained a considerable number, and up to the present time nests have been seen in at least half-a-dozen other counties, particularly in Kinross, Fife, and Stirling shires, as also in the Island of Arran.

The blackcock and his mate the greyhen, so well known in nearly all parts of Scotland, are becoming scarcer and scarcer as the seasons roll on, which, in respect of their being table birds of really good quality, is much to be regretted. Several reasons have been given for the decrease of their numbers, but there is one on which nearly all sportsmen are agreed, and it is that the shooting of these birds is timed to begin a full fortnight too soon, at a date in fact when the young ones are unable to protect themselves. Blackcock ought not, it is thought, to be shot till about the middle of September, as the present time of commencing finds the

---

* 'The Capercaillie in Scotland.' By J. A. Harvie-Brown, F.Z.S. Edinburgh: David Douglas.

birds immature and quite unable to fight for their lives, in other words they are heavily handicapped in favour of the sportsman. At maturity for sport the black-cock is a strong and cautious bird, well able to take care of itself, more especially after exposure for a season to the gun. The cock bird is a free lover, and fights desperately with his companions when there is a lady in the case. As breeding time approaches the cocks in crowds seek the hens, and then begin their quarrels; the birds being at times terribly pugnacious. Blackgame breed abundantly, the hen laying about nine eggs on the average; nests are made in rushy fields near a plantation. Eggs of the greyhen have been sold for those of the plover; in some districts this has tended to the decrease of the birds, which used at one time to be abundant in many of the counties of Scotland, living on the borders of plantations and among thick scrub in rocky places, nesting comfortably on the ground pro-tected by a tree or bit of rock. So long, of course, as the close time is fixed to terminate on 20th August, blackcock may then become lawful prey; many gentle-men say, "We are willing to let the bird have a fort-night's grace, but that would be of no avail unless our neighbours agree to join us." The proper plan would be to get the close season legally extended.

In the southern counties, where blackcock were once abundant, they are less plentiful, having some years ago been massacred in large numbers on a systematic plan. A respectable Scottish game-dealer being in-terrogated on the subject was good enough to inform me that he does not nowadays receive one blackcock and greyhen for the half-dozen he used to obtain some sixteen or twenty years ago.

The "white grouse," as ptarmigan are sometimes called, are found above the snow line of the mountains of the northern and western Highlands ; these birds are not very plentiful in Scotland, although the females are pretty good breeders, laying on an average eight eggs, which are hatched in about twenty days, the nest being usually found on the bare ground ; and in the summer time it requires a practised eye to discover and shoot them on the hillsides, they look so like the stones among which they shelter and form their rough nests. In winter time the ptarmigan assume white robes, and live a life of solitude among the snow. It is an exceedingly beautiful and chameleon-like animal. Once upon a time, when skirting a mountain in the Highlands of Scotland, I alighted from the dog-cart to pick up a beautiful stone which I saw in the distance ; just as I got to the spot that stone became covered with feathers, and endowed with wings, arose and flew away—that stone was a ptarmigan ! Now a man may be in the very midst of a flock of these animals and not know it, they look so much a portion of their surroundings, and at all times it takes a cute sportsman to stalk these birds. Ptarmigan, as stated, have become scarce, from what cause it is, however, difficult to say. This bird is really pretty just before it begins to cast its summer plumage and assume its winter feathers. "Ptarmigan-stalking," as some sportsmen call it, is "fine fun," so many mistakes being made ; but so far as aiding the commissariat may be an object with those following the bird, there is nothing commendatory to be said.

As a table bird the ptarmigan is rather a failure, its flesh being dry and strong, not nearly so palatable indeed as the flesh of many wild birds that can be obtained with much less trouble; " but then it is bad to find and ill to kill," which gives zest to its pursuit, and the food question is never, therefore, a factor of any consequence with zealous sportsmen. The bird, in fact, is so scarce, that it can only be got in certain places; and to get one at a time, and not many, is all that can be hoped for. Moreover, the close time prevents it being sought for after December. It is interesting to know that ptarmigan were at one time found on the hills of Galloway, but it is about fifty years since any of these birds were seen in the south of Scotland, which is to be regretted. As an object of natural history no other member of the grouse family presents so many features of interest.

CHAPTER VII.

NATURAL ECONOMY OF A GROUSE MOOR.

I.

As all who are interested know, it has been legally ordained that grouse shooting must not begin till the 12th of August, and that it must end on the 10th of December is imperative. But birds on some moors in favourable years are ready for the gun, positively " wild " indeed, before that day, and might be shot in the last week of July, while on some areas of heather grouse are not ready till September has begun. It would not be easy, however, to fix upon a day that would be suitable for every moor in Scotland, and it is better therefore to let well alone, and stick to the day that has been ordained by statute ; but much can be said as usual on both sides of the question.

" The case " for an alteration has been " put " by an economist in the following fashion. Grouse shooting, it must be kept in mind, has become more than mere sport. Even very wealthy gentlemen, in view of the large outlay involved in leasing a moor, are compelled to send a large number of their birds to dealers, in order to aid their accounts by a credit entry from the game dealer, which, to speak the truth, never comes to much. The case then as regards a hard-and-fast line of commencement stands as follows : men whose grouse are ready for the gun, and who are themselves eager to commence, begin most punctually on the 12th, and, if prices should rule high, they secure a good figure for the early birds. On the other hand, if men whose birds are not ripe for the gun, begin to shoot them at the appointed time, their grouse would not command a good price; while if they delay for a week they run the risk of the markets being glutted, no uncommon occurrence in these days of rapid transit.

Some of my ideas about the economy of sport are no doubt a little behind the age; one of them is that whenever the commercial element obtains an entrance, sport ceases to be sport in the fine old-fashioned sense of the word. What, for instance, is the difference between " grouse driving " and the capture of salmon in wholesale quantities by a net ? To me the difference does not seem difficult to define, and to avow the simple truth, I am against " driving," as has been stated in the case of the deer. It is in no sense *sport,* to have the birds you are to shoot driven up by a zealous crowd of beaters to the very muzzle of your gun ! To sit in a hut and fire at a flock of birds resistlessly forced to pass a given spot is, in my humble opinion, only poulterers' work even at its very best; and those who make a practice of " driving " are but feather-bed sportsmen. It is always a pity when the commercial element is allowed to intrude itself into sport; it would be far better if men would be modest in their desires, and so regulate their expenditure as to leave it a matter of no moment how many head of game they and their friends should kill, or at what price birds were being quoted in Leadenhall Market. If birds were not marketed, it would not matter much to a man whether he began his work on the 12th or the 20th of August.

Some of the more easily discerned features of grouse
life have been described in the preceding chapter, but
much yet remains to be discovered and related. For
instance, we are all so ignorant of its natural history that
none of us (in saying *us* I allude both to sportsmen
pure and simple and men like myself, who dabble a
little in the natural history of sport) seem to be able to
explain how birds should be plentiful one season and
scarce in another. That grouse possess an unequalled
faculty of recuperation is well known. On occasions
when moors have been largely depopulated by disease,
they have become within two or three seasons more
populous than ever they were. It is certain that in the
course of every winter a large percentage of birds die
in consequence of the inclemency of the weather, and
from various other natural causes ; yet in the course of
the next shooting season some positively gigantic bags
will be made. What I want to know is, how that
comes about ? I have studied and observed, and asked
till I am tired : all I can make out of the situation
is, that after all moors only breed and feed a limited
number of birds, and that when that number is exceeded, and the heather becomes overstocked, and food
is scarce in consequence, Nature at once begins her
remedial measures. Till moors are full the work of
reproduction assiduously goes on, there being plenty
both of food and space for the wants of the birds, and
so long as these conditions continue, the sportsman
may enjoy sport to the top of his bent. The severe
storms of December and January probably help to
purify the heather ; they certainly weed out the weak-
lings of the flock.

It is difficult to determine what number of birds can

be bred and fed on a hundred acres of heather. We can only guess; but this much has been ascertained, namely, that a moor situated in a lowland district, which was literally without a single brace of grouse one year, quite swarmed with these birds in the third season following.

A few years ago Mr. Andrew Lamb, a well-known game-dealer in Scotland, made up for my use the following statement, the figures and conclusions of which may be held as being on the whole pretty correct, taken, of course, for merely illustrative purposes. They refer to the moor just alluded to, in which the gentleman referred to had a pecuniary interest.

Supposing not one brace of grouse to have been left on five thousand acres of heather in the year *one;* comparatively few birds were seen in the year *two;* but two hundred and seventy brace were shot on said moor in the year *three.* Taking it for granted that some fifty pair of birds migrated to the vacant heather in the autumn of year *two,* and that each pair successfully bred and brought up a covey of ten young ones, that would have yielded a stock in the year *three* of five hundred birds, which would not be nearly enough to afford the number shot and leave a breeding stock. It would require at least one hundred brace of grouse to have begun the replenishment of the moor; but it is abundantly curious that barren moors are speedily found out by the birds and quickly re-stocked. In some seasons certain moors became so thickly populated with birds as to have been estimated to contain dozens to the acre! We know really little about the grouse; it is a shy bird, and recedes as far and as fast as it can from the haunts of man.

Year by year grouse become more and more abundant, and many there be, both sportsmen and naturalists, who marvel at their reproductive power. In some winters the mortality is known to be excessively high, but lo! on the twelfth it is announced that birds never were so plentiful. Anon an epidemic courses through the heather, and grouse die in hundreds or even thousands, but in a year or two the moors, we are told, are positively over-stocked. How was it with these birds a hundred years ago? Then there was a larger expanse of heather for their accommodation than there is to-day, and if the moors were as populous then as they are known to be at present, what became of the birds? Were their foes more numerous or their food more plentiful a hundred years ago than in the present year? As shall be shown in the proper place, hundreds of thousands of these birds now reach the markets.

Sixty years since, in the days of Sir Walter Scott, "moor-fowl" were seldom sold; a few were given in presents, and a hundred or two might reach the markets. Now there is an incessant demand at what may be called fair prices, and in consequence, much is done to provide a constant and increasing supply; and to ensure this supply, enemies of the bird are being carefully and constantly extirpated with remorseless vigour. The "bird of sport" has numerous foes. The peregrine falcon is constantly teasing them all the year round. That dreadful vagabond, the "hoodie crow," is death upon the grouse. So say those who know. One naturalist writes, "I have heard of an estate on which, in 1864, there lived in great peace and prosperity a colony of crows. One year 400 of these were killed, and in that same season there were only about 100 grouse on the

estate ; after the lapse of a season or two, when the
crows had been so reduced that only a colony of 40 was
left, over 400 brace of grouse were obtained. *Moral*—
If you grow your crows you exterminate your grouse !"
All statements as to the havoc played by crows and
other vermin in the game preserves have usually two
sides to them, and must therefore be accepted with
caution. An endeavour will be made in a future
chapter to show which of the vermin are really dangerous on the grouse moors and partridge preserves.

On many of the chief points of grouse-moor economy,
very different opinions are known to prevail; no two
persons, for instance, will agree as to what number of
birds a hundred acres will breed and feed. A clue of
a somewhat dubious kind is afforded by the rent exacted
from tenants. Each brace of grouse is supposed all
over to cost the lessee of a moor one pound, and the
rents of moors run from tenpence to half-a-crown an
acre, with houses on them. Many sportsmen put the
average at two shillings (which is, perhaps, rather high),
but for illustrative purposes that figure will serve for
the present. At this rate a shooting of one thousand
acres will cost in rent alone a sum of one hundred
pounds, and that area of heather ought to yield one
hundred brace of grouse, whilst fifty brace should be
left as breeding stock. Counting that there will be
about a hundred nests on a thousand acres, and that
each of these will contain seven or eight eggs, that will
give a total of say 750, but as a matter of course a large
percentage of these will be lost. The account at the
termination of the hatching season should about stand
as follows :—Addled eggs, 34 ; eggs lost in consequence
of accidents to parent grouse, 46 ; eggs destroyed by

the forces of Nature, such as rain, snow, &c., 52 ; eggs which fall a prey to vermin of various kinds, 48 ; total, 180, which leaves 570 to produce young birds, of which 200 are shot, the remainder being left as stock, leaving the parent birds and those over from sport to furnish food to their numerous enemies, or to be destroyed by " the disease " and weather influences ; the percentage doomed to destruction may look large, but there are men who, from long observation, will say the number is not exaggerated.

II.

Few persons know much of the economic considerations which govern the letting and the leasing of a grouse moor or a deer forest. On behalf of the leasing class, it may be well to state a few of the more pertinent facts which are incidental to taking and occupying a grouse moor. There are moors and forests of many sizes, ranging from fifty or sixty acres to an expanse that has to be measured in miles. The rents exacted are suitable to purses of every kind, and the conditions of "tack" vary considerably. A stretch of heather may be shared with one, or, it may be, several brother sportsmen, or one may become the exclusive lord, for a season or two, of ten thousand acres ; as the showman has it, " You pays your money and you takes your choice." Your moor may cost but forty pounds a year, or it may be ten or twenty times as much ; it is all a matter of extent and bargain.

Having, as the saying goes, " made his market," the tenant, it may be assumed, will be on the ground in good time to begin the business of the season. Till "the twelfth" dawns he is quite in ignorance of how his bargain may turn out. On the eventful day, or soon after, he may discover to his great mortification that he has been "done," and that on *his* moor there are very few birds to kill. Such events have happened pretty often—indeed these things are always happening, although they are seldom brought under public notice. And on occasion barren moors have been let in complete good faith, the heather having been shot bare by the preceding tenant without the knowledge of either proprietor or factor. There are still left a few members of the old pot-shooting band, who used to go about in search of moors on which to perform their deadly mission. Those are simply "poultrymen," with them "sport" is of no moment, their ideas of shooting being sordid in the extreme. They stain the heather with the blood of every bird they can find. I remember when many of the lesser Scottish moors were taken during several seasons by gangs of men who shot only for profit; they were not particular as to times or seasons; to get the grouse they killed early to market, so as to secure the top prices, was what they cared for —to harry the ground was essential for their success; they had no care for those whose destiny it was to follow them; if they could help it, not one brace of birds would be left to provide a stock for future sportsmen.

It is not to be wondered at in the face of such doings that lairds and factors became stern and unbending as to terms of lease, of which there are many kinds, most of them, however, containing clauses regulating the annual slaughter of the birds. As a rule, in the case of the shorter "tacks," lairds insist upon their own keepers and gillies being employed. Some shootings, it is well known, are rented on the conditions of a lease being granted extending over several years, other stretches of heather are only taken for the season, hence the precautions hinted at. Happily, all over Scotland there are moors on which the birds never fail, and seem to know no diminution, no matter how briskly the sport may be carried on. There are delightful stretches of heather on which it is at all times a pleasure to take one's daily modicum of sport. There dwells in the chambers of my memory three or four pleasant shootings on which grouse have never even been attacked by the disease, and where large numbers have been killed in the past, and where, let sportsmen work their very hardest, there seems as if there would be no falling off in the future, bar such a calamity as "the disease" breaking out. When such a calamity does occur, the grouse in thousands fall a prey to that mysterious malady, for which, as yet, there has not been found a cure, the origin of which is unknown, and the end difficult to foresee. Like the potato blight, the salmon disease, and other mysterious calamities, the malady which occasionally attacks the "bird of the heather," so far as cause or cure is concerned, or, what would be still better, "prevention," remains to be dealt with. As most sportsmen can doubtless remember, there were seasons when the grouse were so thinned down by "the disease" that no sport to speak of was obtained. But, as has been indicated, the recuperative power of the bird is so wonderful, that in the course of a short time the heather becomes again alive with its familiar occupants.

Speculation has of late been excited as to how breeds of grouse might be improved, and so strengthened as to render them constitutionally impervious to disease. But when the hand of man is intruded on such occasions it sometimes does mischief. In the case of wild animals " in-breeding " cannot be prevented, and to in-breeding, among other evils, the periodical outbreaks of grouse disease have by some economists been ascribed ; but it is a fact within the ken of natural history students, that wild birds circulate themselves by force of instinct, and it has been found in the case of a depopulated stretch of heather, that birds flock to it during the next breeding season even from distant moors, so that the breeding stock speedily becomes sufficiently augmented to provide the necessary population, and in four years birds may be again as thick on the heather as they were before. Grouse of different districts can easily be distinguished from each other. A dealer will readily tell a Caithness bird from one grown on the wilds of Wigtownshire ; just as a fishmonger can easily distinguish a salmon of one river from that of another.

The strengthening of our breeds of grouse has, in the face of the periodical outbursts of disease, been recommended by all who take an intelligent interest in sport. The extinction of that bird, which it was at one time feared might happen, would prove a serious calamity to Scotland, and it is well that several gentlemen have already begun experiments with a view to " changing the blood." His Grace the Duke of Hamilton has been a moving spirit in experiments of the kind. With the view of improving his birds, his Grace on two occasions transferred a number of grouse taken from his moors on Lanarkshire to the heather of the Island of Arran, at the mouth of the Clyde, and happily success

H

attended the experiments; his island grouse soon became
"as good again as they used to be," I was told by a
keeper who had helped at the business, and I have been
also told that the Arran birds have continued ever since
to feel the beneficial effects of the new blood. Several
similar experiments in the way of placing birds have
been made during the last three or four seasons, but
with what result has not become public.

Various modes of effecting a "change of blood"
among the grouse have from time to time been discussed,
with pretty much the usual result, however, namely,
that no uniform plan has as yet been agreed upon—
those operating in the matter doing what seems in
their opinion to be the right thing, but it is thought
that some plan of dealing with the eggs is the likeliest
to prove successful. A hill shepherd with whom I had
some conversation on the subject is of that opinion, and
shepherds as a rule know far more about the grouse
than keepers or gillies, and the shepherd of the grouse
hills is a man to be cultivated—he has much in his
power.

The person just referred to is Sandy Coghill, a
man to whom at various times I have been greatly
indebted for reliable and out-of-the-way information
about sporting matters and the natural history of the
birds and beasts of the chase. Sandy has passed all
his days on the heathery braes of Glenshangie, and has
been engaged in many different avocations in connection
with country craft; he began the working time of his
life as a herd boy when nine years of age, and, as became
the son of a crofter, had a trial at "the fishing," and
had been "at the herring" for several consecutive years;
then he was employed as gillie, and carried the bag,

or rowed a boat on the salmon water for nearly all the tenants of Glenshangie, till in the decline of his days he settled down in charge of a flock of sheep. He is familiar with the sights and sounds of nature, by day and night, in all seasons of the year. Sandy has seen the sun rise and set day by day, and known the vast stretches of purple heather when they were bright as the morning and beautiful as a painting, and he has been on the moors when the fierce winds of winter were sweeping over them with a power that was irresistible, and when the heather was buried in snow his footsteps were deeply printed on it. Sixty-three " twelfths " have dawned on Glenshangie since Sandy first saw the light of day, and he has followed to the grave in the old kirkyard the coffins of two lairds and of a host of friends; but Sandy himself is well preserved, and talks as briskly as ever he did.

"I can tell you, sir," were his words to me on one of my visits, "how you can do that job best; it's not by bringing strange birds to strange moors that you will do it, for the beasties will die before they have time to know where they are; if they are chicks, the old ones will most likely kill them, or vermin will get at them, and their time is up. The right way is to change the eggs; that can be done easy enough, and will be likely to succeed, because if an egg or two be dropped into a nest the bird will never know the difference, and will hatch them with her own. I'm sure there is not a better way of doing the thing, and that will be seen when it is properly tried; but I am really not sure if it's worth doing at all; you may be quite sure, sir, that the Creator of the birds provided for all the contingencies and vicissitudes of their lives."

H 2

But in grouse breeding, as in everything else, " doctors differ," and there are men who hold that the mission of " Nature " is only to show the way, and that whenever possible we must follow up her teachings, and, guided by our intelligence, complete the wondrous tale of creation. But in doing so I fear we fall into errors. We sent the rabbit to the Antipodes, where it has become a curse ; we gave America the sparrow, and now America reviles us for the gift.

My friend Sandy has also expressed on various occasions some very pronounced opinions of his own as to " the disease," and about heather burning, of which he is an ardent advocate. His opinion that the disease is " a belly question," in other words, that it arises from the eating of improper food, is now coming to be a belief in the minds of numerous intelligent sportsmen : and a preventive, and it is an easy one, consists in systematic burning of the heather, not of course all at once, but bit by bit, here and there, so that a yearly succession of tender buds may be at the service of the young birds. Burning, as a rule, is rather late in being accomplished ; would it not be better to burn on extensive moors just as the sap descends from the rank old heather, say at the end of December and beginning of January instead of in March and April, as is now the custom ? By the present mode young shoots are few and far between till a year has elapsed ; new roots have, however, been found in the summer immediately following burning. On a moor covering an area of, say, two thousand acres, the burning may extend over three, four or five years — neither lairds nor tenants being agreed as to time—the space burned in any one season being, say, from four to six hundred acres in patches of from fifty to a hundred, at several places as may best suit the contour of the ground. In this way a constant succession of palatable young heather might be obtained, and how the tender buds delight the chicks can be seen by men who are on the tramp about the time the little ones have commenced to run.

"It's the fine young sprouts o' the heather, sir, that's best for the birdies," said Sandy, "and when there is a fine natural year, that is, as ye ken, when the spring does not come on till the proper time, say in March, you're sure to have a fine supply of meat for the wee chirpers that leave their nests in May and June, because, ye see, there is no interruption to the growth of the heather ; but when the buds come too soon, and then get nippit by the frost, it's a very bad case for the birdies both old and young."

Of late years "the disease" has happily been rare, considering the enormous head of grouse on the Scottish heather. Many economists hope that, by constant systematic burning and by means of intelligent "mixing" of the breeds of distant districts, the disease might be altogether prevented, a consummation devoutly wished for both by landlords and lessees. As to "how to shoot a moor," who shall dare to give directions ? It is a point on which few of those most interested can be found to agree. In the "hurry scurry" that now takes place at the opening of the season, some men rush to those parts of their moor which are known to be crowded with birds, and these are remorselessly shot down, the next best beat being then selected, and so on throughout the twelve or twenty days that can be afforded for the sport. There are economists who plan their sport in a different fashion, and who prefer to take first of all the outlying beats, or what may be termed the fringes of their moor; these gentlemen shoot home, and are contented with smaller bags, perhaps, than their neighbours. On many moors it has now become a fashion to conclude the sport of the season with two or more drives, at which great execution is often done, hundreds of birds being killed.

In Scotland the arithmetic of grouse shooting has never been very precisely expiscated, and in England the figures, unless those pertaining to a few big bags, are still less known. In the "land of the mountain and the flood," an economist has calculated there are about 3000 shootings, great and small, which on the average of years will yield from 300,000 to 400,000 birds. "This," he says, "is the way I arrive at my conclusion :—Assuming, on the average, that five persons will have a few days on each stretch of heather, that gives fifteen thousand sportsmen; and, were each gun to bring down twenty-five brace, that would make up the grouse harvest of an ordinary year. An average of only five persons may seem a rather scanty number; but many moors are so small as scarcely to yield sport for even one gun. On the other hand, relays of visitors arrive at larger shooting-lodges, in a hundred of which there may be assembled at one time a dozen death-dealing shots."

This estimate, viewing it all round, is, I think, moderate; it simply means little more than a hundred brace for each Scottish moor, and one would think that number might be easily obtained, seeing there are moors which yield three to six times the number; in some instances a thousand brace—ay, and more than that. The liberal figures given by the press as to

the abundance of the grouse supply have often been
called in question; but, read in the light in which
I have just placed them, they have certainly not been
over-stated, five hundred thousand brace of grouse having
before now been put down as the yield of the Scottish
moors, which means, of course, one million birds, and a
million, as every person knows, represents a vast
number, as will be obvious when it is stated that one
man shooting at the rate of fifty brace per diem would
require 10,000 days, or about thirty years, to kill such a
quantity of grouse !

CHAPTER VIII.

The Political Economy of Sport.

Sport has of late years been much discussed in political circles, and it is not perhaps too much to say that these discussions have been carried on in a rather "dog in the manger" spirit.

Repeated attacks have been made in Parliament on the owners of "forests" for occupying land with deer which might be turned to more valuable uses, but the area given up to the stag is unfit for cattle or sheep-feeding; as an outspoken member of the House of Commons said, "it would take thirty acres of such ground to graze a snipe!" As sheep-feeding areas the deer forests will never be of much account, five acres of such land being required as a rule to afford food for one sheep. The contention as between cattle and sheep-feeding, or the continued use of the land as deer forests, has of late been elevated into the region of sentiment, but the whole question lies in the matter of rent: no proprietor of a deer forest can be expected to accept ninepence an acre for his ground as a sheep run, when he can obtain a shilling or more for it as a deer forest. A red-hot Radical, a landed proprietor recently elected to represent an important Scottish county in Scotland, was accused at the time of his candidature of being in possession of a deer forest; his reply was, " The ground is only fit for wild animals, and as a deer forest it is put to its best use."

It has been proved that very large sums of money have been expended in the Highlands by owners and tenants of deer forests; one gentleman gave it in evidence, that his expenditure over a period of eighteen years embraced a sum of £105,000 ; another gentleman expended eighty thousand pounds more than that. Quite as many men are employed on a deer-forest estate as there would be on a sheep run of the same area, and at rather better wages. The persons employed in the forests and on the grouse-shooting grounds are drawn chiefly from the crofter population, and they like their employment, many of them, indeed, being able to save small sums of money, which in other circumstances they would not have been able to accumulate. It is, perhaps, not necessary to remind the reader that had it not been for the " sporting interest," the Highlands of Scotland would have differed little to-day from the condition they were in a hundred years since. By means of railways and the steamboat the country has been opened up so widely that all parts of it are now accessible to the tourist and the sportsman, whilst hundreds of persons find employment in connection with the traffic at remunerative wages.

Some fifteen years ago the figures in dispute as between deer forests and sheep runs were carefully worked out by an economist, who took great interest in the question, and who has frankly admitted, on the strength of his own figures, that deer forests are more productive than sheep walks. The same writer was among the first to expound what may be termed the political economy of the question, in respect to whether deer forests or sheep runs would be of most benefit to the poor labourers of the Highlands. His contention was (he died three years ago) that the tenant annually spends a sum equal to his rent; his—the tenant's—commissariat is derived from immediate towns or neighbouring farms; he gives employment to a numerous band of servants and hangers-on, watchers, gillies, &c. ; money is liberally expended in repairs and buildings, roads have also to be maintained. All who labour in the districts are benefited sooner or later by the tenants of the shooting lodges. Benevolence abounds: the ladies are charitable, and the deserving poor obtain the benefit. With the land under sheep or cattle, no expenditure on the lines indicated is called for, while for each shepherd or cattle-herd that might in such case find work, the deer forest employs two or three men.

Following in the line of the foregoing statements, it may be now remarked that out of Parliament there are politicians, or rather " agitators," who insist that grouse-shooting and deer-stalking should be " put down." These persons, it is almost superfluous to say, speak in ignorance. " Perish all such sports," says one sentimental Member of the House of Commons, in speaking of hunting and other field sports. That gentleman is one of those "friends" by whom the working classes suffer so much. He would, by his " putting-down " process, probably deprive fifty thousand persons, who are now earning wages by means of the sports and pastimes of the country, of their livelihood. That legislator has forgotten, or probably has never known, that heather is only a home for grouse, or at its best affords scanty food for a few flocks of sheep, and also that the almost boundless tracts of land in the heart of the Highlands devoted to deer would be of less value—that is, they would produce less rent—as grazing ground for cattle. The economic aspect of these vast areas has often been discussed, and it is well that two Members of Parliament (on the Liberal side of the House) have recently had the courage to tell the "plain truth" regarding deer forests for breeding and feeding oxen, or for farming. It is perfectly true that in some forests there are scattered areas of fine pasture grass ; but were cattle to be fed upon these, that circumstance would militate very much against the letting of the whole tract as a deer forest, the proprietor thinking, and thinking no doubt rightly in his own interest, that it is better to obtain at the rate of one shilling and sixpence per acre for the whole of the area than to let two or three hundred acres at the rate of a pound each, and have the remainder left on his hands, because cattle and deer will not herd together. On the grouse moors, however, sheep may be fed, where these animals can find food, without detriment to the birds ; and in all districts of the Highlands sheep are still being largely fed.

Although the information obtained by means of Lord Napier's Committee has now been at the service of politicians for several years, they seem determined not to make use of it. As a matter of fact, it tends to confute their long-cherished "imaginative" facts and figures, and leave them destitute of much of the capital with which they carried on their work of agitation. Their fine-spun theories and sentimental deductions were undoubtedly shipwrecked by the report of the Committee in question, but they refuse to see it. That five acres of the kind of land "devoted to deer instead of to the use of animals that would contribute to the food of man" are required to feed one sheep has been proved beyond doubt. "We believe," says the report, "that on the best forest land it takes about four acres to graze a sheep, and on the worst perhaps eight acres; but these are both extremes, and over the greater portion of the land devoted to deer forests we believe the average number of acres required to graze a sheep cannot be less than five." That statement effectually disposes of the absurd contention that sheep can be grazed throughout the Highlands on a space of an acre and a-quarter for each animal.

It is not the case, as some "agitators" have been maintaining on various political platforms, that deer have totally superseded sheep in the Highlands, considerably over two millions of these useful contributors to the national commissariat being still (chiefly) summer-fed in the northern counties. Want of space forbids me to enter into full particulars of Highland sheep-feeding, although it would probably prove interesting to describe the economy of that particular business, the incidence of which has been changing considerably throughout the last ten or twelve years; a visit to some of the "wedder farms" of Ross-shire, places where ewes could not be fed, would prove interesting. The wonder of strangers used at one time to be greatly excited by the lengthened trains of sheep in course of being transported to the Lowlands for winter keep. "Ah, sir," said a small farmer to the writer, "sheep-farming hereabout is not so good as I can remember it, the border farmers don't find the business pay anything like so well as it once did either for flesh or wool; I have been told that they can nowadays bring mutton all the way from the other side of the world at a cost of a ha-penny the pound, and you can grow sheep in New Zealand till they are fit to kill for three or four shillings each."

Were the red deer of Scotland to be totally exterminated or to become greatly reduced in numbers, and sheep to be put on the land at the rate of one to every five acres so gained, that would only mean the addition of 400,000 more sheep than there are at the present time, or a total for the four Highland counties of Argyle, Inverness, Ross, and Sutherland of say two and a half millions. But more sheep, it is said, are being at present bred and fed in the north than can be sold at remunerative prices. Far-away countries are sending us their cheaply-fed mutton, and are able to undersell our home breeders in their own markets. About all this the Napier Commission made painstaking inquiry and gave a reasonable deliverance of their opinion, the gist of which was as follows:—" We believe that if it were not for deer forests, and if the present condition of sheep farms is prolonged, much of the land in the Highlands might become temporarily unoccupied or be occupied on terms ruinous to the proprietor."

In other words, the conclusion bound to be arrived at is exceedingly simple, and resolves itself into the very easy question of which party can afford to pay the biggest rent. If a proprietor can obtain 1s. 6d. per acre for his land to be occupied as a deer forest, would it be just to compel him to let it for any other purpose at 1s. per acre? On this point the Commission gave no

uncertain deliverance: " We have considered it our
duty," they said, " to record unequivocally the opinion
that the dedication of large areas exclusively to the
purposes of sport, as at present practised in the Highlands, does not involve a substantial diminution of food
supply to the nation, and we have amply recognized
the various benefits which are in many cases associated
with the sporting system, where it is exercised in a
liberal and judicious spirit."

Another much-made-of contention of the agitators
was shown by the report of the Committee *not* to be
founded on fact. A few lines dispose effectually of
the matter. " The number of persons permanently
employed in connection with deer forests as compared
with sheep farms is about the same, the persons employed all the year round being foresters in the one case
and shepherds in the other; and in regard to temporary
or occasional employment the advantage is in favour of
deer forests."

The conclusion of the whole matter as regards the
vast area of land now occupied as deer forests may be
summed up by the assertion that it is put to the most
profitable use for its owner that could be found for it.
Of that fact no other evidence is required than that
sheep-feeders find it would not pay them to offer a
higher rent than what is now paid by sportsmen.
There can be no doubt whatever that an increase of
twopence an acre of additional rent would at once
be accepted. The whole question involved in the controversy of " Sheep or Deer " is simply one of rent, and
with mutton and wool at present prices the flock-
masters are unable to compete with the deer-slayers.
Nor would the people as a whole, as I have endeavoured

to show, benefit so largely from Highland sheep-feeding as they do now from deer-stalking.

I noticed lately with some regret that a politician, a Member of Parliament, who runs a popular weekly newspaper, busied himself in sneering at lessees of grouse moors who sell a portion of their birds. But what, I wonder, could be done with them, other than send them to market? Birds are liberally enough given in the way of presents; but when the lessee of a grouse moor has at his command twelve or fifteen hundred brace of grouse, what can he do with four-fifths of them other than sell them for what they will bring—although the sum received will not probably be a fifth part of what they cost him? Nor can the heather be turned to any better use. In some parts of the Highlands portions have been, or are in course of being reclaimed, but, as a rule, reclamation does not pay. As one of the sporting lairds said a year or two ago, " I should be very glad indeed if I could change a few hundred acres of my heather into fields of golden grain or into potato or grass land, but alas, for my ambition to do so, it can only be accomplished at the rate of about thirty-five shillings to the pound, and I cannot afford it." As to the selling of superfluous grouse, I cannot see why a gentleman who publishes and sells a sixpenny newspaper, even though he is a Member of Parliament, should take objection or think the doing so an ignoble act.

It is sport that has been the largest factor in the present prosperity of the Highlands, where may now be found in many places, at one time untrodden by the foot of man, schools and churches well attended by an intelligent and God-fearing population, as well as

houses and whole villages, the building of which and
the construction of the necessary roads from place
to place has afforded remunerative employment to
hundreds of the population; and to-day sportsmen
require an army of retainers who earn a fair living
for themselves and families. Those employed on the
moors and in the deer forests—gamekeepers, foresters,
and gillies—are nearly all men and boys who have
been reared on the scene. The persons indicated and
the mechanics and tradesmen dependent on them for
employment or the sale of their goods, would be unable
to keep up their schools and churches were it not for
the large contributions which the rates derive from
sporting tenants. Many additional pages of this work
might be devoted to arguments and illustrations for and
against the continuance of deer forests, but there is one
factor of the case that cannot be set aside; it has been
already referred to, and represents *the* logic of the whole
case, namely, that graziers can have as much land as
ever they like at the same rent as sportsmen.

"Down with fox-hunting!" is assuredly one of the
most absurd cries that a Member of Parliament professing friendship for the working man can start a
career of agitation with. Fox-hunting is one of the
sports that requires to be ministered to by a perfect
array of artizans, saddlers, bootmakers, tailors, black-
smiths, weavers of horse-cloths, hatters and others;
whilst the erection of kennels and hunting stables has
been largely a means of giving employment to the
building trades. Farm servants are employed in raising
fodder for the hunting horses, for which a regiment of
attendants are required at fair wages all the year round.
And yet there are men actually elected to serve in

Parliament by working men who exclaim, "Down with fox-hunting!"

Other sports might be mentioned that have come in for denunciation by political agitators, who, having themselves no soul for sport, would reduce all to their level. No kind of property is safe from these levellers. One may have bought, at a cost of many thousand pounds, a fine deer forest, only to find himself confronted by a Bill in Parliament to open up his land to all and sundry, and to give over his trout and salmon streams to those who like to fish them. This may seem an exaggerated way of putting the case, but it is founded on fact. Some of the " dog in the manger " men, who do not care for sport themselves, and seem not to be able to endure that other men should possess these sporting amenities for which they have paid, are zealously advocating the opening up of other people's moors and mountains (to those who did not pay for them), and the handing over of their streams to men who would speedily make short work with the fish, which are everywhere in need of more protection than is now afforded them. It almost looks as if in late years the law-breakers in sporting districts had been encouraged by men who ought to have known better; it was painful to read a little time ago of the sympathy accorded to the deer-slayers and salmon-poachers of the Island of Lewis, and the sad want of sympathy evinced to the lady who owns the land, for whom not one of the " agitators," or liberal newspaper writers, had one word of commiseration, although she could not get payment of her rents from her crofters, who lately did their best by their lawlessness to scare away the big tenants who did so much for the island by the payment of the heavy

taxes exacted from them. The crofters of the period
have been adopted by the "agitators," who have made
the very most of them, they have been sympathized
with as having in the past been rack-rented, the fact
being that most of them only paid a very small portion
of the rent agreed upon, and have now been legally
relieved of about half of the sums which had accumulated in the name of "arrears." More than that, some
of the "agitators" desire that the holdings of their
protégés should be increased, and that men who have
not capital enough to crop and cultivate eight acres of
land should have twelve or twenty acres handed over
to them!

CHAPTER IX.

ON THE HEATHER.

THE incidence of grouse-shooting, as is well known, has undergone some changes. I remember when many of the moors began to be occupied in the beginning of July, or even earlier where there was good fishing, and on which the tenants would remain till October, and often enough till the middle of November, whilst very keen sportsmen, with an occasional break of a fortnight, would make out the whole period during which it is lawful to shoot.

Nowadays, not a few of our very best sportsmen are well content with ten days at the grouse, whilst a six weeks' sojourn is a long time for many of them; but as a gentleman of my acquaintance says, " Such flying visits won't do for my money; I must have a couple of months at least on the heather, and to that resolve my wife says ditto, whilst my young folks would make a longer stay if they were permitted. My railway fares to and fro, for self and household, cost me over a fifty-pound note—it would be hard, wouldn't it, to expend such a sum in travelling for a mere ten or fifteen days on my grouse moor ? "

Signs of the " Twelfth " begin to be noted here and there in the North at an early date, when some active member of a southern sportsman's family comes to spy the land and "prospect" the hill-sides of his father's shooting in order to find out how the birds are thriving. But even earlier in the year, some time in June most likely, the keeper will have forwarded a homely report to his master as to how the old birds have wintered and how the young ones are thriving, or the lessee of the moor may *in propriâ personâ* have visited his shooting about the end of May, impatient to know how matters are looking. Near the grand day in some places, family parties arrive on the scene. The three great lines of railway leading to Edinburgh and Glasgow soon begin to indicate that the twelfth is well in view. Sporting dogs, bundles of fishing-rods, guns of many kinds, and other paraphernalia which will be called into use when they get "there," are seen on the platform. Ladies in happy parties may be descried in the carriages shaking their children and themselves into comfortable positions, men-servants are making themselves useful, whilst the gentlemen of the party, with fragrant cigars in their mouths, are taking it coolly till the signal to start is given.

From Manchester, Bradford, Leeds and Sheffield, contingents, as August draws nigh, are seen *en route* to Scotland, on their way to the moors. Note, for instance, the address on yonder trunk; it is "Mrs. Lancashire, Glen Hoolichan Castle, by Killin, Perthshire," and besides the trunk a full score of other boxes and packages, similarly addressed, are to be seen, and there are a dozen persons in the party, counting maid-servants and men-servants, likewise masters and misses, radiant with delight, of course, as befits the occasion.

It will be worth while to follow this party.

The Glen Hoolichan heather is well worthy of a
visit; it is thirteen miles from the burial-place of the
Macnabs, and rich in grouse and other "material for
the gun"; not infrequently a fine hart, and every now
and then a roebuck, appears on the ground, and after
"the first," on the lower districts the metallic twitter
of a covey of partridges is full often heard. Then
there is the Loch of Hoolich, with its occasional salmon
and its wealth of trout, fine two-pounders that, seeming
to know their value pretty well, tax the powers of
those who angle for them. As for the miscellaneous
birds and beasts, they are almost numberless, and
Robert Lancashire exacts tribute from the lot with
persistent punctuality.

"Some of them wild birds," he says, "are better to
eat than grouse."

At Edinburgh the party are met by Sandy Fraser,
a favourite gillie, whom the ladies and children
examine and cross-examine rigorously about all the
living things at the Castle—dogs, cows and pony-pets;
not forgetting the Castle retainers of all degrees. Sandy's
face breaks out into one great all-over smile as the
train slows into the station. Jumping on to the platform, the children have fifty questions to ask about their
favourite ponies and dogs, and the gillie, nicely got
up in his "Saabath day's" grey kilt and dull red hose,
needs all his wits to make his replies. Mr. Lancashire
has also questions to ask, nor is Mrs. Lancashire silent,
whilst one of the young ladies falls in love at first
sight with Sandy's splendid deerhound. As for Mrs.
Lancashire's own maid, she has been all the time quite
in a fever to attract the notice of the handsome
Highlander.

A night at Grieves' comfortable Waterloo Hotel
affords refreshing rest, and in the morning children
and servants and a couple of fine dogs depart, under
the escort of Sandy, for their autumn home on the
heather.

Mr. and Mrs. Lancashire remain a day or two to
visit the Forth Bridge and to see other things in which
they are interested, as well as to wait for a lady and
gentleman to accompany them to the Castle.

The route to Killin by Stirling and Callander is
exceedingly picturesque, as all who go to fish for
salmon in Loch Tay, or to seek the great lake trout in
its beautiful home of Loch Awe, are aware. In going to
these parts of Scotland the traveller is enabled to feast
his eyes on the finest of scenery. Dunkeld and
Aberfeldy, though not on this route, are grandly placed,
and their surroundings are beautiful, exceedingly so indeed ; but of all the county of Perth the same may be said.

Before reaching Killin the travellers will have passed
through Glen Ogle, and looked upon the heaven-kissing
hills round and about the base of which the Callander
and Oban Railway has been constructed. There can
be no more beautiful railway route ; it skirts Loch
Lubnaig and Lochearn Head, and the train dashes past
streams well filled with speckled beauties ; rapid
running streams populous with lively fish, causing
many an angler's mouth to "water," as the saying has
it. Then among the beech-trees and hazlewood copses
there may be discovered an occasional pheasant, or "a
covey" may be descried on the edge of a field, whilst
not far off the "bird of sport" itself, the red grouse of
the country, awaits the sportsman on the bonny blooming heather.

The drive to the Castle is always delightful when the day is fine ; the route is picturesque, the road winding along the heath-clad glens of the district, and by the side of little streams of brown and foam-speckled water that rattle every here and there over a miniature fall. The children on their ponies, eager to welcome papa and mamma, come into view, as the open carriage containing the master and mistress and their two friends dashes round the base of Ben Hooli-chan, and the Castle is seen in the distance, with its grey crow-stepped towers and its plantings of waving birch-trees.

Mrs. Garnish, a culinary artist from Glasgow, who has successfully held the post of cook and housekeeper at the Castle for a period of five years, awaits her mistress. Dinner is timed to be early, and already, with Mrs. Lancashire's two brothers, who have been fishing for a week, there is quite a party, twelve persons sitting down to table. To-morrow is Saturday, and after a morning at the trout, Mr. Lancashire proceeds to make up his calendar. The dates of arrival and departure of every guest are carefully entered, the different beats to be shot, and the days on which there is to be fishing only are marked out, and all arrange-ments made in the most business-like fashion. Mr. Lancashire prides himself on being a man of method, and acts accordingly.

Mrs. Lancashire also gets through her part of the arrangements. After breakfast she interviews Mrs. Garnish, and makes a tour of the store-room, kitchen and other offices, which is generally satisfactory. The days on which there is to be a dinner-party, at which some half-dozen of their neighbours will be present, are fixed, and a general plan for the first two or three arranged. The concurrence of " Robert " has, of course, to be obtained; but that is a matter about which no difficulty is ever experienced by Mrs. Lancashire. The wine cellar is well filled, and Mr. Lancashire is a pleasant and companionable host.

All attend the parish church on Sunday, and listen with an attentive ear to the Reverend John McWhirr's homely discourse—an excellent one of its kind. After sermon, the party walk to the Manse and partake of a taste of Athol Brose and eat a morsel of oat-cake. Then, after inviting the reverend gentleman and his wife to dine at the Castle on the twelfth, the carriages come to the door, and the drive home of two miles begins: on arrival it is time to dress for dinner, which on Sundays is always set to be an hour earlier than on week-days.

At length comes the red-letter day of the season, by which time two more guests have arrived. Breakfast takes place at an early hour. Sandy, Allister, and old John and his son, have been waiting with the dogs and guns for half-an-hour; by half-past eight o'clock all are on the march to a fine stretch of heather, fully three miles from the Castle, on which it has been resolved to commence the business of the season. For a period of three hours and a half the sharp report of the fowling-pieces is sure to be heard, and the blood of many a braw moorcock will stain the heather. By lunch time, as Sandy is careful to show, there has been a death-dealing rain of lead, and four-score grouse are spread on the heathery carpet to be viewed by the ladies, who have arrived on the scene.

Sport in the afternoon is not so briskly carried on as

it was before luncheon, over which, enlivened by the
presence of the ladies, the men linger longer than is
usual; but the surroundings are inviting, especially that
delightful view of a long strath, in which meanders a
narrow stream of water, the eternal hills in the distance looking almost Italian as the strong August sun
glints upon them. But to one of the sportsmen there
is a greater attraction. With the other ladies and the
children has arrived on horseback Miss Cairns, the
lovely daughter of the laird of Drumshougie; and as
young Bob Lancashire gallantly lifts her from the
saddle, it is not difficult to prophesy that at no distant
date church bells may ring a merry peal on the
occasion of a union between the houses of Lancashire
and Cairns.

When the men turn their faces to the Castle the bag
soon assumes larger dimensions, and, in addition to
sixty-five brace of grouse, "all fine birds whatever,"
according to old John, there is the usual miscellaneous heap of other wild fowl, as also two couples
of brown hares and more than a dozen of rabbits.
"Not so bad for a beginning," says Mr. Lancashire, as
his soft-stepping butler hands round a dram in the
entrance hall to Sandy and his assistants, as is use and
wont at the fine old Castle of Glen Hoolichan. For
dinner the flag falls at seven, and it is a rule of the
house that all must be in the dining-room to the
minute.

It is not necessary to chronicle what takes place
during this dispensation of the sacred rites of hospitality; the dinner bill of fare is, happily, one of Mrs.
Garnish's brightest efforts. About ten the minister
and his wife are sent home in one of the Castle

carriages, and along with them two brace of grouse, a couple of rabbits, and a good heavy hare. The night wears on; young Mr. Lancashire lingers in the drawing-room; Miss Cairns, who is to remain at the Castle for a few days, being there. The other men are playing billiards and enjoying at the same time their pipes and grog; in the pauses of the game they shoot their birds over again and recite stories of the successes of former seasons. Seated in his business room, Mr. Lancashire, attended by Sandy and old John, is busy with the arrangement of the morrow's campaign. Anon two or three of the men will spend an hour at nap, and then to bed. By the time one strikes on the great bell in the stable yard all is quiet.

The rules of etiquette are not very strict at the Castle, Mrs. Lancashire wisely considering that it is as well to dispense with much dressing and a good deal of ceremony; but on two nights of the week full dress is *de rigueur*—on these nights outside guests come to dinner.

I know another Castle—it is in another county—where etiquette and ceremony reign from morn to night, and a visit there before its close comes to be rather wearisome; one man, I have been told, became so tired of his stay that he wired to a friend to wire for him to come home at once on urgent business: a Belgravian mansion with all its airs and graces in the heart of the Highlands is too much. When people go to the country they want simplicity and are anxious to dispense with form and show. Nowadays, in some shooting boxes, there are pines and peaches, and choice vintages of France and Germany, along with other tempting luxuries of the table.

The other Castle to which I have alluded is that of
Sir Paul Ludgate, the well-known bill discounter and
bullion broker of Lombard Street. There life is as
stately and as much hemmed round with etiquette as
in their residence in Grosvenor Square. Her ladyship—
she is the only daughter of Lord Ingot—when a friend
of my own happened to be visiting Sir Paul, came
down to breakfast in a beautiful robe of painted muslin
bedecked with dainty ribbons, her fairy-like feet in
French-made slippers of bronze; then after breakfast
she arrayed herself in a fancy dress in which to visit
her dairy and hen-house; next she came out in riding
or carriage costume; five-o'clock tea saw another
change, when she made her appearance in a Marie-
Antoinette robe and coquettish cap; in the evening
(dinner at eight o'clock), full dress was, of course,
necessary. Poor Ludgate had to give in to all his
lady's whims, and was compelled to dress in three or
four different costumes every day. At five-o'clock tea
he appears in velvet shorts and black silk stockings ;
but, as he tells his friends in confidence, "it is best
to give in, less trouble, you know, than fighting
her."

Thus time passes on the heather. But all sportsmen
cannot afford to live in a castle, and to rent an area of
11,000 acres of land to shoot over, and have a trout
loch and salmon river thrown into the bargain. There
are shootings and shootings, and life on some of
them is *not* luxurious. I have in my mind's eye a
" shooting-box " so called, which once upon a time was
a corn-barn ; but three merry fellows spent a long month
in it and greatly enjoyed themselves, their attendant
being a ploughman's wife, who acted as housemaid and

"did up" the place as soon as they had taken their departure to their shooting-ground. They lived chiefly on tinned meats, and were glad to obtain the services of a boy of thirteen years of age to go to the post-office for their papers and letters and carry their birds to the railway station. Life on the moors is varied, but the sport has a fascination that is all its own, and no fear of personal hardship will ever deter its votaries from indulging in it.

Mr. Lancashire was not dictatorial, he never dictated to his friends how they were to shoot. His ideas on the subject were simple exceedingly. "You have got your bird to kill," he would say; "well, then, kill it as clean as you can, but don't attempt to bring down more than one at a time, or you may come off second best," which was good enough advice of its kind. There are lots of critics (men, I presume, who have themselves failed as sportsmen), who are always ready to lay down the "law," and dictate as to how you ought to hold your gun, how you should take aim, and the precise moment at which you should fire, as also how you should command your dogs and teach your keepers. But there exists a race of men who disregard use and wont and refuse to be taught, and who most determinedly insist upon carrying on their sport in their own way, and not in any cut-and-dried fashion. These men will not work their heather in any stereotyped manner, but will come and go pretty much as they please. Style they leave to others; the birds are what they want, and they like better to see them fall on the heather than fly away. In shooting, as in most other things, experience is by far the best teacher. As an old keeper says, "This is a game which it is best to let everybody play in their ain fashion."

Mr. Lancashire always wound up the season with a drive or two. "I pay for my pound of flesh and I shall have it," he says. "All I can do, even with the aid of my friends, does not produce my tale of birds, as nominated in the bond, and therefore I hold a drive to get the number made up; but for personal enjoyment I prefer to go out with the dogs."

One of Mr. Lancashire's friends, an enthusiast about matters of sport, lays down the law of an evening, whilst enjoying a pipe after his glass of grog. "Now let me tell you this, gentlemen; the best mode of grouse-shooting is to tramp the heather, with your dogs well in hand. Never mind how you handle your gun, let others *pose* and look picturesque, attend you to the business in hand, manœuvre to get well at your birds, and then be sure you kill them. Give me a fine glowing day with a nice gentle breeze blowing, and let me grass a score of grouse; that amount of sport will satisfy me. Others may have an ambition to kill double or treble that number; let them. I shall not be led into that temptation; a five-mile tramp out and a five-mile tramp home, and a bird every here and there, satisfies me in the amplest possible fashion. So also on the stubbles. I have no ambition to be a partridge butcher, nor in the park preserves do I desire to pot more than a couple of dozen pheasants, even when they are brought to the gun in hundreds."

Here is what "Christopher North" once said on the subject. It was one of his breakfast mornings, when, clad in his shooting-jacket, he was entertaining a little party of his students, in his house at Gloucester Place,

to good cheer and cheerful chat, as was often the case
during the University session.

Some of the men being due on the moors on the
coming twelfth, to make their *début* amid the moor-
fowl, he thus addressed them :—

"Now, my lads, don't be in a hurry when you go on
the heather, don't attempt to shoot all your birds in one
season. Go to work deliberately, and don't make a toil
of what is a pastime. *Sport* is implied not so much in
quantity as in quality ; play a waiting game ; you are
young, and in the fulness of time you may see many a
year come round on the heather-covered moors. Let
your eyes follow the birds you raise with tenderness,
let no spirit of revenge enter into your mind as you
view your moorcock, do not fire at the bird as you would
at some wild cat or wolf ; bear in mind the days to come,
there will be for you a long procession of to-morrows.
Don't think it poor sport if you only bag a score of
birds for your day's work ; remember you are sportsmen,
not poulterers. And I pray you look well around, and
study and learn all you can. Be on the look out for a
lesson if you can get one. Shoot, by all means, and
take the necessary pains to shoot well ; attune your
thoughts to the scene, keep your mind's eye open, there
are other things on our vast stretches of heather
than grouse. The forester (and his gillie as well) is
most probably a character worth your studying ; he
may entrance you during luncheon by the narration of
some wonderful old legend or awe-inspiring story of
second sight, or he may read the clouds as they float
along over the distant mountain-tops, their edges gilded
by rays of sunshine, and foretell, perhaps, from their
weird-like and ever-changing shapes some lines of your

destiny. I confess to many such experiences. Ian or Donald may not be scholars as you are, not learned in logic, and ignorant of what Reid or Hamilton or Brown has made plain to you, but both Donald and Ian have much acquired knowledge. Donald, with the rudest possible machinery, can lure the trout from its home with an ease and precision that the best upholstered angler could never hope to compete against, while Ian will find you at three minutes' notice a grouse or blackcock with unerring instinct. Donald, with a quick glance at the heavens in the early morning, will foretell the weather for the next twelve hours as correctly as if he had the making of it; and both men have a presence of mind in situations and times of danger that excites the wonder of all who have occasion to know the fact."

CHAPTER X.

L. S. D.

I.

IT will be as well to include under one heading such information of a reliable kind regarding the cost of sport in the deer forests, and on the grouse moors and salmon rivers as I have been able to gather from reliable sources, and is likely to prove interesting to the general public, or to sportsmen intending to visit Scotland for the first time. The expenditure incidental to these sports has of late years grown enormously, and is annually increasing. Only men, indeed, who have the good fortune to possess plethoric purses can afford a month or two on the moors or in a deer forest. As for salmon-fishing, it is the most costly of all Scottish sports, small fish even costing the fisherman in some districts the better half of a five-pound note. As to the expenditure incurred in shooting, fishing, or stalking, much depends on the shrewdness of sportsmen, one man being known to pay a hundred pounds for that which another had at one time obtained for half the money. In out-of-the-way localities, in some of the more distant counties or islands, tolerably productive areas of heather can still be leased at moderate rents, say from fifty to eighty or a hundred pounds per annum. Shootings, however, which are nearer at hand — those, for instance, in the fine sport-affording county of Perth—require still to be paid for at about the usual rates, tenpence to two shillings an acre, according to accommodation and amenity, and in accordance with the number of birds guaranteed or likely to be shot by the tenant and his friends. An area of ten thousand acres, well stocked with birds, along with a roomy shooting-lodge, can seldom be leased under five hundred pounds per annum ; whilst, if there be also a right of salmon-fishing, and a plentiful supply of ground-game, as well as a fair stock of blackcock and a few partridges, if there be turnips or stubble at hand, it may cost an additional fifty or sixty, or mayhap a hundred pounds ; and, even although a liberal rent may have been fixed, the tenant will, as has been stated in a preceding page, be rigorously tied down to severe conditions, the number of grouse he may kill will be set forth with due accuracy, and all that he may do, or may not do, while taking the use of his moor, will be duly nominated in the bond.

All classes of sportsmen can nowadays be accommodated in a manner suitable both to time and purse. Gentlemen who are simply desirous of having a turn at the grouse, by way of whetting their appetites for the work of the partridge preserves, may want only a fortnight on the heather. They can get it, and do not require to pay for any longer period, as some other gentleman is pretty sure to want the place for September, to be succeeded perhaps by a tenant who prefers to be on the moors in the fine shooting month of October. There are enthusiastic sportsmen, indeed, who remain in the Highlands till Martinmas, or even

K

till the close time begins. As bearing on what has
been said in a preceding page, I may here allude to a
case of abject pot-shooting on the moors which was
some years ago exposed in the newspapers of the day.
A party of three Highland " chairmen " (street porters)
from Edinburgh made their appearance one " Twelfth "
on a Wigtownshire moor, which within three weeks'
time they cleared of every bird upon it, and, by dexterously laying down a few " stooks " of corn at the
boundaries of their own heather, they managed likewise
to obtain a hundred brace from adjacent shootings.

These chairmen, it was said at the time, made " a
very good thing of it," while others, of higher
social position than Highland chairmen, have been
known to combine a little business with their sport
and so ensure payment of rent and other expenses.
Such conduct has often led to much unpleasantness.
Lairds, not aware that their heather had been harried,
let their moors next years as usual ; and tenants, finding
birds to be rare, thought they had been swindled of
malice prepense, and stormed accordingly. Honourable
sportsmen, however, experience no trouble in getting
all they ask, and many gentlemen do not hesitate
to take a lease for three or four years of a stretch of
moorland they may fancy.

The rental of a choice deer forest, and the working
expenses of such a luxury, can only be borne by the
few. There is, however, one gentleman now stalking in
Scotland for whom one forest does not suffice, he has
leased some five or six ! These vast tracts of country
now bring to those owners who let them twice, and, in
some instances, three times the sums obtained for them
twenty-five or thirty years back. The tenants of such

sporting estates do not get any more than they bargain for, the right of killing as many stags; the privilege of stalking, in short—as has been shown, a most fatiguing pastime, and in a monetary sense absolutely profitless. On a deer forest outlay is the order of the day; there is no income, red-deer venison being of very little value; in some great Highland houses, it has been said of late that the domestics have declined to eat hashed venison, or even venison pasty, just as in the olden times apprentices are reputed to have bargained against being compelled to eat salmon oftener than once a week.

An English gentleman who recently rented a pretty extensive forest was very glad when his lease came to a conclusion. He gave the following summary of his experiences : " I am more than thankful to announce to you that my lease of Benmackwhappie deer forest and grouse moors has at length come to a close. I have had the confounded place now for three seasons, and it has cost me in that time not less than ten thousand pounds all told, in addition to no end of small sums of which I grew tired of keeping a note. Believe me, I have never before worked so hard—not even when I wore the clogs in my father's dye-shop—as I have done at deer-stalking. Had I time to narrate all my experiences, comic and serious, you would get many a hearty laugh out of them. For a couple of hours at a time I have walked with the water of a running stream well over my boots. A suit of clothes has been done for in a day's time, twice or thrice I have sunk up to my chest in a moss, once I fell over a precipice and startled a herd of deer, much to the disgust of my forester, Allister Mackenzie, whom no quantity of whisky

would pacify. He sulked over the event during the
remainder of the day, and doubtless he thought my hurts
were well deserved and not severe enough for the sin I
had committed. On one occasion whilst out fishing on
Loch Whappie, I fell overboard, and was not fished up
till I was nearly drowned. On another occasion, when
I was creeping about in a plantation of young larches,
I was fired at by one of my own gillies, who said he
mistook me for a 'beestie,' of what kind I know not,
but I fancy I had a rather narrow escape. *Per contra,*
I have on five occasions brought down a good stag,
at an extra cost all round for my baptism. So much
for my career as a deer-stalker in the Highlands of
Scotland."

The "miscellaneous" expenditure incidental to Scottish sport is now very onerous, and has increased within
the last quarter of a century by some 30 per cent.
The Southrons are considered fair enough game by
many of the Highland people, who make them pay
pretty well for any service rendered. No amount of
money seems to satisfy the persons who let out boats,
and their servants are always looking for more than
they are given. Thirty years ago, if you asked a
Highlander the road to any given place, he would take
great pains to show you; he thought it no trouble
to walk a mile or two with you, to see that you did not
take a wrong turn; and had you offered him a gratuity
he would have felt offended. To-day, if you were to
ask a little boy if that building is a church, he would
expect you to give him sixpence after he had said,
" Yes, sir." If the total rent-roll of the Scottish deer
forests were to be included in the cost of sport,
that of itself would prove a formidable item. There

are one hundred and ten of these forests in Scotland, occupying an area of land of about two million acres, as can be seen from the list already given, the rental of which varies according to size. From £2500 to £4000 is not an uncommon rent; but the best way to obtain the figures of rental is to average the area occupied at a given sum per acre, which may be taken at 2s. 6d. all over, making a total for the vast acreage stated of £150,000. The cost of living, and the extra outlay of different kinds, will certainly increase the amount by the sum of £50,000, showing a grand total for deer forests of £200,000.

Grouse are found in every county in Scotland. It has been calculated that each brace of birds shot costs the owner or tenant of a moor one sovereign. The number of grouse moors cannot be stated with precision. In several instances two or more are occupied by the same tenant, whilst a few big moors are divided into two, and in some instances into three or four sporting estates. There will, however, not be less than 2400 shootings, in addition to the deer forests, on most of which grouse and other birds of sport are found. In the charming sporting county of Perth—the best in all Scotland for varied sport—there are about 400 distinct estates.

The head of grouse annually killed in Scotland is large, in a good season it has been calculated that 500,000 brace will be shot. Supposing each of the 2400 grouse moors to yield on an average only 200 brace of birds, which is a modest calculation, that would represent 480,000 brace, or 960,000 single birds, which at the old-fashioned price of a sovereign per brace would represent a rental of £480,000. Travelling and living expenses must, of course, be provided for.

Taking it, as has been estimated, that there are 2500 shootings and stalkings in Scotland, and that each in the season (striking an average) is visited by only ten sportsmen, we would thus have 25,000 persons (many of the sportsmen being accompanied by ladies, children, and servants) paying travelling expenses for themselves and their impedimenta. At the rate of £20 each that will add £500,000 to the account. These figures are simply stated by way of "illustration," and like those given by an economist on a preceding page, must not be taken for more than they are worth.

A wonderfully large sum of money is nowadays expended on "fishing." To catch the salmon of Loch Tay involves an expenditure of thirty shillings a day, and no fish guaranteed. While passing a few days in the hotel at Killin I heard a gentleman say that the salmon caught by him during his fortnight's fishing had cost him not less than a shilling an ounce! But there are places where anglers are charged for the privilege of fishing, and have to give up all they catch to the landlord; this, however, is an experience that I have never personally encountered. It has been computed that there are about forty thousand anglers in the kingdom who will expend at least on an average one shilling weekly in railway fares to and from the place of their pastime. Supposing they do so for twenty weeks in the year, the amount as a whole becomes considerable, and, if the sum annually expended on fishing gear of all kinds be added, it may not be far short of the truth to estimate that as much as a hundred thousand pounds are disbursed every year in this pleasant pastime.

Coming now to consider the question of domestic

expenditure, I am able to lay before my readers the advice of an old sporting hand. The following is worthy of all attention :

" Make your moor as nearly as possible provide your table. Don't spare your keepers or other out-of-door servants ; they ought not to be idle, where there are trout in the lochs and streams, as well as hares and rabbits running about everywhere, ready to be killed. A liberal table can always, by good management, be spread in your shooting lodge, almost nothing of what is served being immediately purchased. You have plenty of vegetables for your hotch potch, choice joints of black-faced mutton—than which no flesh can be more delightful. You have an occasional salmon trout, fresh from the water ; you have rabbits to curry, and barn-door fowls to roast, in addition to mountain hares for soup, and, as the redoubtable Meg Dods, of the Cleikum Inn, used to say, ' What soup is better, tell me that, if you can ? ' You have your grouse, of course—the shattered ones for soup and pasties ; you have black game and an occasional taste of venison when a stray stag comes upon your land, and, if you have selected your location well, you will not lack for a brace or two of partridges when September comes upon you. The miscellaneous birds will be found in scores on your marshy lands, many of which are delightful and well worthy of a place on your table ; in short, there need be no commissariat better furnished than that of the lessee of the kind of shooting I have tried to picture. Your cow you will be able to dispose of at a profit when you flit, and from the bee hives in your garden plenteous supplies of honey will be made sure."

II.

Shooting lodge expenditure has of late years been much increased by the cost of extravagant luncheons served on the heather. This is especially so where constant relays of visitors are arriving; happily the practice has begun to be frowned down, certainly not too soon. I read a few months ago of a shooting on which about a dozen of champagne was consumed on the moors daily during the grouse-shooting season! It goes without saying that, when champagne is sent on to the heather in such quantities, the luncheon served will be in keeping therewith—hot and *recherché*, and, as a matter of course, costly. Such absurdities are sure to bring about a change; luncheon on the heather should, in the opinion of all sensible men, be a most simple affair, and it is gratifying to know that many good sportsmen are striving to make it so.

The following ideas on a kindred subject were promulgated several years ago by a fine Scottish sportsman of the olden time, Mr. Sharpe of Hoddam, in the steward's room on Musselburgh racecourse. He was addressing the son of a friend who had recently come of age :—

"Beware of those heavy hunt breakfasts, my lad, and eat little and drink sparingly. You cannot without danger go into action after a hearty meal—the less inside weight you carry the better day you will have; I am an old stager and speak from experience, as your father will tell you. Avoid the hock and seltzer, the tumblers of 'phiz' and the goblets of claret. If you want a great big drink, wait till you have accomplished your work. Take breakfast at home an hour before you ride over to the meet, and see that you make a good meal, then reading your *Courant* will while away an hour, after that the canter, take it leisurely, to join the dogs will be advantageous. Dine when you return, and have a friend or two to partake of your hospitality. An hour or two at billiards or pool before going to bed will do you good."

Dismissing Mr. Sharpe for a time, a word or two may be said about breakfast. The sportsman when at work on the heather should fortify himself for his day's labour by making a very hearty meal. In all Scottish shooting lodges a splendid breakfast is served in plenty of time. Salmon steaks and other kinds of fish, cold grouse pie, savoury omelettes, a roasted grey hen, ham and tongue, poached eggs, tea, coffee, porridge, honey, marmalade, flour scones, oat cakes and plenty of cream, with daily changes equally wholesome and palatable too numerous to mention. It was happily said by an English bishop while staying in a Scottish country house "that the breakfasts of Scotland are better than the dinners of England," which may be taken as a great compliment. Scottish breakfasts have been celebrated since the days of Bailie Nicol Jarvie of Glasgow, and why not? "A Scottish breakfast, with its cold corned beef and sheep's-head pie, its kippered herrings and finnan haddies, its grilled ham, its marmalade, heather honey, and bramble-berry jam, its delicious cream and oaten cakes, its fresh baked flour scones, its porridge and sweet milk, and its varied background of potted meats of all kinds, would create an appetite in the most dyspeptic of mortals." So said the bishop. After making a satisfactory meal the walk or drive to the place agreed on for the work of the day should be reached in leisurely fashion—but in good time for business, as an early hour or two among the birds is valuable ; it is the period at which most is done for the filling of the bag.

Having so breakfasted no sportsman will require very much in the shape of lunch, and that species of refreshment cannot be too light or too simple. Much has been of late written about this phase of life on the heather, and the conclusion that is being generally arrived at is that what is most wanted is an hour's rest, a drink of good pure water, and a smoke by lovers of the weed. The best time for luncheon is when the heat has sent the grouse into deeper cover than usual, say between one and two o'clock. An hour's cessation from work will then be grateful. No elaborate " spread " is required, " let each man look after his own wants " is now the rule of some shooting places. A choice of " luncheon matter " is laid out in the dining-room and each guest carries a piece in his pocket according to taste ; one will take a couple of rolls cut open and spread with marmalade, another will make up three or four sandwiches. An excellent sportsman recently told the writer that he always gets best through a hard day's work when his luncheon consists of a piece of buttered oatcake well spread with gooseberry jam, washing his mouth afterwards with half a tumblerful of cold tea. This gentleman long ago gave up the whisky-and-water which used to follow his mid-day repast on the heather or while in a field of stubble. He even eschews water, and can pass the purling brook with great resolution. There is reason in this. Man cannot work well upon an overloaded stomach ; when he attempts to do so, his

eye becomes dimmer than usual, and the trigger-finger
more nervous than when he is abstemious.

Speaking from experience, it is generally "thirst" by
which sportsmen are most overtaken on the moors or
stubbles; when it can be obtained, there is almost
nothing better for that troublesome visitant than to
masticate a fresh pulled turnip, casting out the *débris*.
A good juicy apple has also proved effective, but of
actual food really little is needed, and that taken should
be of the simplest possible description. An egg sand-
wich, composed of fresh bread and very thin slices of
hard boiled eggs, is often selected. Nothing that is
sprinkled with condiments of any sort should be taken,
as "that kind of thing" is provocative of thirst. As to
what should be provided in the way of liquor opinions
differ very much, a mixture (half and half) of cold tea
and milk, without any sugar, is often recommended by
old stagers, "whisky-and-water for me" is the motto
of others. Pure water in which has been placed a
handful of oatmeal is also a very good thirst assuager.

On moors, where extravagant luncheons are sent to
the heather, the dinners are of course in keeping—they
are also costly. Some men seem to come to the moors
of Scotland in order to live more extravagantly than
they do at home, and in consequence they have
messengers always coming from the station with fine
things for the table ordered from London or Edinburgh. These men make no change in their mode of
life, and, except that being in search of sport they are
more in the open air than when in London or Manchester, the "racket" goes on just as it does at home.
I am speaking here of "certain persons" only who
are, as it may well be supposed, new to the work.

These remarks may perhaps be deemed impertinent, as those who pay the piper have certainly the best right to call the tune, but, as an advocate of a simpler mode of life on the moors than that which is prevalent in many of the shooting lodges of the period, I deem it proper to protest.

Mr. Sharpe, to whom allusion has already been made, used to say that by far the nicest dinners were those devised by the aid of the local larder.

" Let your moor keep you, and you will be all the more able to keep your moor," was his philosophy : and the laird was a philosopher. I have preserved in a note-book one of his plans for a good dinner. First of all have salmon—in two ways if the party is large— boiled with parsley sauce and in cutlets. For entrées you can have curried oysters, a salmi of snipe, stewed partridges, and plover *à la Bonaparte.* Follow these with pheasants and a haunch of roebuck, let grouse and capercailzie then appear; in addition to which, if you' want it, have a black-game pie; apple-pudding, pan-cakes, and other sweets succeed; then a dish full of " melted " cheese with a supply of oat cakes. Have plenty of sound wine ; Amontillado Liebfrau-milch, Roederer's champagne, and claret. This *menu* will perhaps not compare with some which might be put down on paper by a professed diner-out ; but, although it may lack variety and want that light and shade so dear to the educated *gourmet,* it has the advantage of being real and undoubtedly most sub-stantial, and better still, of being in great part stored in your own larder. I forgot to say that Mr. Sharpe recommended no soups other than those of Scotland. Hotch potch, lockie leekie and hare, all of

which can be confectioned from home-grown " material."
As to the wines, they, no doubt, come to money, but the
presentation at table of many expensive vintages is not
in my opinion necessary. There are persons who think
that in the Highlands nothing suitable for food is to
be obtained but oatmeal ! That, of course, is an error
due to ignorance ; even in the far north of Scotland, on
the islands of Ross or Inverness-shire, fine vegetables
and tempting fruits are to be found, and, as has been
suggested, the sportsman should create his own commissariat.

CHAPTER XI.

PHEASANTS AND PARTRIDGES.

No one whom I have asked has been able to tell me in what year the pheasant was introduced into Scotland. Several of the oldest keepers in the country have been questioned on the subject, but with no result other than some occasional recollections of an interesting nature as bearing on the growth of sport throughout the country. A near relative of the writer could remember that in Berwickshire, in the beginning of the century, the pheasant was looked upon as a rare bird which the peasantry would walk long distances to look at.

I remember when pheasants had not in several districts of Scotland become "birds of sport," and were not in consequence killed wholesale, as they are to-day. Sixty or more years ago the pheasant was looked upon as an ornithological curiosity to be confined in an aviary, and thought to be too beautiful to kill, whilst its fine food qualities were known only to epicures. Mr. Muirhead, in his time a well-known Edinburgh poulterer, once related a little anecdote of a lady who received a brace of these birds from an English relative residing in the county of Suffolk. "She sent the pheasants to my shop in Queen Street (Edinburgh)," said Mr. Muirhead, " and then called in the course of the day to ask what

she was to do with them, as they were a little too far
gone (wasted) in the feathers to stuff, 'and I suppose,'
the lady said, 'they are not for eating.' Of course I
told her the truth, which was that, in my humble
opinion, there was no finer table bird in all the three
kingdoms."

I have seen it stated that the pheasant originally
became "wild" in Scotland by the escape of three or
four from confinement. Many of the Scottish peasantry
were wont, at one time, to trap or shoot the cock
pheasant that they might get it set up to ornament their
best room; none were poached at the time referred to,
there being no market other than of the kind indicated,
and, as a matter of fact, none among them thought
the bird was "for eating;" even some in Scotland, who
must have known from their reading that the bird was
greatly esteemed in France and in England also, entertained such an amount of prejudice against the pheasant,
that "they would not," as one old lady graphically
stated, "put a mouth upon it." To-day in Scotland the
pheasant is, comparatively speaking, a common bird and
may be seen in all its beauty from Maiden Kirk to
John o' Groat's. It is at home on almost every gentleman's estate, and hundreds are now bred every year, even
in one or two of the sea-laved islands of the west and
far north. In the course of the last quarter of a
century an enormous number of pheasants have been
hatched throughout Scotland, and to-day seven of these
birds are in all likelihood brought to the gun for the
two of twelve or fourteen years ago. A large dealer
recently told me that pheasant shooting had increased
fivefold during the last twenty years.

It is not the custom of good sportsmen to do much

in the way of pheasant shooting anywhere till October
is well advanced, so that the birds may be stronger than
they would be if indiscriminate shooting began with
the month.   Happily the pheasant in Caledonia is a
strong bird ; the modern system of annually importing
the eggs of " the bird of Colchis " from English game
farms and breeders has kept up the breed in all its
strength, so that tolerably good sport is ensured in the
preserves.   Many of the young pheasants bred by
keepers escape, almost as soon as they are liberated
from their coops, to distant parts of an estate, where
they breed, if they do not get killed, and become in
time the parents of fine broods.   Of late some of these
birds have taken to " wandering," and have been known
to make their way to distant preserves.   The total
number of eggs annually purchased by gentlemen, who
breed a few dozens or it may be hundreds, is very large,
and is increasing as time goes on, hatching being accomplished under the personal superintendence of the
keepers or their wives, chiefly hitherto by the aid of
domestic fowls, as many as eighty and even eighty-five
per cent. of chicks being obtained in many instances,
but over all it is thought good work to hatch seventy-
four eggs out of each hundred.   Keepers on some
Scottish estates are now trying various hatching
machines, of which there are several kinds on sale.
Of those brought into use in Scotland two or three have
proved satisfactory, as many as sixty-five and, in one or
two instances, seventy eggs having each yielded a
chicken.   By the means indicated, the supply of
pheasants can be kept up to any required number,
and thus gentlemen are enabled to show their friends
fair sport of a kind, when the partridge supply has

become a failure in consequence of the activity of the poachers, who seem to centre their affections very much on that bird and the hare. The pheasant, being in the home preserves, obtains better protection than the partridge, the game thieves not being yet so bold as to venture into the best-protected part of an estate, although I dare say that time is coming.

The natural history of the pheasant has been often discussed. The wild pheasant is a careless mother—frequently making her nest in exposed places, so that the "industrious poacher" is pretty sure to find her eggs. When hatched under natural circumstances, the chicks have at a very early period to look after themselves and fight their own battle of life. As soon as his mate begins to sit, the male pheasant deserts her, and whenever the eggs are hatched, or the majority of them, two or three being often left in the nest never to be hatched, the mother begins to move about, quite careless as to whether or not her progeny are able to accompany her.

To breed these birds for the gun costs money. Some gentlemen in Scotland who like to give their friends a day in their coverts pay a considerable amount every year for eggs ; the game dealers supply thousands every season. There are persons who make a business of providing eggs, keeping a large stock of birds for the sole purpose of laying. Each bird knocked over in a battue will probably not be of less value, in money actually expended, than three shillings, and yet in some seasons pheasants are so plentiful that they may be purchased by the public at the price of two shillings or half-a-crown each. As a rule, those who breed pheasants will not, for those they send to market, probably be paid more for them all over than two shillings or a few

L

pence less for each bird. The orders received for eggs exceed in some years the number that can be supplied (I am writing here of Scotland, where, as I have already hinted, the bird is yearly growing in favour with proprietors of estates on which keepers can always have it under their personal observation). Pheasants, as a rule, never suffer from "disease" in the same sense as the grouse. "The gapes" and one or two infantile troubles can be pretty successfully dealt with, and a constant change of breeding ground is said to have much to do with the successful rearing of the young broods, whilst the interchange of blood that is accomplished by means of the importation of eggs is doubtless beneficial to the different stocks of birds. An attempt is, however, being made to bring to this country, with a view to still further strengthen the pheasants we breed at home a supply of these birds from the land of their origin, the present bird of the coverts being the result of crossing.

It is not a little curious that, whilst it is not more than seventy or eighty years since the pheasant became common in Scotland, the "bird of the battues," as it has been called, has been known in England for nearly a thousand years, and was never known to be so abundant as it is at the present time, three or four thousand being annually shot on several of the larger English estates. A Midland gamekeeper on a nobleman's estate, who was recently applied to for some facts and figures about pheasant breeding, stated that he would be able, between wild and home-bred birds, to bring at least six thousand to the gun before New Year's Day. The rearing of so many birds is a troublesome industry for all taking a part in it. The quarters

of the keepers being turned for a time into a pheasant
factory. There will on some estates probably be as
many as two hundred barn-door hens employed in the
business of hatching; and what with bad eggs, refractory
hens, delicate chicks, gapes, gripes, and the other ills
which pheasant flesh falls heir to, the head keeper and his
women-kind are kept in a constant state of anxiety:
from dawn to dark he is ever at work; and his wife, too,
from June to the end of September, is quite as anxious
as her husband.

The present writer some few years since communi-
cated to the *St. James's Gazette* a paper on the pheasant
supply, but he cannot do more than guess the probable
number of these birds which are bred in the United
Kingdom. There are at least a dozen estates on which
from three to five thousand pheasants will be grown for
the gun every year, and there are three or four score
on which at least a couple of thousands will be
annually hatched.

If the inhabitants of London and the stranger sojourn-
ing within the gates of that great city consume, taking
the figure simply as being illustrative 190,000 of these
table birds per annum, and the residents in all the
other large towns of the kingdom as many more, or,
say, 365,000 in all, what stock of breeding-birds would
be necessary to maintain the supply? The eggs must,
of course, be provided, or we could not have the birds.
Hatching-mothers being found among the domestic
poultry, some of the hen pheasants have been known
to lay a goodly number of eggs without stopping, not
being encouraged to breed. If 20,000 hens were each
to lay twenty eggs, that would yield 400,000, and
would allow a certain percentage for all kinds of

L 2

fatalities. Twenty eggs are, however, a large number to give, as naturally the bird seldom lays above fourteen or sixteen; but in the way indicated great numbers are obtained, and twenty is an easy number to reckon by. Such figures must, however, be taken with the proverbial grain of salt; and there are practical persons who will have it that more eggs ought to be got than the number stated, but the mortality in pheasant breeding, taken all over, is exceptionally high, often as much as 30 per cent.

There must always, of course, be a breeding stock left, not less than 50,000 hens and as many cocks. As to the real strength of the egg-producing power of the pheasant-mother there has been much controversy, and so far as my inquiries have extended, I cannot find that any standard figure of production has been agreed upon with any degree of unanimity. The chief misapprehension about the laying power of the bird seems to have arisen from the well-known fact that several hens have been known to use the same nest, so that in some of these egg depositories as many on occasion as three dozen eggs have been found, a number which no bird could successfully hatch. Nests containing as many as seventeen eggs and coveys of young birds numbering from eight to twelve have been counted. Mr. Tegetmeir, who is allowed to be an authority in such matters, is of opinion that the eggs laid are "usually about eight or nine in number." Another writer puts the quantity at from eight to fourteen. Gamekeepers interviewed give the number laid as being fifteen or sixteen. One keeper told the writer that pheasants in the open are tempted to lay a greater number of eggs by depriving them of some already laid. During the

season he visits day by day the wild nests he has discovered, and, watching for a favourable opportunity,
purloins an egg from each, placing those acquired under
a barn-yard fowl to be hatched. Treated that way,
the pheasant lays a larger number of eggs, but great
care is requisite in carrying on these thefts, as old hen
pheasants will often, under such circumstances, " for-
sake " their nests, but young layers are not so particular.
Care has also to be exercised to begin the thefts almost
at the very outset of the nesting season, so that the
eggs in the nest may be kept as long as necessary
under the number on which the hen would begin to sit,
which she might do on an accumulation of nine or ten
eggs after once or twice being robbed. To take these
eggs is, say some keepers, a really meritorious action,
because, in all probability, the sitting pheasant would
not hatch above two-thirds of the number laid, nor can
she cover comfortably sixteen eggs.[*]

[*] " Curious speculations have from time to time been entered
upon about the powers of laying possessed by pheasants and other
wild birds. A hen shot by accident while sitting on nine eggs, on
being dressed for table, was found to be clean in her ovary, whilst
another one, also killed by accident, and which was known to have
laid seven eggs, was found to contain a great many eggs in every
stage of progress, from one or two ready to lay to others about the
size of a bean. Other pheasants at the beginning of the laying
season have contained large numbers of eggs in various conditions
of progress. These facts have been mentioned to more than one
person who ought to be able to explain them but has failed to do
so. The point to be elucidated is by what principle the laying
power is regulated—is the bird provided with a 'lachter' (layer)
containing only a given number of eggs, to be laid from day to day,
or can the bird go on creating eggs for any length of time? if so,
by what rule is the rate of production governed, and at what stage
of their growth are the eggs rendered fertile? "

As to the partridge, I have not much to tell that is new or interesting. In Scotland it was at one period a plentiful bird, but during the last ten or twelve years the supply has much decreased both from natural causes and in consequence of the excessive poaching which prevails.

Twenty years since, and even at a later date, these toothsome birds could frequently be purchased at the modest price of a shilling each, and certainly were not dear at the money. Why the "paitrick" became for a time a scarce bird, especially in Scotland, has never been fully explained; it has been said, however, that the reaping machine has had, in its time, a good deal to do with the falling off in the partridge supply, hundreds of young ones having, from time to time, been killed while the hay crop was being cut. Poaching, too, has formed a factor in the scarcity. Partridges and poachers seem somehow to be allied to each other, not that poachers confine themselves to that one bird.

At present there are indications of the rehabilitation of the partridge, which is a favourite with the votaries of low ground sport, and adds a feature to that October shooting which many sportsmen are so fond of. The "bird of the stubbles" used to be plentiful in all the lowland counties of Scotland, "thousands upon thousands" being at one time taken off the fields of the three Lothians and in Roxburgh and Berwick shires. In the counties of Fife and Aberdeen the partridge is pretty plentiful—indeed, there are few of the thirty-two counties of Caledonia stern and wild on which partridges cannot be found. At one period some of the Scottish farmers and economists made a dead set at the bird, but altogether without reason, because it is the friend and not the foe of the agriculturist.

Both partridge and pheasant afford fairly good sport of a kind—not equal, though, to grouse-shooting. Many sporting writers decry the big pheasant "shoots" of November and December, but, for all they have to say against them, not a few of them would be glad if they were asked to share in the sport. Although in the case of both birds driving is constantly resorted to, they have a fair allowance of "law" and many escape the gun. A keeper of experience thinks that not much more than a third of the birds brought up in the course of a big battue will be grassed, the others making their escape. He is probably right, because it requires several shoots to exhaust the supply. One feature of such sport may be alluded to in passing; it is that, whatever its demerits may be, the pheasant kill of the season provides for the use of the public a large supply of very palatable food at a cheap rate.

Harking back to the economy of the partridge preserves, it remains for us to say that partridges are prolific layers, coveys numbering from thirteen to sixteen birds being common enough. In several English counties the bird is wonderfully numerous, and forms a favourite object of pursuit, the operations of the poachers being in some degree counteracted by protected breeding. By means of occasionally hatching the eggs of partridges under common fowls, bantam and other hens, the number of these birds now got ready every year for the guns of the first of September has been much increased, and if partridges were to be allowed another fortnight's law that would tend to strengthen the breeds very considerably. It will, doubtless, astonish many of our agriculturists to be told that the partridge is one of their best friends; at all events, these birds do more good than harm. It has been found that one hundred partridges will, in the course of a season, eat 10,000 insects which otherwise would have lived to prey on the crops of the farm.

A little time ago great numbers of partridges fell a sacrifice to the reaping-machine at hay-cutting time. The wet weather of some years killed a great many thousands, whilst on some estates an increase of vermin led to the destruction of quantities of eggs and multitudes of the young birds, at a period when they were unable either to flee from their enemies or show them fight. " People may talk as they like, sir," said to me, on a recent occasion, a provincial game-dealer of experience, " but I do not put two-thirds of the partridges through my hands that I used to do in former years ; they are not on the land, I assure you."

My informant was speaking of Scotland, and I am quite able to corroborate what he said. Some sixteen years ago one could fill a pie-dish with the best parts of eight or ten birds—and a well-made partridge pie is not to be sneezed at, hot or cold—for as many shillings, whilst during some late seasons these birds could not be purchased, almost anywhere, at less than five or six shillings a brace.

It may be taken for granted that partridges have once more become pretty plentiful, whilst a few years ago a Scottish poultry seller told the writer that all the partridges he was selling were English birds got from the London market. " Lanarkshire," said this dealer, " and also Dumfriesshire, were wont to yield an abundant supply, but the poaching miners have done

for them entirely ; of late they have swept the fields
so completely that, speaking comparatively, scarcely a
partridge is now to be seen ; one Scotch estate on which,
sixteen or twenty years since, a thousand or twelve
hundred of these birds were usually shot in the course
of a season, does not at the present time yield fifty
brace."

The eggs of partridges, it may be stated in conclusion, are now being hatched throughout Scotland in
considerable quantities by the aid of barn-door fowls,
which, in time, will help to increase the number of these
birds.   Hitherto, from want of the proper sort of
hens, not much has been achieved by this mode of
procedure, but now that a light-bodied breed of sitting
fowls, suitable for the work, has been hit upon,
partridge-breeding will, in future seasons, be systematically entered upon.

CHAPTER XII.

OTHER BIRDS OF SPORT.

I

IT may be affirmed as a general rule that all the wild
birds found in Scotland afford food for powder. Days
at " the crows " and " pops at the pigeons " in turn find
favour. The rapidity with which shooting pastimes
have grown throughout the country is really remarkable. Nearly every third man one encounters is "something of a shot," which the Volunteer movement of the
past twenty years has chiefly to be thanked for. A
well-known gun-maker told me last year that he now
sells a much larger number of sporting guns as compared
with his trade of a quarter of a century ago, and the
demand continues to grow. Upon asking him how he
accounted for the increased number, he said it was
owing chiefly to the love of miscellaneous sport which
had of late become a sort of craze with young men ;
" As you know," he observed, " the seaside is within an
hour's walk, and on the sands you will often find a
dozen guns at work on the miscellaneous birds of sport ;
up the Forth in particular there are men constantly
shooting, and the desire seems to grow with what it
feeds on." This view is confirmed by an extensive
dealer, who receives consignments of various wild birds

from active pot-hunters who find their quarry on that river above Queensferry, and from others who seek their sport on the banks of Clyde "down Dumbarton way." The kind of birds referred to—there are many of them—secure a ready market in our larger seats of population, where they form an acceptable addition to the commissariat, and not a few of them are good for food when properly cooked. It has been computed by men who are extensively engaged in their distribution that the total number sold in the course of the year in Great Britain, counting the larks and other small birds disposed of in London and the larger English cities and towns, will not be fewer, taken at a fair guess, than four millions, but that figure is only stated as being illustrative, no official statistics being collected.

In Scotland, when George the Fourth was King, the woodcock was a rare bird. Fifty years since a flourishing Edinburgh poulterer of that time attracted crowds to his shop by displaying a couple of brace in his window, which in due time made their appearance on the dinner-table of a well-known gourmet, cooked by an artist brought from London, who also sent to table one or two other *plats* not usually at that time seen in the dining-rooms of the modern Athens; but these birds are now regularly shot in many parts of Scotland in annually increasing numbers, having evidently become acclimatised to the country, and never evince any migratory instinct. This is a fact which many persons will endorse, and from inquiries made I think it is certain that we have that bird with us all the year round; in some seasons they appear to be more plentiful than in others. During the awfully cold winter of 1879–80 they were killed in some parts of the kingdom in literal thousands, and in London were sold at sixpence and a shilling per bird. Woodcock within my recollection were very expensive, and when seen in the dining-room the event gave rise to some gossip : ten shillings a brace was not so very many years ago a common figure for these dainties of the table.

As sportsmen know, woodcock as a rule are fond of " the solitudes." They feed much in the night-time, and are prone to lie in concealment during the day— they "love the merry moonlight." They have become rather scarce during late years, consequent chiefly on the increase of killing power and the inroads of land reclamation desires ; woodcock are fond of marshy ground, and much of that being in the hands of draining contractors accounts, as has been hinted, for the growing scarcity of the bird. The woodcock is generally found where decaying leaves are forming into mould ; near at hand there is sure to be water, in which the animal washes itself with great regularity. So far as I have observed, the bird makes no long flights, and its movements are startling and clumsy. Dogs, strange to say, do not seem to care about " handling " woodcock ; why they evince such a repugnance to that particular bird not any of my sporting friends are able to tell me. The bird is short-sighted, and sees best in " the gloaming."

Numbers of snipe are annually shot by grouse shooters ; but, as a rule, those killed are very young and inexperienced birds which frequent the marshy places of the moors, and frequently rise with " the bird of sport." Woodcock are rarely shot in August or September. The Wild Bird Acts have greatly aided in preserving woodcock and snipe, and indeed all wild birds.

In searching for what I call "book-information" about woodcock and snipe, I came across the following about what an old naturalist designates the "woodcock-snipe," *Scolopax rusticola,* and, considering the remarks made to be of some interest, I have transcribed them. The date of the book is 1812 :—

"Sir John Callum, Baronet, appears to have been a very keen observer of the habits of these birds, as the following abridgment of his notes will show. Woodcocks, he says, come over sparingly in the first few days of October, the flock of that period being a sort of advanced guard which precede the two great brigades which are usually timed to arrive in November and December. They always come after sunset, and the time of their arrival is determined by the state of the wind, and not by the light of the moon, as has been often stated. It is probable that the moving power in the migratory instinct of the woodcock and other birds is the desire for food ; they seem to know that if the commissariat gives out in one place it will not fail in another. Love and hunger are the two great instincts of the animal creation. If the flight of the birds has been favoured with a fair wind, and they arrive on the coast comparatively fresh, they at once proceed to their haunts ; but sometimes, when their progress has been retarded by strong opposing winds, they will rest for a day on the shore of the sea, and they are occasionally so very much exhausted on their arrival as to be quite devoid of strength to resist capture, and so fall an easy prey to all kinds of enemies. The birds come in little detached lots, and not in a great multitude. When the red-wing appears on our coasts in autumn, woodcocks are not far distant. The departure of these birds seems

magical in some years. One day they may be seen in
hundreds, the next day they are gone, and not one left
apparently for the sportsman's pastime. Between the
middle and end of March, these animals repair to the
coast ready to embark, if the simile may be allowed, on
their voyage of departure. Should the wind prove
favourable they linger not, but go at once ; sometimes,
however, they are detained and remain among the furze
and brushwood of the seashore till a favourable season
occurs for flight. At such times sport becomes fast and
furious, the spoil falling to the guns being commen-
surate."

Snipe are earnestly hunted by many of the pot shooters
of the period. The bird is easily found by those
best acquainted with its haunts, it faces the wind and
flies before it. I have heard it said by sportsmen that
snipe and woodcock will fly to you and insist upon
being killed ! Personally I do not know much about
them, but, in one of his occasional sermons or religious
lectures, Sir James Simpson, the discoverer of chloroform,
said to his hearers, " Look at the snipe, they have not
been armed with their long bills for nothing. Nature
knows no superfluities, we must acknowledge, as we
see this bird thrusting its long bill into the soft earth in
order to find its food."

The " mysterious Moorhen " deserves a few words in
passing, it yields a good deal of what may be described
as sport of a rather tantalising sort, and very often,
when a fellow thinks he has killed one, he finds himself,
metaphorically speaking, " done." The bird has only
been laughing at him ; when fired at, it is not of course
always killed, but often feigns death, and by doing so
escapes. It is affirmed that these birds do not breed in

"England" (I presume the United Kingdom is meant),
but I rather think they do, and a naturalist has assured
me that he entertains no doubt of the fact, having seen
both eggs and young ones in this country. The male
birds are exceedingly pugnacious, and fight with a
vigour and determination that only the death of one or
other of the combatants can put a stop to, nor are these
birds afraid of man. They feed greedily on garden
stuff and possess a vast capacity for devouring all kinds
of small fruits. Writers on natural history describe
how they build. "The female acts as the master
mason, and places the materials in the proper form;
the male bird performing the part of labourer, searching
for and bringing the stuff of which the nest is formed to
the builder. When a nest is built over a bit of water
that may rise a little during a flood, it is built a
couple of feet or so above the surface; if the water un-
expectedly rises upon a nest already formed, it will be
removed by the birds to a higher level."

II.

Of the many millions of miscellaneous birds which are
annually secured for the commissariat, the pigeon—all
kinds of pigeons—yields a very large proportion. There
are probably as many as twenty thousand pigeon-houses
in Great Britain contributing their quota quietly
without the intervention of the poulterer, and as to the
wild pigeons of many kinds which come to market in
the course of a season they are numbered by hundreds
of thousands. In various countries pigeons seem to be
much-appreciated birds, and have formed the theme of
numerous essays or other articles. Of late years the

pigeon has given rise to controversy, the points chiefly
in dispute being, whether or not the food value of the
animal will cover the damage it does, or is supposed to
do, in the turnip or other fields. The ring-dove, or, as
we call it in Scotland, the "cushie doo," is to be seen
at times in flocks comprising many hundreds, thousands
in some instances. Now, this is a really valuable table
bird, abundant supplies of which are at times to be
found in all the markets of the kingdom for use as food ;
it is far preferable to the inhabitant of the dovecot,
which, daintily dressed or covered with rich paste in a
pie-dish, is so often seen in the dining-rooms of the
wealthy. But in matters of sport no hard-and-fast
lines need be laid down ; whether the pastime pursued
be pigeon-shooting or deer-stalking, each man follows
his own method of dealing with his quarry, and disdains
to be dictated to by his neighbour. On a partridge-
shooting day, on a well-furnished estate near Edinburgh, I can remember of a gentleman "taking the
pet," because some men would shoot after a fashion of
their own, instead of doing as he bade them. "I shoot
as I please," said recently a Scottish sportsman of
repute, "I hate rules. I simply want to kill my bird
without hurting my neighbour ; that is my way, others
may do as they like."

Pigeons, as is well known, yield sport and pastime of
different kinds. "Pigeon flying" is now becoming
quite an institution in Scotland, there being many
societies throughout the country devoted to that mode
of recreation, and some day, perhaps, in Scotland, we
shall be as eager about homing birds as the people of
Belgium. Those who are familiar with that country
know that the sober-minded Belgians have a mania for

pigeon-flying; so far as I could ascertain from personal inquiry, it is the one pastime which the people really heartily indulge in—there are in the course of the year set races in which thousands of pounds are placed at stake, the King and the members of the royal family subscribing to the funds. Everybody in the little kingdom seems interested in "the carrier," all talk of the pigeon, and some men make the training of them the business of their lives. There is a newspaper devoted to the sport, and some of the matches are more spoken about in Brussels than the Derby or Cesarewitch is in London. Every child in Belgium takes an interest in the sport, and the Belgian ladies, from the princesses to the peasantesses, if I may coin a word, delight in the pastime of pigeon-flying.

As has been stated, this mode of innocent recreation is regarded with favour in Scotland, where some men have indulged in it for many years, more especially the coal-miners of Lanarkshire, of one of whom the following story was published a few years ago. The man was ill, dying in fact, and his parish minister, a good man, was painting to him in vivid language the home of the angels, to which, if he died repentant, he might perhaps be admitted. The dying pitman, who had been in his day a keen pigeon-fancier, grasped at the idea, he liked the description of the angels with their grand spreading wings, which was given to him by the clergyman.

" They will be grand at fleein'," gasped the man.

" No doubt of it," was the reply.

" Will you be in heaven too, minister ? "

" I hope so, my friend," was the answer.

" And have wings too ? "

M

"Most likely, I trust so."

"Tell you what, minister; when we meet, I'll flee you for a pound note!"

Matches at pigeon shooting were at one time more frequent in Scotland than they are at present. Throughout the "forties" and "fifties" there used to be frequent pigeon-shooting handicaps, both in Midlothian and elsewhere, but I fancy the Volunteer movement has had something to do with the falling-off that has taken place in this kind of sport. "Doo-Davie" was a man in Edinburgh who used to buy all the pigeons which were killed in the handicaps, and hawk them around for sale at a cheap figure; in one season he said he sold over five thousand.

Wild pigeons afford excellent sport to those who know how to avail themselves of it. Many a man who cannot afford to "take a shooting" has in his necessity fallen among the pigeons, and, finding them good for powder, has returned again and again to the pastime from choice. These birds can be taken singly, that is to say, they may be stalked individually, or you may intercept them to great advantage when they are flying in flocks from their feeding-places to their roosts. On gusty evenings they generally skim low, and can be easily killed from a secluded hiding-place. Some who peruse these pages will doubtless be more able to teach their author how to shoot pigeons than he is to teach them; but, to those who know no better, it may be said that to bring down wild pigeons when in flight is not exactly child's play: to do so requires a sharp eye and a firm hand. Much calculation is necessary in order to do execution, and good flight shooting is not to be had every afternoon. Some sportsmen get at their pigeons by means of a decoy from a hiding-place ; a couple of tame birds may be used to attract the others, or the ground in the neighbourhood may be baited liberally with such kinds of food as the season affords, in this way a bag may often be well filled.

As to the destructiveness of pigeons on the fields of the farm, I am of opinion that too much has been made of the accusations advanced against our wild pigeons ; they mostly get what we call " Jeddart Justice," being shot first and then tried for their offence. Rightly or wrongly, " the cushie doo " has been accused of being the farmers' foe, but I think the charge made ought to be received with caution. No doubt wild pigeons have often been killed in the stomachs of which were found " suspicious vittels," but in hundreds of instances nothing has been seen other than what should have been there, namely, the seeds of weeds and various grubs and other things that, had they been permitted to develop, would certainly have done harm to the crops. Persons invested with a little brief authority are often rather severe on many of our feathered residents : the sparrow is experiencing a hard time of it, but it should not be forgotten that even the sparrow has been of use.

Coming now to the crow family, who has not eaten of rook-pie ? Rook-shooting for a very lengthened period has been a pastime of the Scottish people; but rookeries are not now so numerous as I can remember them to have been, although there does not seem to be any diminution in the flocks. Many of Scotland's greatest sons have begun their battle of life by herding crows in the fields of our farmers. Even in such an occupation much has been learned and the foundation laid of after celebrity. One of Scotland's best preachers had in his young days to do duty as a herd, but unfortunately, as his father thought, he paid greater attention to reading such books as he could obtain a loan of than to the scaring of the crows. His mother, in answer to the complaints made by his father the farmer, used to say, " Weel, weel, Tammas, we canna help it, he'll just have to be made a minister."

The rook in common with the wild pigeon has always had a bad reputation ; but those who have seen these birds hopping after the plough, seeking what they can devour, and industriously picking up all that comes in their way of worm or grub, will not endorse the bad character that has been bestowed on them. The rook is undoubtedly in many respects the friend of the farmer by eating the wire worms and the destructive larvæ of the cockchafer ; each of the birds, it has been calculated, will require four or five ounces of food per diem, and the kind they prefer is that stated.

As a matter of fact, rooks and many other birds claim a percentage of seed corn as it is being sown, but that the claim does not after all amount to much the thickly growing grain in the fields will testify. Nor does his rookship scruple to capture and devour smaller birds. I have seen one pounce on an unsuspecting newly fledged sparrow, and holding it tight by means of its claws pluck it, behead it, pick the flesh off its bones, and then carefully bury the remains in the earth ! The defence of the rook being undertaken upon one occasion by a parish minister in an important agricultural county, he took with him to a particular farm on which he knew that sowing and ploughing would be both in operation a small jury of half-a-dozen persons ;

first, visiting the sower there was not a rook to be seen, but the three ploughs were attended by scores of these industrious grubbers all hard at work, picking up worms and the larvæ of beetles, cockchafers, and other animals. "Now, then," said the reverend gentleman, "what say you, have I proved my contention that the rook does more good than harm?" "You certainly have," was the unanimous reply of the half-dozen witnesses. Farmers who have the good fortune to be near a rookery never suffer from the wireworm.

Rook-shooting is in my view rather fatiguing sport; all sport is, of course, more or less fatiguing, but what I mean is in relation to results. Rooks do not possess much pecuniary value, and to point one's rook-rifle straight up and take a sight at the branching birds is not unlike task work, most of the animals falling to sitting shots—the poor young crows in many instances are not allowed much chance of escape ; however, as many think, it is better to have a day in a rookery than no sport. It is satisfactory to know that the rook, if not esteemed as quarry by men who can command a grouse moor, is growing in favour, and likely in time to come to be better protected than in times past. I could spin many a long yarn about rooks and rookeries, but that the exigencies of space demand me now to notice one or two other birds.

Among the earliest of my "lookings on" at other people's sporting, I can recall various visits to the Bass Rock and its Solan geese. The Bass Rock is situated off North Berwick in the mouth of the Firth of Forth, and has for centuries been an historic landmark. It is still crowded, but not quite so crowded, with gannets as it was at the time of my boyish visits, when the firing of a gun would alarm the birds to such an extent as to cause probably as many as twelve thousand to rise from the island. A party in a boat with a couple of guns could shoot as many as they required, and I have seen us return to Canty Bay with three or four dozen of these birds. The "gulls," as some call them (but they do not belong to the family of the gulls), are also taken by other means, but are not of very great value for table use, the palates which are able to tolerate the Solan goose being rather uncultivated. One or two strong-minded *gourmets* of my acquaintance tell me that the Solan goose is really a tolerable table bird when properly treated by being steeped in hot water frequently renewed and then roasted; so cooked a Solan goose, they say, provides excellent eating; as to whether this is so or not I cannot offer an opinion—forty-eight years have elapsed since I partook of roasted gannet and thought it first-rate food, but I was then a hungry boy.

At one period it was the fashion at dinner parties in Edinburgh to serve a roast Solan goose first of all by way of whetting the appetites of the guests. I have often seen these gannets offered for sale by the poulterers of "Auld Reekie" at one shilling and sixpence each, the average weight of the Solan geese is about $7\frac{1}{2}$ lbs. Gannet, it has been affirmed, follow the shoals of herrings, devouring vast quantities of these fish. It was Professor Playfair, if I am not mistaken, who made the following calculation of the herring-eating powers of the gannets of St. Kilda, based on the supposition of there being a population of 200,000 on the island; "assuming that each bird remains on the island for seven months and eats five herrings per diem, that number will amount for the whole body of gannets to one million of these fish. In the 214 days, therefore, which these fowls pass on the island, they will consume 214 millions of herrings." Valued at the price of one half-penny each, a total sum of over £445,833 will be thus represented. On Ailsa Crag, and at St. Kilda and one or two other places in Scotland, gannets are numerous, existing in thousands.

It may not be out of place to say a few words here about the wild birds of "lone St. Kilda, high up in the melancholy main." There are not at the time of writing more perhaps than ninety people all told on the island, living a simple and primitive life and carrying on, when their feathered friends arrive, the business of bird-catching, in order to obtain food and exchange their feathers for other necessaries of life; indeed, the providing of feathers in quantity sufficient to supply their landlord is the tenure by which they hold their poor dwelling-places, the rents of which are mostly paid in feathers. "Imagine the number of birds which must be killed before you can accumulate 260 stones of feathers," once wrote Sir Thomas Dick Lauder, after a visit to the island; "it represents hundreds of thousands of fulmars and other sea birds of every kind." At St. Kilda those sea birds are incredibly numerous in their season, when "feathered fowls are like as the sands of the sea."

No bird, says Pennant in one of his dissertations, is of such use to the St. Kildeans as the fulmar; "it supplies them with oil for their lamps, down for their beds, a delicacy for their tables, a balm for their wounds, and a medicine for their distempers," and the oil of this bird is also a cure for rheumatism. The men of St. Kilda "fowl" on the neighbouring islands of Soa and Borrera, as the feathers can only be obtained, by constant industry during the period when the birds are on the island. Every able-bodied man on the island must contribute his labour to the general stock. The men of St. Kilda will collect and kill ten thousand birds in a very short space of time, but they are so numerous that such a number subtracted from the general stock is of no moment. Each rock and crevice of the great sea-walls of the island, and the adjacent " stacks," is inhabited by sea-fowl, chiefly gannets, and if an alarm be sounded, in the shape of firing a gun, the display of birds is something wonderful.

The gulls may now be noticed, they are the ravens of the deep. As the poet Crabbe says,—

> " Inshore their passage tribes of sea-gulls urge,
> And drop for prey within the sweeping surge;
> Oft in the rough opposing blast they fly
> Far back, and then turn and all their force apply,
> While to the storm they give their weak complaining cry;
> Or clap the sleek white pinion to the breast,
> And in the restless ocean dip for rest."

"These birds are ill to shoot Ellangowan," said Captain McGaw to me one day as the *Iona* was entering Loch Fyne. The captain's observation was a true one. Every year a detachment of them may be seen on the river Clyde, accompanying the steamboats from about Greenock to the entrance to Loch Fyne; flying in the wake of the vessel, or circling round it as it voyages to its destination, waiting for the cook or steward to throw overboard the *débris* of the dinner table or cooking galley. I have seen many a shot fired at these birds from boats, but very rarely have I seen a gull drop to the gun. Gulls—there are many kinds of them—are clever, both at eluding enemies and finding food ; they will carry high up in the air a small crab or lobster, and then dropping it from on high it is smashed into pieces, and is then eaten shell and all! I have been told on good authority that a gull cannot be shot unless you have a clear view of its eye. Whether that be so or not, it is splendid practice for young sportsmen to try their 'prentice hand on the gulls. I should say, from the little I know of gull-shooting, that if a man, unaccustomed to the sport, hits one in thirty-five, he will prove a splendid shot, for he has not only to study the eccentric movements of the bird, but has to mind the motion of his boat as well. It is a feature of gull life to join together to flout the common enemy. "When Greek joins Greek then is the tug of war" (an oft-misquoted quotation). I have personally seen a small flock of gulls put another bird to death, pluck off its feathers, and then eat it !

The following curious little anecdote has been related by a gentleman living on Loch Fyne side : "A flock of gulls frequenting a certain ferry will circle round the crossing boat with great fearlessness, except on any occasion on which there is a gun aboard ! If there is no gun to be seen, the birds will almost touch the passengers, so familiar do they become, but once let them obtain a glimpse of the death-dealing fowling-piece, and, lo ! they are out of range in a moment."

III.

What is called wild duck shooting, "sporte in ye marrisches," so far as my knowledge of it extends, is decidedly "miscellaneous." I have *seen* a good deal of it, having more than once been a spectator of that kind of bird killing which has become familiar by means of many books and the numerous descriptive essays devoted to it, but no exhibition of penmanship can exactly convey what one sees on such occasions. Like angling in reality *versus* angling on paper, there is a difference. Upon one occasion of looking on at the shooting of some wild ducks, I was greatly surprised a few days afterwards at being asked if I had " seen it." " Seen what ? " I naturally replied. " Why, the description of our adventures of the other evening, of course." " Certainly not," was my reply, " I didn't know we had encountered any." But I was soon undeceived ; there had appeared in a local paper a highly painted narrative of an evening's shooting in which was stated a vast number of incidents that, if they really took place, had passed unheeded by me ; it was very difficult to refrain from laughing at what was said, and at the wonderful cleverness displayed by my friend in killing and securing his birds. Ever since, printed narratives of sport of any kind, no matter where they appear, seem to me suspicious. But the shooting of wild ducks is a topic on which no amateur has a right to enlarge, or to offer much criticism, seeing it is, as one may say, a distinct branch of sport, with a following and a literature all its own ; the tales, real and imaginative, that have been told about duck-shooting would about fill fifty volumes. It has one point in its favour, it is without doubt a pastime of the most picturesque description.

It would not be difficult to give a long account of these particular birds of sport, in the natural history of which there is much that is interesting ; without meaning to be verbose, the writer may give a few odds and ends about them which he ascertained many years ago; as to the "punting," nothing shall be said, in case of my being accused of doing that which I have accused others of doing. Evenings in the wild duckeries are as a rule worth a trial, and there are men who are particularly fond of the sport of duck-shooting. With a tent at hand in which is kept up a good fire, and plenty of boiling water, tea or toddy can be made as required, the nights at the end of October and beginning of November being on occasion extremely cold.

The *mallard*, if I am not in error, is the *true* wild duck, and the name should be applied to both male and female. The bird is usually described as being migratory, but it has been stated, on good authority, that it is to be seen in Scotland in each week of the year. Many interesting details might be collected about this bird and others that are all commonly classed as "wild ducks." It plays on occasion a wonderful part during the breeding season, being able to remove its eggs from place to place when danger threatens, and she (the female that is) can carry about her newly-hatched young ones balanced on her great broad feet! The young birds, however, are so soon able to take to the water, that they must at a very early age indeed be able to get out of the way of their enemies. Enormous numbers of these wild ducks (mallard) annually come to market, the female being a prolific breeder. When Pennant travelled and wrote about these animals, vast supplies of them were found in Lincolnshire, then, as now, the great centre of wildfowl in this country. In one of his tours, Pennant informs us that, " in one season, and in only ten of the decoys in the neighbour-

hood of Wainfleet, 31,200 wild ducks of various kinds
were taken.   At the time indicated (about 1805)
men were willing to contract to supply wild ducks at
tenpence the couple, teal and widgeon to count only as
half birds."

In her simple nest the hen lays a lot of eggs.
Instances of fourteen are known.   That the mallard is
exceedingly fertile may be asserted from the numbers
annually slain ; from the moment they come upon the
scene, usually about October, their destruction begins,
and legions of them are shot, not individually, but
" at-a-go," the duck-shooter being usually ambitious or
killing a whole flock at a time, for which purpose he
uses a particular gun, and resorts also to many devices
in order to ensure a big bag.   The number of these
birds now being brought to market has increased
enormously in consequence of the protection afforded
during their close times.

The wild duck or mallard is the parent of our
domestic strain, some of which, as is well known, are of
great commercial value.   Many months elapse before
the young mallard becomes of table value, and even
when the bird attains maturity it scarcely, on the
average, feathers and all, weighs three pounds.   By
many persons the wild duck is much liked as a table
animal ; on the other hand, there are not a few who
dislike it.   When, however, they can be caught and fed
for a time in a garden or barnyard, they become
exceedingly good for food ; and when they can be bred
from—paired with the domestic duck—the ducklings
are excellent.   Mr. St. John was able to accomplish
this.   " Some few years back," he tell us, " I brought
home three young wild ducks ; two of them turned out

to be drakes. I sent away my tame drakes, and, in consequence, the next season had a large family of half-bred and whole wild ducks, as the tame and wild breed together quite freely. The wild ducks which have been caught are the tamest of all; throwing off all their natural shyness, they follow their feeder, and will eat corn out of the hand of any person with whom they are acquainted." The gastronomic value of this animal is discussed in another page.

Mr. James Allan of Glasgow, a very extensive dealer in game and domestic poultry, has favoured me with the following note of prices—Wild duck sell in November and December at about 2s. 6d. to 3s. each, retail price, and during February and March at from 3s. to 5s. each, according to the supply. The best and largest supplies come from Holland, and are consigned to the London market, from whence they are distributed all over the country. The wholesale price fluctuates according to the state of the weather in London. " This season (1888), on the 1st February, I had 4s. 6d. each for birds; while, on the 21st, I was supplied with finer birds, and in any quantity, at 1s. 9d. to 2s. each." Big prices, as a matter of course, bring in tremendous supplies; causing, as is usual, a great glut, so that prices fall with considerable rapidity, as much as 50 per cent. reduction being noted in three days.

Much of what has here been said about the mallard is applicable also to widgeon and teal, but I have not space at my command to do more than mention these birds of sport. Good teal-shooting is always being sought, and when found is much prized by sportsmen.

One of our other wild birds, however, is deserving of some little notice, not because of any claim it has to

be considered a bird of sport, but because of its adapt-
ability to the spit, and also from its being the source of
a much-appreciated table delicacy of the present time
—that bird is known generally in Scotland as " the
peesweep." The lapwing and others of its kind are
good for food, and much relished by those who know
that. Plovers' eggs are invariably in great demand in
the early days of the London season, and fetch a high
price in the great metropolis, to which considerable
quantities are annually sent from Scotland—commencing about the second week in April, or earlier should
the season prove genial. On special occasions as much
as a pound per dozen has been paid for these eggs, and
when the demand is brisk they can seldom be procured
under six or seven shillings per dozen. Although
plovers' eggs were known to the epicures of sixty years
ago, they did not become fashionable till about thirty
years since, upon the occasion of Her Majesty the
Queen taking luncheon at a nobleman's house where
she was staying for a few days. Being much pleased
with a plovers' egg salad which was brought to table,
the Queen desired that particulars of how to make that
dish should be sent to her *chef*, and from that time the
eggs have always been in much demand for wedding
breakfasts, luncheons, and ball suppers. Reader, when
you ask for plovers' eggs be sure you get them, as the
eggs of other birds are often substituted.

CHAPTER XIII.

Poaching.

I.

Of poaching, much that is interesting might be told; as a " business," poaching in Scotland may be said to have originated when steam-vessels began to ply between Leith and London. Previous to that period there was almost no illicit commerce in game: men only killed for their pots, or knocked over a few hares for the sake of their skins, which were at one time valuable. Grouse and partridges were not so much appreciated half a century ago as they are to-day, and the pheasant, when it became known in Scotland, was only surreptitiously killed in order to be stuffed and exhibited as a household ornament!

Game used to be forwarded to London by the smacks, but these vessels were, on many occasions, so long on the passage, that the stuff on their arrival in the Thames was found to be unsaleable. At the time referred to, men who tried their hand at poaching had to be contented with nominal prices, except at the time when fur of all kinds was in much demand, and when hares and rabbits were killed and skinned on the fields, the carcasses being there and then buried. I remember when hares could be purchased for sixpence each; sixpence,

indeed, was a common *wholesale* price, and no wonder—
a quarter of choice grass-fed lamb could often be purchased in the summer months at the same price. Hence
poaching, as a business, had not assumed the extensive
ramifications of the last twenty-five years. As a pastime,
however, poaching has prevailed from the earliest days.
In some Scottish counties gentlemen were slow to
recognise the fact, and great demoralisation ensued
before efficient steps could be taken to stop it. Had
some of our landowning magnates been quicker to act,
poaching would never probably have attained the
dimensions of these later years, during which it
has taken place on a larger scale than our forefathers
would have thought possible.

With the introduction of steam carriage from Scotland
to London, the commissariat of the great metropolis
began to be enriched by the game birds and fish of old
Caledonia. As the demand for these choice additions
to the metropolitan bills of fare increased, poaching
increased also, and numerous persons speedily took
part in carrying on the illicit traffic, great care being
taken by such dealers to avoid discovery; much
caution was therefore exercised by those who came
into direct communication with the poachers, who
received the game in small quantities as opportunity
offered. The spoil was usually hidden in back shops, or
"planted" in cellars till the time arrived for transference;
while much of the game of that period reached individual
customers and country hotels by circuitous routes and
peculiar messengers, direct from the poachers. The lax
morality of well-to-do shopkeepers, and even merchants
of capital, in purchasing poached game, furred or
feathered, was not a little remarkable; it was of kin to

the extensive dealing which everywhere took place at an earlier period in smuggled whisky and in brandy and tea, upon which no duty had ever been paid.

Before the railway era, heavy goods from country districts were usually sent to towns by means of common carriers, and that being so it was not the practice for any quantity of game to be transmitted at one time, because of the limited carrying capacity and slow rate of progress of the carriers, who, as a rule, were well known; their routes and the kind of goods they carried being patent to all along their line of travel, and, although some of the body might be unscrupulous, the majority were undoubtedly respectable men, who would have refused to countenance any organised system of poaching. Nevertheless, many a poached hare and salmon found their way from country to town by means of the carrier's cart. In larger towns, when facilities of transport became greater, "collections" were made by various persons "in the trade" to be forwarded to Liverpool, Manchester, and London. These consignments of game were so disguised in packing as to deceive persons on the outlook for them, who were not so sharp in those days as their successors of the present period.

Cash payments in all poaching transactions were the rule, and the person who took the most trouble and had the greatest risk in the matter, namely, the poacher, was very poorly paid for his dishonest dealings. For a hare he would get sixpence, for a pheasant ninepence, and for partridges about tenpence a brace; the profit on these, on their being handed from the receiver to the collector, would average all over about three halfpence a head, and the person who sent them to market took his chance. If game was scarce, his profits

N

were large; if there came a glut, he might sustain a loss.

Coming down to a later period, I used to be in the confidence of a poor waif who was often loafing about the Edinburgh livery stables in " the thirties," his name was Jamie Skinners, and he knew perfectly every rood of ground in Midlothian ; at one time he was employed in the stables of Mr. Ramsay of Barnton, and he also found employment of various kinds through the kind-hearted coachman of Mr. Allan, the banker, on the neighbouring estate of Lauriston ; it was in the harness-room of Lauriston Castle I first heard related many of Jamie's poaching adventures.   This poor man was thought by some to be " daft," but if so his madness was not without method ; at all events he enjoyed the reputation of being one of the cleverest poachers in the county, no man was more " knowing " when there was a hare to be snared or a pheasant to " smeek." The home park at Dalkeith Palace was one of his hunting-grounds, he quite looked upon the Duke of Buccleuch's game as being " as much mine as his ! " The plantations of Barnton, too, yielded him tribute on two or three nights of each week, after the short days had set in.

Poor Jamie was in reality a sort of simpleton ; had he not been so, he might have made money by his poaching. So far as I know, he never came under the ban of the police, not then so active, however, as they are to-day. Skinners had a number of patrons whom he supplied with occasional hares or rabbits, poached of course ; for these he was paid in kind by grocers and butchers, as also by keepers of public-houses, who were good customers ; a few ounces of tea and a pound of sugar

for a brace of partridges, and a bit of beef or mutton for
a hare and a pair of rabbits, was what Jamie preferred ;
it was a saying of his that "they things were not
worth money." Such spoils of Barnton and the neighbouring estates of Cramond and Lauriston, in the shape
chiefly of ground game and partridges—pheasants were
hardly then so plentiful as they are to-day—were
bartered in the manner named by Jamie. In Jamie's
time county policemen had not been called into requisi-
tion ; at all events, if they had been constituted, they
were seldom seen, and did not think it any part of
their duty to put disagreeable questions to persons who
certainly looked all over like poachers, their pockets
being distended by a few birds or a couple of hares—
rabbits no man thought of concealing. That being so,
Jamie flourished for years in the poaching line, and
long continued to be a sort of oracle in the smiddy of
Jemmy Jack at Davidson's mains, to which allusion has
already been made in the pages devoted to coursing.

No bribe or promise of reward would induce poor
Jamie to meddle with domestic poultry of any kind ; it
was only "wild beasts," as he called game, that he
meddled with. It was known to his credit that he
more than once pointed out to the farmers' wives
places where their turkeys had made nests and were
"laying away," as the phrase goes. Upon one occasion
when a grocer's wife commissioned him to get her a pair
of ducklings, his reply was prompt, "Buy them,
mistress, buy them ; ye can get them for siller, ye ken ;
what I bring are no worth money, and if I was to bring
ye ducks it wad be stealing, ye ken, and stealing's a
great sin." But, all the same, Jamie exacted tribute of
hares and partridges from Mr. Ramsay of Barnton.

Skinners was a stout man, rather flabby-like taken all over, walking with a slouching gait and usually clad in some one's old clothes. The Laings of the Royal Horse Bazaar in Edinburgh were kind to him in this matter. No person knew where Jamie slept; the poor waif had no home, and did not even sleep in hay-lofts to which he had access; he was a "mystery" during the years I knew him, and a mystery he remained to the end of his days. Where he died, or of what disease, or where he was buried, no one could tell. The last I saw of him was in Cramond Churchyard, when one fine June Sunday he sat listening to the service, the church doors being open. The poor fellow used many a time to sit and look long and wistfully at a particular grave in that old kirkyard, which some of the wise folks of the parish said was the grave of his mother. In the days of Jamie Skinners, the grounds of Barnton, and the adjacent estates of Lauriston, Cramond, and Dalmeny were a very paradise of the poaching fraternity. Being within four miles of Edinburgh, a ready market was at hand for the disposal of the game, so that there was little trouble and almost no chance of detection. A good story was told of a coachman of the period ('tis many years ago) who was very obliging in the matter of watching the churchyard, a sad necessity of sixty years since, when "bodies" were eagerly sought by medical men for dissection. Well, this good coachman, who could at any time be relied upon to take a neighbour's turn of duty, never came home on such occasions without having a hare or two, or a brace of whatever birds might be in season, in his pockets. He was, in fact, an accomplished poacher, and, whilst supposed to be on duty in the watch-house of Cramond Churchyard, he was often enough engaged in "finding" a hare, or "smeeking" a pheasant.

In one of our most popular polemical publications there appeared two or three years since what might well be termed a defence of poaching; at any rate the writer of the paper propounded the idea that poaching was not a moral offence! If that be so, it will require a clever casuist to draw the line between moral and other offences. If, for instance, a person pays three hundred pounds a year for a grouse moor, and by so doing obtains the sole right to the birds thereon, how can it be no moral offence for a band of poachers to net that gentleman's heather and send away a portion of his stock of birds to be disposed of in London or Manchester for a good round sum of money? To continue the argument, when, may it be asked, do game birds become property? Suppose, for instance, that a dealer purchases a covey of poached partridges, would it constitute a case of theft to take them from his shop, and if so, would that be a "moral offence"? If it was no moral offence for the poacher to take these birds off the fields, surely it could not be a moral offence to seize them in the poulterer's shop and carry them away. Again, the same writer, putting his arguments, so to speak, in the mouth of a working man, deprecates the keeping of an army of policemen for the detection of poachers; but, as proprietors of land pay taxes like other people, ought not their property to be protected? But, in the eyes of this writer, policemen are evidently men for the protection of warehouses and shops only. This logic cannot last, at all events it will not be generally endorsed. A country manufacturer objected that he should be taxed for policemen to apprehend salmon

poachers ; then said a county gentleman who was
present, " We will just go quits, for I object to be taxed
for the watching of your weaving shop. You have just
said that I ought to pay for the protection of my salmon,
and therefore I repeat your own argument—pay for the
protection of your manufactory." Under the auspices
of the writer referred to, we might very soon have a
new edition of the old story, altered of course to suit :—

" At a meeting of the poachers of the United Kingdom, the following resolutions were unanimously proposed and adopted : 1. The earth is the Lord's, and the
fulness thereof. 2. He has given it to His people. 3.
We are His people."

Many sketches of the men who certainly do not
consider poaching a " moral offence " might be given in
these pages, but one will perhaps be thought enough ; it
is typical. The name of this man was Bob Sykes
(perhaps he is still alive) ; he was born in Lincolnshire,
and continued to live in various parts of that county
for many years. At an early period of his life he had
been convicted of poaching, having been detected in
snaring two hares. The conviction taught him to
proceed with caution, and, although closely watched, his
future expeditions were so well planned that he escaped
detection for years, and once, when pulled up, the case
could only be made out one of trespass. Bob for a
time had the reputation of being an habitual drunkard,
but the drink was a mask to cover his misdeeds. On
such nights as he became intoxicated at the village ale-
house and was helped home, he had business in hand,
and after he was supposed to be in bed he would be a
couple of miles or so distant from his house busy at
work, and long before daylight come home to bed.

He never brought any game home with him ; the fur
and feather killed by him were invariably " planted " at
a place agreed upon and carried off by his pals, who
sent them to London, receiving in due course a remit-
tance for the jobs. Bob moved about from place to
place in the county, generally within a radius of some
twelve or fourteen miles, and, in conjunction chiefly
with a small innkeeper who managed the business part
of the transactions, made a good deal of money. Another
of the same, and living in the same county, was Bushell,
who called himself a rat-catcher and vermin-trapper.
In his early days as a poacher he was more than once
caught and punished, since which he has acted with
great cunning. No person employs him or his ferrets,
but for all that he lives well, pays the rent of his house
regularly, and never seems to be in want of anything.
Remittances of money come to him every now and
then from London and Liverpool, and he is frequently
absent from home for a week at a time, leaving usually
in a spring-cart which comes to lift him.

Such men as these and their " pals " find plenty of
" work " cut out for them in the course of the season,
which being short, requires that they should be industrious. They have to earn their year's keep within three
months. They devote themselves largely to partridge
poaching, these birds being annually netted in spite of
all precautions. On grass fields and stubbles which
were known in the breeding season to be populous with
young birds, the shooting, when the time arrives, is
lamentably scanty ; and no wonder, seeing that the
ground has been gone over by an organised gang of men
who have lifted off a few thousand acres many
hundreds of the best birds. In several English counties

there are still families noted for their skill in poaching —men who can outwit the most astute keepers and shrewdest watchers, and carry away a covey almost before their eyes. Considerable sums of money are earned by some of these persons during the partridge season, and many of those who engage in the illicit trade are cunning enough to live far away from the scene of action. They can reach the field of operations from a distance of twenty-five or thirty miles by means of a dogcart about nightfall, and before dawn they will have filled the game bags and departed, leaving no trace of whence they came or whither they have gone. Partridges do not bring such a figure in the market as grouse, but a pretty good total can be run up with the dealer before the close of the season, especially in those years in which the birds are abundant. Poachers are not, of course, pleased when prices become too low; they like to realise a shilling a bird at least. The professional poacher, when he has done with the partridges, begins with the pheasants, hares, and rabbits he finds at all times ready to his hands.

Grouse poaching continues in spite of all the precautions which can be taken. The epicure must have his bird on the "Twelfth"—it must be "high," too— and, as a matter of fact, grouse are to be seen in the poulterers' shops even before breakfast-time on that day, ready for all comers who possess the wherewithal to purchase them. There is, of course, only one way of accounting for this readiness of accommodation on the part of our game-dealers; the early birds must have been obtained in some way from the poachers, and, as it is a general rule to keep grouse for a time before cooking them, the birds must undoubtedly have been

taken eight or ten days before it became legal to
kill them. And even in the case of birds not ready
for the spit, but which can always be found for
sale early on the morning of the "Twelfth," it is
only reasonable to conclude that most of them are
poached birds, seeing there are no stretches of heather
so near London as to admit of grouse being shot
and then sent on by railway train to be on sale
by nine o'clock in the morning; besides, the birds in
question are nearly all of them Scotch birds. In very
early seasons, grouse are most industriously netted
wherever there is a chance of its being successfully
done; hundreds of birds being forwarded to the large
seats of population to be in readiness for the high prices
which are usually obtained during the first two or three
days of the grouse season, when it is utterly impossible
for birds shot in Perthshire or on the more distant
moors of Inverness-shire on the "Twelfth" and succeeding days to be in London, Birmingham, or Manchester.

The sums derived from the sale of poached birds are
tempting—probably 6s. or 7s. a brace; and the poachers
who are cunning enough and sufficiently active are able
to make a "good thing" of it during the end of July
and the beginning of August by their illegal traffic. It
is already well known to the initiated that a very large
number of the birds which were on sale at an early hour
on last "Twelfth" could not have been shot, but had,
in fact, been netted by industrious poachers some week
or two before, and had been sent to London and Manchester by train, probably packed in herring barrels or
salmon boxes, such packages being pretty well known
by the officials on two or three lines of railway as "fish
with feathers on them." That saying was originated, I

believe, by a little boy, the son of the station-master on a northern line of railway, who, being curious to see what kind of fish were contained in a certain box, found on inserting his hand that they were covered with feathers—that, in short, as the station-master at once discovered, the box was filled with grouse. A considerable sum of money is annually earned by not a few of the gangs of grouse poachers, as was made known in the course of a recent prosecution. Some industrious grouse poachers in the north of Scotland thought it an exceedingly poor season if they had not a sum of £150 for division after a couple of months' work. As these men obtained half-a-crown each for their early birds, the number they were able to send off soon came to money. They were, however, greatly put to it in the end to disguise from the railway authorities the commodity in which they dealt; but their difficulties were frequently overcome by the ingenuity of their wives and daughters, who packed the birds in clothes trunks and crockery hampers. At the present time, during the season, over two thousand brace of grouse will be sent from Scotland to England packed, as has been hinted, in herring barrels and salmon boxes ; but not consigned, for reasons of prudence, to poultry or game dealers.

It was stated a year or two ago in a game law debate that three men living in Derbyshire could earn in July and August during good seasons about £70 each by poaching; before the 8th or 9th of August they would have a hundred brace in London, and perhaps as many in Manchester and Birmingham. The poacher, it may be remarked, is a great student of the market; his birds always arrive in time to command the highest prices which are to be obtained; never by any chance does he send a consignment at a time when there is likely to be a glut; and the poacher's birds are always "A 1" in quality, for the very good reason that, as he takes them alive, he is able to select the best and allow the others to escape, knowing that he will be able to capture them when they are in better condition for the table. No poacher is so stupid as to send "cheepers" or "piners" to his merchant; as a rule, poached birds are the best on the moor to which the poacher who knows his business has access.

The persons engaged in the following little plan will not surely be defended by the writer who thinks that poaching is not immoral, but it is so difficult to draw the line, one never knows; at any rate the following series of frauds were really perpetrated in the way described :—" A curious scandal in connection with the grouse trade was disclosed a few years ago. It was occasioned by the cunning of a family (a father and two of his sons) who acted as guards on one of the northern lines of railway. These men bought from keepers, through the agency of a confederate who shared in the profits of the swindle, all the poor grouse which could be obtained—" cheepers," " piners," and " cripples" especially. These birds, by arrangement, were carefully packed and consigned to a dealer in the south. Half-a-dozen hampers, we shall say, having been filled with these outcasts of the moors, and duly labelled and sent to the station, were operated upon as soon as ever the train started by two brothers who regularly travelled by the train as guards; these men opened all the hampers of grouse sent by the same train, and, selecting the largest and fattest birds, replaced them with "piners" or "cheepers." Boxes consigned to private

individuals were first operated upon, because persons
who receive presents of grouse do not usually look their
gift-horse in the mouth, and therefore, in acknowledging
receipt of such a present, say nothing about the quality
of the birds.   Dealers, of course, are not so reticent, and
credit the account of the senders with the prices only
which the birds are worth.   The "oracle" was, however,
worked in this way—the grouse sent as presents to
private persons were first selected ; and, if there were
not enough of these, the birds were changed and changed,
all round, till even the dealers could hardly make a
complaint.   The fine, heavy half-dozen brace of plump
birds consigned to Lady A. were at once seized upon by
the two guards ; but they could not put in their very
"starvelings," because Lady A. was a judge of grouse.
So they operated on all the other hampers till they
"worked round," and in the end, of the thousands of
birds sent forth by that particular train, the *crême de la
crême* of the lot were found to be consigned to Messrs.
O. P. and Q., the consignees being X. Y. Z., of Inverdeen.
The price paid for the "cheepers" was at the rate of
about 6*d.* per bird, but the price credited to the
manipulators was nearly 7*s.* per brace—a most excellent rate of profit certainly ! "

II.

Having as a Tweedside boy "enjoyed" for several
years a fair run among the fish poachers, I think I am
competent to say a few words about the illicit traffic in
salmon which was largely carried on half a century ago,
and is still actively pursued when opportunity serves,
which indeed has become a trade of considerable

magnitude, not less than a hundred tons of unseasonable
fish of the salmon kind being, it is thought, annually
exported from Scotland to England and France, where,
after being nicely flavoured by competent cooks, it is
sent to table in palatable guise. For every couple of
salmon legally caught another one is reported to be
poached. On Tweed and its tributaries, as many as
from six to eight thousand fish annually fall a prey to
the "black fishers" at the period of their greatest
value—namely, just as they are about to spawn, and
even sometimes in the very act of spawning. All this
means, in plain language, that the public have to pay
about a third more for the salmon they consume than
would be the case if there were no poaching.

"These picturesque scoundrels, the salmon poachers,"
as the late Mr. Buckland said, "give no end of trouble."
That gentleman was right; there has been more ill
done and more annoyance given by fish poachers than
by men who wreck the partridge and pheasant preserves
or "work the oracle" on the grouse moors. The river
Tweed has for longer than a hundred years proved a
profitable preserve for the poacher. None but persons
having personal opportunities of becoming acquainted
with the facts and figures of capture are able to
estimate the evil done to the fisheries in the spawning
season by the ruthless slaughter of breeding fish.

I was told by a Tweed poacher that to take eighteen
or twenty big salmon in a night was looked upon as
"poor sport." These fish—I am speaking of a period
which embraced from the year 1852 to 1865—were
sold to English buyers, some of them being boiled and
disposed of as potted salmon; but the majority found
their way to the Continent, a practice which I have

been informed still continues. Tweed and its numerous
tributaries have from the days of the old border feuds
been infested by poachers; indeed, there is scarcely a
dweller on Tweedside who does not consider that "the
fish" are as much his property as they are the property
of the proprietor of a fishery or his tenant. No man on
Tweedside looks upon poaching as a crime or even an
"offence," and there are families thereabout in whom
the poaching blood has circulated for many generations.
Mr. Alexander Russell (of the *Scotsman*, author of 'The
Salmon') used to tell a story of four generations of the
same family being "had up" all at one time for illegal
netting! To pay the wages of watchers and the cost of
prosecuting poachers, the Tweed salmon fishery proprietors assess the rentals they receive to the extent
annually of 20 per cent., by which, on a rental of about
£13,000, they obtain a sum of nearly £2500 a year
with which to fight the "picturesque scoundrels" who
make war upon the fish chiefly within the close season.

In one or two of the border villages the women have
been known to play their part in the poaching of the
period as well as the men. Not only can they lend a
hand in capturing the fish, they are clever in hiding or
disposing of them as also in the art of throwing the
watchers off the scent, so that one part of a stream
might be spoliated, whilst the bailiffs, having been lured
to another locality, were powerless to interfere. Many
tales might be told of salmon poaching under difficulties;
of border frays and terrible encounters with the water
watchers; but they are all of the same kind, and must
end in the confession that even now, with a wide-
awake body of river police educated up to all the tricks
of the business, the poacher has still the best of it.

One great feat, performed by a woman who was known from her colour as " Quadroon Bell," is still a sore point on Tweedside. Under the pretence that she was assisting a daughter engaged in domestic service "to flit," *i.e.*, to remove to a new situation, this clever woman obtained the assistance of a Tweed bailiff to hurl on a wheelbarrow a heavy trunk to the railway station ; that trunk, it is needless to say, contained a few salmon packed in ice, which ultimately found their way to Newcastle-upon-Tyne ! This incident reminds me of an Edinburgh story, in which a thief-taker in search of a stolen hundred-pound note was made by a notorious woman to carry about in his hand the stolen treasure as he searched the house, the note having been previously wrapped round the end of a tallow candle inserted in a ginger-beer bottle. Other tales of salmon smuggling in which the Tweedside women played a part might be related, but the above is one of the best.

In the matter of salmon poaching, it is a fact now pretty well known that the fishermen honestly engaged during the season in carrying on the net fishing on both Tay and Tweed " keep their hand in " during the close seasons. Several of them have been detected and punished, and very properly, seeing they obtain remunerative and easy work during the six months of the fishing season. As that class of men are versed in the habits of the fish, as well as being familiar with places where they can be advantageously captured, they deserve no sympathy for the fate which overtakes them when their sins are found out ; they are men who poach for the markets and not for their own pots.

About thirty years ago there were a number of

persons travelling who were able at all times to supply "fish." These men were more or less "characters," and not a few of them made money by their nefarious practices. As being typical of his kind, "Fish Tam" may be briefly described—he was well known in the South of Scotland. Nominally he was a "mugger" (gipsy hawker), in reality he was a poacher of the deepest dye, but, strange to say, never had been convicted. His head-quarters were at the gipsy colony of Yetholm, a few miles from the town of Kelso, from which place he made frequent excursions through the country, going as far on occasion as Edinburgh, where he was known to dispose of large quantities of kippered salmon, chiefly at the inns frequented by carriers and stage-coachmen. His salmon were of good quality, and when "kippered" after the fashion of a recipe known to the gipsies (who decline to let the formula be known) commanded a ready sale. They were all poached fish, Tam being descended from a race of poachers—men who held poaching to be a virtue, or at least no "moral offence"; and, although no case was ever proved against him, it is certain that in his day he had been the death of thousands of fine Tweed salmon. It is not many years since Tam died, leaving behind him a sum of £700 and two small houses.

Another of these characters was known as Salmon Job. This person acted ostensibly as a fish cadger, travelling between Perth and Edinburgh, taking as many towns on his way as he possibly could, having in his cart barrels of salted herrings and bundles of cured cod and ling fish; but, as was well enough known to his customers, he supplied salmon all the year round at a cheap rate to those in "the know" of his trade, which, as has been said, was carried on between Perth and Edinburgh, doing in the modern Athens a large business in poached fish, his price being at the rate of threepence a pound weight. Fond of money, and of saving habits, he accumulated quite a little fortune, all made, as he used to say, by his own honest industry ! Salmon Job was possessed of one special virtue ; he never dealt in " black " fish, and singularly enough he had a happy knack of finding clean salmon, both in the Forth and Tay, when other people could only capture " Bagots " or " Kelts." Job was, unfortunately for himself, drowned in the river Forth in the exercise of his vocation, his body being found in the river a little above Stirling; he had been originally a weaver at Kinross, and after his death it was found that the money he had earned by his "honest industry," amounting to no less a sum than £1700, a large figure for the period, was left to his granddaughter, a poor girl, who, as they say in Scotland, had a " want "—in other words, was deficient in intellectual power—an affliction that did not prevent her from getting married so soon as her claim to the money was established. It is not a little remarkable that Job, however much he might be suspected, was never found out ; he continued to sell his poached salmon to the day of his death, and often had more orders than he could supply. He had a numerous body of assistants, but, wise in their generation, they kept their own counsel.

Many anecdotes might be related of salmon poaching. Once upon a time a gang of sixteen or seventeen gala water weavers swept the salmon " redds " of one of the Tweed tributaries so effectually as to secure twenty-nine fish, several of them with their spawning matter

dripping from their bodies; such an occurrence was by
no means uncommon, and poaching of that kind has not
yet ceased in Scotland. It is hardly necessary to say
that the catching of salmon by those who have no right
to capture them goes on all the year round on most of
the rivers of Scotland in which these fish are to be found,
in the open season as well as during the close time.
Even so-called " honest anglers," while ostensibly intent
on trout fishing, have been known to bag a salmon. This
has been again and again found to be so on Tweed and
other streams as well, on many of which there are long
miles of water which it is impossible effectually to watch,
and on these the poacher keeps his eye, the occasional
capture of a sixteen or twenty pound salmon being, in
his opinion, a good reward for his industry and cunning.
A farm servant and his family living on one of the larger
northern rivers used to earn a sum of £30 every
year by poaching, finding a ready outlet for his fish
(they were in his case clean salmon) in a manufacturing
town to which he used to send nearly all that he
captured.

Returning for a moment to Tweed, it may be
mentioned that " sixty years since " nearly every
family that dwelt within sight of its waters laid up
for winter use a stock of pickled or kippered salmon.
At that date, however, poaching had not become a
" profession," it was simply a pastime in which many
took part. " Burning the water " and killing the fish
by means of a leister was a favourite mode of sport,
but is no longer legal, although it is still sometimes
practised. Tweed anglers have a busy time of it
ventilating their grievances, which, if we can believe
them, are very numerous. " Russel, of the *Scotsman,*" in

his day a capable and able writer on all angling questions, and notably about salmon, used to scout the idea of such a person being in existence as an "honest" angler, and of all who dwelt on Tweedside he held the idea, once promulgated by Sir Walter Scott, that "all men, and women as well, of the peasant class born within sight or sound of the silvery stream think they have as much right to the 'fish' as the lairds have."

The poacher of the olden time—the poacher of the days of Walter Scott—was a respectable man; that is, he did not, to the utter neglect of his daily labour, make poaching the business of his life; the occasional capture of a fish meant simply recreation, and not, as now, a trade; indeed, poaching as understood "sixty years since" was condoned by all concerned, especially when it took the shape of "burning the water." A night's sport of that kind, such as used to occur in the olden time, when the lord of the manor and his plough-man would take each his part in throwing the spear, just as if engaged in a curling match, was a picturesque scene, productive of hearty enjoyment to all engaged. Few fish were captured, for "burning the water" was a sport, and not a commercial speculation. It was only engaged in during the winter months, when the nights were dark and the fish had ascended to the upper waters. Poaching is now a most abject trade—it is no question now of home supplies of salmon, but of a whole-sale trade; and the spoils of the poachers are commen-surate with the improvement which is everywhere distinguishing the salmon fisheries. The salmon, being a migratory fish, going from the salt sea to the sweet waters of some delightful rural retreat, becomes an easy prey to its human enemies, and thousands of these fish are annually killed just at the time when they have become of increased value ; for, however great a prize a thirty-pound salmon may be on the slab of a Bond Street fishmonger, it is immeasurably more valuable when it is about to multiply and replenish its kind.

These reminiscences and anecdotes might be largely extended, it would not indeed be difficult to fill a volume with good stories about poachers and their adventures, many of which, as is well known, have had a sad ending, seeing that the gibbet has more than once claimed a victim from among the fraternity. It is impossible, however, to say much more about poaching in these pages, having already devoted so many to the subject. The great argument of those who defend the poachers is " that running animals and flying birds are not the property of any particular person," but in the opinion of the writer they cannot be considered the property of the poacher—his logic does not go that length. Surely hares may reasonably be assumed to belong to the person on whose land they breed and feed. Partridges and pheasants, as has been shown in another part of this volume, are bred and fed in thousands at a considerable outlay of money, and, that being so, why should they be surrendered to the tender mercies of the poacher ?

The following story of how a gentleman was cheated in stocking his preserves with hares, although it has previously been briefly told by the author in another place, shall conclude his illustrations of the arts of poaching. A certain person having bought an estate, and having a numerous circle of friends, became anxious to offer them good sport. With that view he bargained with a poulterer for a thousand living hares to be sent

to his place. The price being fixed, the dealer at once
set his myrmidons to work—poachers, of course.
By-and-by the game began to arrive, and was duly
forwarded to its destination by the poulterer, the
mortality, of course, being considerable—about one in
five, I think. After some six hundred hares had
been obtained, fur then became scarce; the industrious
poachers, finding their movements closely watched by
suspicious keepers who had noticed their hares becoming fewer, rose to the situation. Determined not
to be done, they hit upon the plan of recapturing some
of the hares they had already stolen from other estates.
They caused a watch to be set upon the transport of
the animals, in order to find out their exact destination,
which was not known to the poulterer, the hares having
been removed in a spring van at stated intervals; but to
a persevering poacher nothing is impossible. The van
was carefully watched to its destination, and, to make
a long story as short as possible, the hares were re-
captured and brought back to the poulterer from whom
they had been purchased, to be again sent forward to
the place they came from! Thus the gentleman paid
for a thousand hares, while in reality he only got half
the number, through the fine irony of the situation.

The cunning of poachers is proverbial, they are the
"sneaks" of the period *par excellence*. When roused,
poachers become terrible desperadoes, especially on
such occasions as they are discovered by keepers or
watchers—then there may ensue a tragedy. After
knowing many of them, and seeing and hearing much
of their ways and works, I feel sure they deserve no
sympathy, seeing they commit their transgressions with
the full knowledge that they are breaking the law. Some

thoughtless people are crying, " Let there be free trade
in fishing and shooting ; " but, if there were free trade in
fishing and shooting, in a year's time there would neither
be a salmon in our rivers nor a moor-fowl on the
heather! So much for the poachers. Keepers have
been also known to be occasionally guilty of many very
shady, or rather criminal acts, and for the matter of
that so-called " gentlemen " do some queer things every
now and again.   Poachers and keepers have been
known to go hand in hand for mutual benefit at the
cost of a too confiding master, the game dealers being,
of course, in what is called " the know."   As to what
others do, a curious case was, on a late occasion, nearly
becoming public, which will illustrate a mean part
played by the owner of a shooting ; he had been so
fortunate as to get a well-known dealer to contract to
take all his partridges at the price of three shillings per
brace, the man having been told these birds would be
scarce. On the contrary, they became plentiful, exceedingly so, indeed, as the dealer, who was held to his
bargain, found to his cost, and what added much to his
discomfort was the fact that they arrived in literal
hundreds every few days. Suspicion was aroused and
inquiry made, and the fact was then discovered that the
" gentleman " was buying partridges right and left
from his neighbours at two shillings per brace, the
market price, thus bagging a profit of sixpence per bird.
To save exposure, a big sum had to be parted with in
name of smart money, the contract being made for
the birds on the " gentleman's own estate " only, and
not for partridges he might purchase from his neighbours to sell at a profit.

CHAPTER XIV.

GAMEKEEPERS.

HAVING said so much about poachers and poaching, it will be proper now to devote a little space to that excellent servant, the gamekeeper, on whom, on all estates of importance, so much depends. It may be stated at the outset of these remarks that the great majority of these men are, as a rule, trustworthy servants who, in not a few instances, perform their duties with their lives in their hands, especially when their employment lies in mining and manufacturing neighbourhoods. Keepers in these districts often come into collision with bands of poachers, and sometimes suffer in consequence from personal injuries of a serious description ; it is not the first time, indeed, that keepers have been murdered by lawless persons, who, as my readers have been told, make a " trade " of their illegal work, the game they obtain being usually sold to unscrupulous dealers at a reduction from the usual price.

Some excellent specimens of the honest keeper are to be found in Scotland, men brought up to the business and who have been engaged in it from their earliest days. Scottish gamekeepers are men of mark in their way, having a wide knowledge of natural history. At

least one of their number (Mr. Thomas Speedy) has
ventured into print, and has produced a remarkably
readable book. One proof of the general good character
of keepers lies in the fact of so many of them having
been for long periods in the same situation, fifteen,
twenty, and even thirty years standing at the credit of
not a a few of them. Keepers on duty in Scotland are
here alluded to ; but there are a considerable number of
Scotsmen on English estates who as keepers are much
esteemed by their employers, and I have no doubt that
Englishmen in the same situation are equally alert and
faithful in the discharge of their duties ; although it
may be prejudice on my part, taking them all round, it
may be pretty safely said that the Scottish-born gamekeeper is the better man of the two ; at all events, he is
usually better educated than his brother in office across
the border.

In an interview which took place a few months since
between a keeper of the right sort and myself, I
obtained some particulars of his way of life, which I
shall venture to make public for behoof of my readers :—

" Weel, sir, I have been in my present place for four-
and-twenty years, but I'm no sure that a day o' my
life would give you much o' the kind o' information
you want; besides, it would be ill to fix when my day
begins, or at what time it ends: some nights I'm never
in my bed, if I get a bit nap for a couple of hours in
the afternoon it's all I get."

" Oh, yes, I get to the kirk on the Sabbath, but I
never feel at ease when I'm there in the pheasant-
breeding season ; ye see we're surrounded here by a
terrible lot o' rough men that have no reverence for the

Lord's day, in fact it's the day they sometimes choose to set their wires for my hares or to rob the wild pheasants' nests. It was the year before last that my wife noticed a bit lassie in the kirkyard that she never saw come into the kirk, and, wondering at the circumstance, we set one of our boys to see where she went, and he soon discovered that she came from the colliers' row; the lassie, ye see, watched me to the kirk, and then ran home to tell her father I was there, and as soon as he knew that he was off to our preserves; but I nicked him clean by a little stratagem I adopted, and he was had up and punished."

" Hares ? Really, to speak the truth, there's not one on the estate for the half-dozens there used to be. The poachers get two shillings now for one of them, and if a man can snare a dozen in the week and net as many rabbits he'll not work at any other kind of work."

" No, sir, my work is always going on, and although I have an active assistant, it needs both of us to keep the supply up to the mark, and provide sport for Sir John and his friends; even in the dead o' winter there is plenty of employment, we have shooting parties up to the end of January, and then when there is frost I have to look after the curling ponds and the skating ice."

" It is all low country game here, but Sir John has a moor, or at least a share of a moor along with his brother and uncle; it is called the Brae o' Ballengeich. I have to be there a fortnight before the twelfth, as well as the other keepers, to see that all is right and find out the best-stocked ground; we always come home in time for the first, but the paitricks, I must say, are not nearly so abundant as I can mind o' them being twelve or fifteen year back."

" Weel, ye see, sir, the pheasants are just as we provide them; we have as many as we like, and they are a fine strong breed here; I get eggs from Lincolnshire in England, and also a few from the estate of Sir John's uncle in Surrey. No eggs are bought from any of the local cadgers, the beggars did me clean some years ago; would you believe it, sir, I found out upon one occasion that I was buying my ain eggs—that's a fact; the wild nests were being robbed by two women who were employed on the estate, they never took away all the eggs from a nest at one time, but only one or two every now and then. They carried their eggs into the town and sold them to a poultryman, who brought them to me as the produce of an English aviary. Did you ever know the like ? And the ingratitude was something awful—Sir John only three months before had paid all the funeral expenses of a daughter of one of the egg-thieves, who had died of a decline. The case nearly drove me mad, but Sir John was obstinate, he would not do anything."

" We have a warren on the property, and I kill no end o' rabbits. I should say there are thousands; I send the surplus to a Manchester dealer; Sir John received fifty-six pounds for the quantity sent last year. I have, generally speaking, over a thousand pheasants— what we sell don't average a couple o' shillings the piece. Anybody on the estate can get a pair of rabbits for the asking, and lots of game of all kinds go to Sir John's tenants, and he never has a shooting party without asking two or three of the farmers to join. When the work is over they dine in my parlour, and all the men who have helped get their dinner as well ; my wife is a capital cook and one of my lassies waits the table."

" Oh, some of the gentlemen who come to shoot are pretty good hands at the work, ithers are mere bunglers. I do the best I can for them, and help them, as I may say, no' to mak' fools o' themselves. Those of the learners that come often soon pick up the airt o' killing a fleeing bird or a flying hare, and one or two o' Sir John's visitors have little to learn—they never miss their bird. As to shooting by any sort of rule, as used to be the way when I was a boy carrying the bag, there's none of that now ; even your novice will hardly let you give him a word of advice. Every man thinks he can handle his ain gun best, and nowadays, you see, sir, with this Volunteer movement, nearly all men are marksmen—I'm a sergeant in our regiment here, of which Sir John is the colonel, and there are a lot o' clever shots in the corps."

" So far as that goes I have the fullest liberty, I get as many rabbits as I please, and any of the pheasants that are too much shot for gifts to friends fall to me. Partridges being nowadays so scarce, I never take one, but I can kill as many cushie doos as I please, and Sir John will send a pair or two of rabbits, every now and then, to any person I name that has done a service ; one or two widow women on the estate get pigeons or rabbits once a fortnight."

" As to vermin, I certainly do kill a lot—they are not ill to kill—but I do not go the length of some keepers, and go in for universal extermination, because, and Sir John agrees with me, that the less we interfere with the balance of Nature the better. It is as well

that there should be always a moderate stock of birds
and beasts of prey on an estate, as they make a clean
sweep of weak game, and that I think is very desirable
in the interest of good sport, but opinions differ—a
neighbour of Sir John's took it into his head one year
to have all the small birds shot on his land, because
they took toll of his fruit, but he soon tired of his
resolution, as the insects increased to an extent that
was unbearable, and that is mostly what happens. It
is best to be moderate in such cases."

" As I've said already, my work is never done, but I
could scarcely make out a map of it. The estate is
large, but I make it a rule to go over it all twice a
week if possible; in the egg seasons my anxiety never
ceases, and if I did not get active help from my wife, I
think I would be driven out o' my judgment altogether.
She is a grand hand wi' the pheasants, and thinks
nothing of sitting up all night when lots o' the eggs
are chipping; in fact she knows far more about the
hatching business than I do, and in some seasons she
has had eighty-eight birds to the hundred eggs, and
that is grand work, sir, I can assure you. Oh, yes,
we keep a cow, and sometimes two—there is a great
demand for milk by the villagers, you see, and it is
most profitable to sell the milk. I have a fine breed
of pigs as well."

" Yes, we have incubators now, but only for poultry;
I don't hatch our pheasants with them as yet; one of
my daughters understands them pretty well, and with a
little practice I think they will turn out profitable."

" I breed all Sir John's dogs, and keep up a lot o'
ferrets for rabbit work; in fact, I've never a moment I
can with safety call my own; but I do not grumble, Sir

John is a liberal master and has been kind to me and my family; my eldest son is in the estate office under Mr. Turnbull, the factor, and has thirty shillings a week. Jenny, my eldest daughter, is housekeeper to Sir John's uncle in Surrey, a grand place for such a young woman —she's not thirty yet, sir—and has forty pound a year."

There were one or two points which I felt a delicacy in dealing with during my interview with " Dawvid," as he is called. I did not ask the amount of his wages, or an estimate of the value of the presents he received; but I ascertained from Sir John that his wages were at the rate of eighteen shillings a week in money, in addition to which he has a house rent free, a garden and grass for a cow, or two if he likes, as also eight tons of coals every year, and one pair of breeches, and two pairs of boots. Mrs. Fleming, " Dawvid's " better half, has an allowance of six pounds a year for assisting with the pheasants. As to the perquisites, they amount, I know, to a considerable sum, occasional pounds, and a great many half-sovereigns, and no end of dollars falling in to the keeper in the course of the year. This I do know, that " Dawvid " is the present holder of ten shares in one of the most prosperous of our Scottish railways—these at present are worth twelve hundred pounds, and they yield him about forty pounds per annum.

As the reader will have noted, Sir John's keeper is a keen game preserver, of the old-fashioned sort; he would give no law to a poacher; " they're all blackguards, every one of them," is David's contention. Although of the old school, Fleming is an excellent servant, and there are many gamekeepers of his kidney in old

Scotland—it is much to be wished they should be all as good and faithful, but there are, as I have had occasion to know, a few black sheep among them. A case recently became public in which a keeper was accused, in conjunction with a dealer, of falsifying his accounts. He sent on to this person much more game than appeared in his shooting-book; in other words, the poulterer on receiving a hamper of, say, fifty rabbits, would only credit the sender with three dozen, the same plan being followed with hares, partridges and pheasants. In return the keeper received every three weeks a hamper containing tea, sugar, and other household necessaries, as well as occasionally a jar of whisky, a bunch or two of Finnan haddocks, and a couple of stones of dried fish, with every now and then a pound-note in the bargain. Such dealings are, however, rare, but I did know a poultry-seller in a large way of business who demoralised nearly all the keepers who forwarded game to him. The following anecdote is apropos :—A keeper was discharged from his situation because his master suspected, although he could not prove, that peculation of various kinds had been going on. Some of the man's friends offered him their sympathy : " You had a good wage, Tom, it is a pity you are leaving." " Oh, blow the wage," said Tom, " that was nothing; it was my perquisites I valued most, they came to double my wage."

As has been shown, keepers have much in their power, and it is to their credit that so few prove dishonest : they deserve fair wages and good treatment, and, generally speaking, masters are aware of their deserts and act accordingly ; as a rule, the keeper is valued as being the most confidential servant on the estate, but there are a few gentlemen who only look upon them as labourers, and treat them as such.

With regard to the vexed question of gamekeepers' tips, which every now and again comes up for discussion, there is, as usual, much to say on both sides. A friend of the writer, who interests himself in such matters, has taken the pains to collect a number of opinions on the subject, and has been good enough to send him the following summary of those ascertained :—

" One landed proprietor says that he deprecates these donations, and wishes his friends when they come to his place for a week's sport, to have it without cost. ' I pay my keeper a fair wage, and he knows very well that my friends will come to shoot, why he should expect them to pay him as well as myself I cannot understand.' Another gentleman, a fine old Colonel, born in the days when George the Fourth was king, told me that his keeper was his old military body-servant, and that he paid him no wages, but allowed him to kill the rabbits and sell them for his own benefit, ' and as for his tips I don't interfere with them ; if my friends like to give him a guinea, that is their business. He makes a deuced good thing of it, I can tell you.' Sir Charles Pomander instituted a box into which he requested all gratuities might be paid, so that the money should not all go to the head keeper ; one of the housemaids, finding she had a key that opened it, helped herself to a portion of the contents ; the footman, thinking he should have a share of the spoil, got a key made for the box and subtracted an occasional half-sovereign, with the result that the division came to be laughed at, and the box given up."

Keepers greatly dislike any one to come between

them and their "rights"; they desire to get their tips, and, after all said and done, they do not in many instances come to much money. "I don't think, sir, I get more than a ten-pound note all told," said one man to me, "but I make a few pounds by dog-breaking, which master does not object to. I have raised a good breed of greyhounds that bring me in some money; my wages come to forty pounds a year, and I have besides a free house and an acre of garden ground, and I am allowed to kill as many pigeons and rabbits as ever I like for the use of my house."

A keeper on the estate of a noble marquis, of whom I have heard, gets about a hundred pounds in tips every season, and has wages besides. Probably I ought to explain that the marquis lives in England, and the curate of the parish has often been heard to say, "I wish I was my lord's gamekeeper." There are keepers who from various causes have to expend little sums of money that are never recouped to them. On one estate some of the more lively visitors used to hold a rendez-vous in the keeper's quarters, and punish his whisky-bottle at a great rate (unthinkingly, I dare say), and never thought it necessary to send him a gallon or two.

Other head servants are sometimes served after the same fashion. Let me here relate a case in point, in which a popular huntsman suffered severely in this way. Many people used to drive out on the Sundays to "the kennels" to see the dogs. Of course the good fellow brought out his bottle and his cake-basket, while it was sometimes a case of "a cut from the round," or a chop, or bread and cheese at least. No wonder this man was poor. His income from his employer was, I think, about eighty pounds a year, with a few etceteras. One or two only of his visitors were sufficiently thoughtful to make him a little return ; a wine merchant sent him a couple of dozens of sherry, whilst two farming friends gave him twice a year a choice bit of pork. That good fellow ought to have had an addition made to his hunt salary of at least fifty pounds a year, and even then he would have been out of pocket. The groom who took charge of the horses got the "tips" which were given by the visitors.

P

CHAPTER XV.

OUR GAME SUPPLY.

I.

FACTS and figures illustrative of the national commissariat, at one time much neglected, are now greatly in
demand, the question, " how are the people fed ? " being
full of interest to all concerned. In respect of the
consumption of game in the United Kingdom, it is
impossible to do more than guess to what extent the
birds and beasts of sport are available for food, no
statistics being taken for the use of economists. We
might with advantage follow the exemplary practice of
some foreign nations ; taking France as an example,
the French so manage that even the supplies of field-
fares and sparrows which reach the markets are carefully
enumerated. Our want of alertness in this respect has
often afforded cause of complaint to members of Parliament and other politicians—but nothing is done.
Such stray facts and figures as have been obtained are
due to private inquiry, and, so far as is known to the
writer, no reliable estimate has ever been made of the
number of the birds and beasts of sport annually sent
to market, ultimately to find a place on the tables of a
luxury-loving public.

In attempting to supply this deficiency, certain figures
have after careful inquiry been arrived at; but these
must not be taken for more than they are worth—they
are at best but a rough-and-ready attempt to supply the
deficiency so often referred to by politicians and others,

who take an interest in the game supply. Only those birds and beasts of the chase have been taken note of that are oftenest in men's mouths, such as hares and rabbits, also partridges, grouse and pheasants. These will be enough for illustrative purposes, but, in the old sense of the word, animals of most kinds individually killed were usually considered "game," or at least were looked upon as affording "sport," as that word was at one time understood ; but sport nowadays has not, I fear, the same meaning as it used to have in "the long ago." As a matter of fact, very few of our wild birds and beasts come under the category of "game," and, as for the hare, it is still without the protection of a close time in Great Britain ; in Ireland, however, that animal is not allowed to be shot during its breeding season.

Game, it may be stated, before going further, can only be legally sold to a licensed game-dealer by a person holding the proper licence to kill game, a certificate for which costs the sum of £3. In the case of hares, these animals can also be sold to a licensed game-dealer by those occupiers of land who are entitled to kill hares or rabbits, or who "occupy" lands under the Ground Game Act. It is well these conditions should be understood, as hitherto great latitude has been taken in the matter of game dealing by many sportsmen, and particularly by poulterers who possess a licence, and who are liable to a penalty of £20 if they deal without having first of all obtained—in addition to the licence of the Justices of the Peace—a proper certificate from the Inland Revenue Office. No close time exists for hares in Great Britain, which is less fortunate in that respect than Ireland, and there can be no doubt that this want of protection during their breeding season has become a factor of importance in the increasing scarcity of the animal. The officers of the Inland Revenue can therefore do nothing to prevent the sale of hares at any period of the year, those entitled to kill them may select.

The various birds of sport and some other birds as well are protected by a close time, during which it is illegal to kill them, and many gentlemen, as a matter of policy, refrain from shooting their blackcocks and pheasants till long after the date fixed by Act of Parliament. Commerce in game is now so extensive as to place it almost beyond the power of the authorities to regulate the sale. At all events their vigilance can be eluded, even in the face of the protection which the Legislature has devised ; and often enough supplies of game arrive at the dealers and are sent away without finding a place in the game purchase book, which by statute every poulterer who buys grouse, and other birds and beasts protected by the law, is bound to keep for the inspection of the proper officers. In the early days of the grouse-shooting season, for example, a dealer in an extensive way of business will receive large consignments of these birds by nearly every train, either in pursuance of contracts he has entered into, or to be disposed of on commission. In a prolific grouse year a dealer told the writer that he would sometimes handle and repack as many as one thousand brace of birds in an afternoon, without even knowing at the time by whom they had been sent.

The following details, apropos to game commerce, having been obtained from a person engaged in the trade all the year round, will be found pretty reliable.

All animals which pass as game, as well as rabbits and several kinds of wild birds, are usually consigned by proprietors or lessees of shootings to dealers, either under a contract as to price, or to be disposed of at the market rates which are current at the time of their being sent. These dealers in the course of business forward from one to another till the whole is disposed of. By way of illustrating the mode of commerce now in vogue, it may be inferred that an Inverness or Perth poulterer has arranged with several owners or lessees of shootings to receive and pay for the grouse to be sent to him at a given price per brace; but these dealers are quite well aware that they cannot dispose of a twentieth part of the birds sent to them in their own towns, and, that being so, at once despatch their grouse and other birds to the south, where are to be found the best markets. The birds as received are carefully repacked, each one being wrapped in its own paper, and sent off by fast train to Glasgow, Edinburgh, Manchester, or London, where they are received by the wholesale men to be distributed to the various retail buyers, who are always ready to deal. The current price, whatever it may be, must be accepted by the persons sending the consignments. Prospects of sale and price in all the chief markets can be ascertained by means of " a wire." When birds are scarce the price goes up, and on any given day may range from 1s. 6d. to 5s. per bird— dealers, it may be stated, account to each other by single birds. When markets become congested nominal prices only are obtained.

The supply is occasionally so great as to cause a serious glut. On occasion lots of the cheaper birds (grouse) are destroyed in order to promote sales : it "pays" in the end, of course, to put out of sight, in some way or another, a few hundred "cheepers" or living ones (decaying birds), so as to enhance the price of those which are left. In very plentiful grouse-yielding years, it is not unusual to find these birds on the carts of the costermongers, which points, of course, to enormous supplies and the payment of nominal prices only to those who have sent the birds.

The days of exceptionally big prices for game of any kind have passed away; even for salmon, "the venison of the waters," occasional cheap days have come. This season (1888) fine fish have been on sale at eightpence per pound. A few years ago, a guinea, and even twenty-five shillings, used to be a common enough charge for a brace of early grouse in the West-end poultry shops of London; such prices have not been heard of lately, except in the early morning of "the twelfth," abundance of birds being usually on sale before the dinner-hour; by the evening prices will have fallen largely, and in the course of a day or two, if birds are plentiful, dealers are glad to sell at any price. The system of telegraphic messages now in vogue has proved of much benefit to commerce in grouse, as persons in the provinces—say at Perth—can ascertain by expending a shilling whether or not it is desirable to send on birds to London, or hold them back for twenty-four hours or longer. One day's delay, or the reverse, in forwarding consignments, may make a difference of a shilling in the price of each bird. Retail dealers in grouse, or other game birds, require in some quarters to give long credit, as also to "tip" the cooks. In years of scarcity as much as 30s. have not infrequently been charged for a brace of grouse by west-end London game-dealers.

As a fashionable and out-spoken poulterer once said to a customer, " You see, sir, if ten persons are each in want of a brace of birds, while there are only six brace to supply the demand, prices must rise accordingly." That is undoubtedly the political economy of such a position, although not always pleasant to purchasers. It is obvious that, between the first and the last price of a brace of grouse, notwithstanding railway charges and commission, there is plenty of room for profit, and game-buyers on the contract system, as a rule and over a series of years, were wont, it is said, to make a very fair return by means of their speculations.

A wonderfully large head of game birds, as well as hares and rabbits, are given away every season by owners of pheasant preserves and lessees of grouse moors. Persons who have not considered the number of hares, grouse, rabbits, pheasants, partridges, and haunches of venison which are given away every year in presents, would, if they gave the matter a little thought, be surprised at the quantities distributed. If we take only the clergy as the recipients of such gifts, the head of game annually presented to the Church must be enormous, and, adding what is given in charity and presented to tenants and dependants, the total figure must be a large one.

Apropos to such gifts many curious anecdotes have every now and again been circulated as to the adventures of thrice-presented pheasants and grouse which have gone the round of half-a-score of friends, and then come back to the first donor ! The following is one true tale of the kind: a venerable old lady having received a present of a brace of birds, likewise a pheasant and hare, at once sent them by her footman to different friends; the pheasant and the hare she sent to her minister, and "the birds" to Lord Parchment, a distinguished judge, who had a greater knowledge, it was wickedly said, of cookery than of law.   In the evening the pheasant came back to her!   The minister had given it to one of the elders of his church, and as that gentleman, a bachelor, was just leaving home for a week, he forwarded the pheasant, with a polite note, to the old lady.   It may savour of a made-up story, but the grouse actually came back to her as well! The judge, living by doctor's orders and on a regimen, was not for a time allowed to eat grouse, and, therefore, kindly sent them on to a brother of the Bench, who had a taste for the good things of the table.   Being engaged to dine with the lady on an early day, his lordship, in a polite note, begged permission to send a brace of grouse as a contribution to her *menu!*   The lady was able to identify both birds—at least her cook was—from the fact of the pheasant having a broken wing, and one of the birds a maimed leg.

This little episode will recall the story of the present of early strawberries sent by a Yorkshire nobleman to a well-known clerical dignitary in York, who passed them on to a rich old lady from whom he had expectations, who in turn presented them to the Archbishop, who sent them to a sick lady friend, who forwarded them immediately to the dignitary of the church who was their first recipient!

II.

Coming now to the figures of the national game-bag, so far as it is filled from our home preserves, the supplies of the birds and beasts of sport consumed in

London has been more than once ascertained, and it may be taken for granted that more than half of all the game killed in the country reaches the great metropolis, either for consumption there or for re-distribution. The season begins on the 12th of August with grouse and ends on the 1st of February, when pheasant-shooting terminates. In the year 1860 the London game supply was very carefully noted, and the figures proved, as far as that could be done!

At that period the resident population, and the strangers within the gates of the great city, were estimated at about three-and-a-half millions of human beings and by this time " that vast agglomeration of persons " has been augmented by an increase of over a million-and-a-half, big and little, making, say, five millions to be daily provided with food of all kinds. If, then, the London of 1860 consumed a certain head of game, what should the London of twenty-five years later consume ? Taking the number, of the former period as a basis, the game consumption of " the mighty wen " has been calculated by an expert in such matters to be pretty much as follows :—

[*The figures pertaining to both periods have been placed side by side for the purpose of easy comparison, in both instances the calculations being only illustrative must be taken with the usual pinch of salt.*]

	1860.	1886.
Grouse and other black game . .	115,000	210,000
Partridges	140,000	176,000
Pheasants	90,000	190,000
Hares	110,000	170,000
Rabbits	1,500,000	4,000,000

These figures may be accepted as a fair representation of the game supply of London, and—as has been indicated—this much can be said regarding them, namely, that they are not the result of any merely rule-of-thumb calculation.

Extending the area of inquiry, we require to search for a basis on which to erect, say, " a theory " of the quantity of game which is annually consumed out of London, but a good guess at the figures is all that can be given. All the great towns, however, are big consumers, and several have a large population, many of their inhabitants being wealthy enough to indulge in the luxuries of the table. Excluding London, it may be affirmed that we have a population of 30,000,000 of all ages to provide for. What quantity of game will these persons consume ? It might be said off-hand, just five times the quantity required in London; but that would be anything but a correct answer, because " the means " of the dwellers in that city, where a very large proportion of the country's wealth is centred, are greater than those of the people scattered throughout the provinces, many of whom never touch game at any period of the year, although consumption to some extent is constant during the season. London is the centre to which the greatest luxuries of the table are forwarded—especially at the moment of their highest value—the first salmon of the season, the earliest laid eggs of the plovers, the firstlings of the lamb flock, the forced strawberries, the first pluck of green peas, the ducklings soonest ripe for the spit, the lobsters that come quickest to shore, and the asparagus and salad vegetables when they are newest and rarest, are all despatched to the grand centre of wealth and luxury.

[*The following figures are offered for consideration simply as indicating the total game supply :*]

	London.	All other places.
Grouse and black game . . .	210,000	300,000
Partridges	176,000	200,000
Pheasants	190,000	175,000
Hares	170,000	260,000
Rabbits	4,000,000	5,000,000
Total	4,746,000	5,935,000

The summation of these two columns of figures shows us that a grand total of 10,681,000 head of the animals enumerated is consumed throughout Great Britain in the course of the season devoted to the gathering of the game harvest, and the estimate is undoubtedly a moderate one for such a population, even assuming that only a third of the number are able to procure (or eat) game of any description. As regards London, a very large head of foreign rabbits may be added to the figures given.

Before attempting to estimate the value of the national game supply, it will be as well for the benefit of the uninformed to give some idea of the weights of the various animals, which may be set down as follows :—

Pheasants from 2½ lbs. to 4 lbs., average 3 lbs.
Blackcock „ 3½ „ 5 „ 4 „
Grouse „ 1¼ „ 2¼ „ 1¾ „
Hares „ 6½ „ 9 „ 7½ „
Rabbits „ 3¼ „ 4¾ „ 3¾ „

The figures vary in different localities, and I do not take into account birds or beasts of out-of-the-way proportions. I have seen both fur and feather that went above these computations. When prepared for the table the figures become, of course, reduced.

As to the money value of these birds and beasts (it is the prices paid by the purchasing public I am just at present desirous of illustrating), the following calculations present a fair idea of the sum paid in the course of a year for game, but the figures offered must not be taken for any more than they are worth; hundreds of rabbits, for instance, will bring two shillings, but, on the other hand, thousands are sold at sixpence each.

510,000 grouse and black game at 4s.	per bird,	£102,000
376,000 partridges	at 2s.	„	37,600
365,000 pheasants	at 4s.	„	73,000
430,000 hares	at 3s. 6d. each,	75,500
9,000,000 rabbits	at 1s. 6d.	„	675,000

Total £963,100

By adding to the above, snipe, woodcock, ptarmigan, mallard, widgeon, teal, plover, and small miscellaneous birds, a further sum of £50,000 might be made up, and quite as much may be added for game given away in presents, so that the figures of our game supply might easily be augmented to considerably over a million per annum. These prices, have been averaged over a period of ten years, and may therefore be considered fairly representative.

III.

The foregoing figures are not in the least exaggerated, but on the contrary modestly stated, although some of them may seem prodigious. As regards the grouse supply of the great metropolis, I contributed to the *Times* a few years ago, after a considerable amount of inquiry, some facts and figures from which the following is an extract: " There are, in round numbers, 1200 clubs, cafés, hotels, restaurants, dining-rooms, and superior public-houses which daily provide luncheon or dinner, but in many of these grouse is never seen, and perhaps not more than 150 of these houses will regularly provide game as a daily item in their bills of fare. But, when the markets become glutted, more than half of them will give their customers a taste of grouse. Buyers go round picking up lots, and on three or four days of the season will get 50 brace of birds at perhaps a shilling a bird, or even at a less figure upon some occasions. As an estimate of the consumption of the clubs, hotels, cafés, dining-rooms, &c., we may take it that 500 of them will average two birds a day on each of the 120 days (including Sundays) of the grouse season, which will require 120,000 grouse, or considerably more than a half of the total number of birds received in London."

Fashionables are, of course, out of town during the grouse season, and many of the birds consumed by those living in London from August to Christmas will be received as presents. A gentleman who has studied the commissariat of the great metropolis intelligently, and who is in possession of numerous out-of-the-way facts and figures bearing on the subject, is of opinion that, without exaggeration, the London grouse supply may be put down at a quarter of a million of birds ; but, as I have a strong desire to keep my statements within the mark, I prefer to adhere to the figures given. As we must provide a supply for other cities, a great many of the grouse and much of the other game which reaches London, it should be borne in mind, falls to be redistributed. Orders for Brighton and other watering-places on the south coast will, no doubt, swallow up day by day ten or twelve thousand birds. As a means of checking the grouse supply, there is the fact that the sporting rental of Scotland is assessed at about half a million sterling, and Scotland, it may be safely affirmed, supplies three-fourths of our total grouse supply.

Foreign ptarmigan are largely imported, and are coming into demand because of their cheapness. An extensive trade in these birds has during late years been organised between this country and Norway and Denmark. In these countries the bird is to be found in literal tens of thousands, and nearly every year shiploads of them arrive at Hull and Leith, near Edinburgh, packed in boxes, which are placed on the tops of large blocks of ice. The birds and ice are simply looked upon as ballast for empty vessels, as during the winter season in Norway a cargo cannot be obtained, whilst captains know that by coming to British ports they can find the wherewithal to load their ships.

Ptarmigan in Norway are not shot, but caught by brona bran gins, that is, a looped hair attached to a pin set in the ground, or attached to some article on which they feed. The price of these Norway birds varies exceedingly. If a large quantity be brought at any time to market, the price, of course, falls; at times in London ptarmigan cost 1s. 9d. each, and at other times they may be bought for a third or a half of that sum. Cargoes of them are frequently purchased in Leith or Hull at the rate of from 2d. to 6d. per bird. A drawback in connection with these Norway birds is their being sometimes packed in salt. They are rolled in paper and then placed in cases containing from 30 to 100 each, each layer being covered with a sprinkling of coarse salt. This plan may be, indeed is, good enough in frosty weather, but the moment the ship enters a

warmer latitude the salt begins to melt and the birds to
" go." If more attention were paid to the packing and
forwarding of these foreign ptarmigan a much better
price would be obtained by those sending them for
sale. I am sorry I cannot recommend these imported
ptarmigan for table use ; as a rule, they all taste of the
pine-tree tops, and have in consequence a rather disagreeable *goût*, but when our game is out of season
ptarmigan may be tolerated.

An extensive commerce is now being developed in
various foreign birds—particularly Russian partridges,
of which thousands are imported after shooting has
ceased throughout the United Kingdom ; and as these,
in virtue of a recent decision, may now be lawfully sold
by British dealers, the trade is likely to increase to an
almost indefinite extent. Although the national commissariat will in consequence be largely benefited
thereby, it is rather difficult to express one's satisfaction
at the fact, seeing what an outlet is presented to the
poacher.

Scottish venison, it must be confessed, is not of so
much account for table use as the park-fed haunches
which sometimes form a feature of an English dinner,
and which are, as a rule, " fed " from an early day of
their lives, so that when they leave the kitchen they
may please the palates of those who are " destined to
dine beside them." The best venison for the table is
that which has, as we may say, been " caponised " ; but
our red deer or roebuck are never so treated, nor do
many of them reach the market. The hinds, which are
annually shot in large numbers, are usually distributed
among the tenants and servants of the deer forest on
which they have been killed. Red deer, therefore, can

scarcely find an official entry in any account current with the national game bag. It has happily been discovered that venison chops are excellent when served *fresh,* and in consequence the cook in some of the stately Highland homes likes to have a beast, as some of the London cheesemongers would say, " on cut." Sir Walter Scott used to lament the fashion of sending to the dining-room a haunch with a very strong perfume. " I am not asked," he would say, " to eat my gigot of Cheviot mutton in a high condition, nor is my roast beef sent to table in a highly-perfumed state ; why, then, should my pheasants and my venison be kept till they are in a condition in which no Christian gentleman or lady should be asked to eat them ? Bread sauce and red-currant jelly I have found out—they are mere disguises."

A note about the supply of hares and rabbits will conclude all that need be said about the game supply. As has been shown, the number of these animals which are sold is really immense, especially in the case of the rabbit. The writer has spoken in the course of the last few years to many game-dealers about the rabbit-supply, and they have all assured him that it is positively wonderful. A London salesman said to him, " This is the way to look at it, sir. I have said that there will be four million rabbits sold in this here city and places around ; well, you see, with strangers, there is a population of over five millions to feed, and, if we cut off two-thirds of the number as not being eaters of rabbits, we cannot allow the other third, at these figures, more than two and a half rabbits each in the course of a whole year ; that ain't much, is it, sir ? "

This seems to me a modest way of setting down the

rabbit supply, and if we add to the rabbit-consuming population of the "great metropolis" that of other large towns and cities, it will at once be admitted that, to put down ten millions of these animals as being consumed in the United Kingdom would not be an unreasonable estimate, seeing there is a population of about thirty-five millions to be provided for. A fair-sized rabbit, without its skin and entrails, weighs fully two pounds, so that if we venture to take the total weight of ten millions of these animals as being twenty million pounds, and estimate the price all over at the rate of sixpence per pound weight, we at once find that the money value of the rabbit supply may be set down at a sum of £500,000. Curiously enough, once upon a time, the coney was more valued for its skin than the meat it produced; early in the century as much as half-a-crown and three shillings used to be paid for single rabbit-skins. A hare which, in its fur, weighs seven pounds, can scarcely be considered dear at three shillings, seeing that it yields four pounds of meat; and if a million of these soup-producing animals could be sold in the course of a year the sum produced would amount to £150,000. It is not, of course, an easy matter to find out how many hares are sold annually, but some who are familiar with the incidence of game commerce put even a higher figure on the quantity brought to market than a million; but I do not care to over-estimate the number, and have therefore placed it at less than half; any one who likes to take the trouble to look at a poulterer's stock can see at a glance that he is showing over a dozen rabbits for every hare he has in stock.

Q

CHAPTER XVI.

Game in Larder, Kitchen, and Dining-Room.

Having killed our game, or bought some of other people's killing, it will be instructive, not to say interesting, to note its after-treatment in kitchen or larder, and as to the much-discussed length of time which should elapse between the death of a bird and its being presented in the dining-room. Tastes differ so much that probably no three persons will agree as to the proper degree of *haut-goût* which game should be permitted to attain before being cooked; but there are sensible men, and happily they are increasing in number, who are beginning to think it a mistake to keep either birds or venison, as has been hitherto almost always done, till they begin to "stink." A very smart Scottish cook, who does not "hide her light under a bushel," as the saying goes, but has published a book,* told me recently a little anecdote apropos to the subject. One of her masters, a very hospitable country gentleman, once said to her upon the occasion of a party of his guests departing, "Mrs. Wren, now that we are to be alone for a few days, do if you please give me the treat of seeing a

* 'Modern Domestic Cookery,' by Jenny Wren. Paisley: Alexander Gardner.

roasted pheasant on the table that is fit for a Christian
to eat. Some of those we have had recently have only
been fit for the dung-heap. That, of course, was no
fault of yours, but I could not taste them."

Many will, doubtless, agree with the desire of that
gentleman; no bird, in my humble opinion, is so much
spoiled by over-keeping as the pheasant, which, when sent
to table in fine trim, is palatable in a high degree. Not
that I advocate its being hurriedly transferred from the
larder to the spit—certainly not, but I only echo good
opinions when I say that pheasants ought not to be too
long "hung." When recently at luncheon in a country
house, a couple of pheasants were placed on the table,
and the conversation, opportunely for me, turning upon
the cookery of game, I feel pretty sure that the fair
châtelaine of that mansion was won over to my views of
game cookery. At any rate, none present who ventured
to join in the argument could give a reason for keeping
wild animals till they became nearly putrid. " No,"
as Monsieur Blazé, one of the best sporting writers of
his time, and an epicure to boot, used to say, " I do not
eat the rotten bird; those who keep a pheasant till it
can change its position without man's aid must permit
me *not* to be of their opinion."

We keep our game till it becomes " high " simply
because our fathers and grandfathers did so before us;
but, as a rule, all the wild animals we kill are so sufficiently "high" by their course of feeding as to render
it unnecessary they should be kept for any great number
of days.

The proper cookery of game is a subject on which
much might be said, but in these pages it is obvious
not more than a passing dissertation can be given,

although a book of many sheets would not contain all that could be said.

Many "authorities" have from time to time given their opinions on the subject of game cookery, but no dogmatic utterances are now offered as in the olden time, when even Sir Walter Scott was afraid to speak his mind on the matter. That sensible woman, "Meg Dods" (authoress of one of our best cookery books), was also somewhat averse to utter a pronounced opinion, but she goes so far as to say : "Necessity, and the vanity of producing at a dinner what is rare and far travelled, must first have introduced among clearly civilised nations the custom of *over-keeping* game, till in time it came to be considered as essential to its perfection that it be kept till putrid, and that what has not flavour may at least have *fumet*."

Alexis Soyer, in his day the celebrated *chef* of the Reform Club, was among the earliest to raise his voice against the system of keeping birds till they became high. To a friend of the writer's he one day, while enjoying a chat, made the following observations :— " There is a wonderful *goût* in your bird" (grouse) " which baffles me ; it is so subtle. It is there because of the food it eats, the tender young shoots of your beautiful heath ; but it is curious, sir, that in some years these birds are better than in others. Once in about six seasons your grouse is surpassingly charming to the palate, the bitter is heavenly, and the meat on the fleshy parts short and of exquisite flavour, but in other years it is comparatively flavourless, and the attentions of my art will not improve it. In the year of its perfection I do eat one bird daily ; roasted, and with no aid : no bread sauce, no crumbs, no chips, no nothing, except a crust of bread to change occasionally my palate. Ah, sir, grouse, to be well enjoyed, should be eaten in secret; and take my experience as your guide, do not let the bird you eat be raw and bloody, but well roasted, and drink with it, at intervals, a little sweet champagne. Never mind your knife and fork; suck the bones, and dwell upon them. Take plenty of time; that is the true way to enjoy a game bird. And, look you, do not allow your birds to be over-kept, because from the food they eat they are ready for the cook in three or four days after being killed."

A cook of the period writes, "The chief object of game cookery should be to preserve the *gamy* flavour, and, in my opinion, it is not necessary to keep birds till they are—I speak plainly—'stinking' to ensure that. Some men like their game 'very high,' but there is a difference between a grouse being *high* and its being a mass of putridity. I only keep grouse myself for a matter of four days or so, which serves to get rid of some of the earthy flavour, and to intensify the bitter of the backbone, which is *par excellence* the 'tid-bit' of the bird, as epicures well know."

As all who are versed in the economy of a well-arranged shooting lodge are aware, the unpresentable, that is, overshot birds, are kept by the cook for the soup pot, and if any of my readers have not tasted grouse soup they should endeavour to do so at the first opportunity— I do not mean the kind concocted and sold under that name at hotels and restaurants. Even in clubs grouse soup is often a failure. It is a misfortune that at many of these places the soups served are all made after one fashion, the same liquor for all; put in it a few pieces of the caudal appendage of an old cow, and, lo! you have ox-tail soup. In clubs and other dining places where soups are wanted in a hurry, that is the rule, and it is only in the very best places special preparations are made. It is a custom of the period to compound nearly all soups from two kinds of stock. Ox-tail soup is simply some particular preparation of stock to which a few joints of the tail have been added; kidney soup is made in the same way.

Real grouse soup can assuredly be made only from the birds, "the more the merrier," and the following hints for its preparation by "an old gastronomic hand" will be found practical : — "Cut off the presentable pieces of flesh and lay them aside to be served in the tureen when the soup is sent to table. Break up the carcasses, leaving out the intestinal parts, and place them in a stewpan with the necessary quantity of water, and with seasoning to taste, as parsley, a little thyme, two onions, and two or three small carrots, with the addition of an apple. Boil till the meat becomes a sort of mash, then strain carefully through a sieve into a clean pan ; put the liquor on again with the flesh previously cut from the birds and boil for half-an-hour, or till the pieces are nicely cooked ; season with a salt-spoonful of cayenne and as much salt as is necessary, and then dish. A *soupçon* of catsup may be added, also a glass of claret if liked ; a thin slice of toast may be thrown into the tureen cut in dice. This soup is easily prepared, and is a really excellent autumn *potage.*"

Grouse soup can be made in other ways, and *gourmets* who like a pronounced flavour may add a slice of lean ham and a little "thickening." This compound need not be decanted through the sieve, but may be served as thick soup ; half-a-dozen or eight birds will be sufficient to make soup for ten or a dozen persons.

" Potage à la Yetholm " (or gipsy broth) was " invented " by the Duke of Buccleuch's cook at Bowhill in honour of Sir Walter Scott; it (the soup) has also been called " Potage à la Meg Merilees." This appetising compound is made as follows :—Boil first of all in plenty of water lots of minced onions, a teacupful at least, a sliced carrot or two, the half of a cabbage (the heart portion only) chopped into small pieces, a couple of whole baking apples, skins and all. When the whole is well boiled, strain off the liquor into a clean pan, and add to it the game in season, let us say a couple of boned grouse cut in pieces, the bones having been previously used in the stock, a blackcock treated in the same way, the fleshy parts of a hare, likewise a partridge or pheasant. It is not at all necessary to brown these in flour and butter, because the soup will be quite as tasty without doing that; but they can be browned by those who like to do so. Season to taste with black pepper, allspice, and salt, and a stalk of green celery if procurable. See that the various meats are tender, but not overboiled. When mushrooms can be procured, boil half-a-dozen of the juiciest in the stock; failing the mushrooms, a tablespoonful of mushroom or walnut catsup may be added seven minutes before dishing. This soup, when properly made, has a delicious flavour, and with a good helping of the game and vegetables constitutes a dinner of itself.

Hare soup may be claimed as belonging to our Caledonian cookery: " rich, ruddy, and reeking, it is most appetite-provoking." There is only one way in which a hare can be thoroughly utilised, it must be made into

soup; "a hare that's roast is lost." Hare soup is seldom
well made out of Scotland, because in other places
unnecessary elements are introduced. Many recipes
for hare soup are found in cookery books; one which I
have read advises that a red herring should be placed
in the pot in order to enhance the flavour! another
says that a bottle of London porter should be added to
the liquor; whilst a third says boil a shank of ham in
the stock. Now, all these recommendations are flat
heresies. Hare soup should have no foreign flesh in it,
but should be made of the hare only. To admit of a
plenteous potful being made of the requisite flavour,
two hares should be provided; it will be as well if they
have not been shot, the blood playing a most important
part in the confection of the soup. Cut the meat off
two hares, and while doing so be very careful to save
every drop of the blood. Use the carcasses of the
animals, minus the offal, as stock along with a couple
of sticks of celery, an apple, an onion or two, a
teacupful of nicely chopped carrot, and the heart of
a white cabbage; boil well, and season with black
pepper and a little salt. Strain into another pot
in which have been placed the cuttings from the hare,
put on to boil, and add all the blood you have saved;
keep stirring with great attention till the soup comes to
the boil, after which let it simmer for about twenty-five
minutes, when it will be ready. A single glass of port
wine may be added before dishing, as well as a snuff of
cayenne pepper. Some persons like a potato grated into
a pulp added to this soup, in that case the potato should
be carefully added so as not to lump; take out a little
of the soup in a basin and gradually stir into it the
pulp, adding the lot to the soup a few minutes before it

is dished. When the king, George the Fourth, was in Scotland, nothing in the national *cuisine* pleased him better than hare soup. As the Ettrick Shepherd said, " His Majesty *admires* the Newhaven fishwives, but he *loves* the soup."

Excellent soups can be also made from the partridge and the pheasant, as well as from the roebuck and the rabbit ; it is not, however, necessary to present formulas for these at present, they can be confectioned in the same way as the others ; the rabbit, it may be stated on the authority of a well-known culinary artist, makes a better foundation for " mulligatawny " than a fowl. The speciality of Scottish soups is, or at any rate should be, that they are compounded directly from their main ingredients, and are not sophisticated by other " materials," and these as a general rule come to table in perfect condition as to seasoning, although there are men who will not take that for granted, but use the bottles of the cruet-stand with great freedom. The cook at Ellangowan House was famed for her hare soup. Mrs. McLardy used to ask the butler, whenever there was a dinner party, " how they liked the soup," and if she were told that any person had dared to use additional season ing she took huff, and would threaten to leave the house ; but Colonel Mannering was generally able to pacify her by reminding her that her hare soup was, according to Sir Walter Scott, " simply perfect." A celebrated French cook blew out his brains because some stupid foreigner, it has been said, put additional seasoning in his potage !

Apropos to the rabbit, which many persons affect to despise as a contributor to the higher *cuisine :* from this animal a most delicious soup may be confectioned

—a potage which I have heard some epicures say is
much better than hare soup, albeit not the same in look
or flavour. In making it no flesh but rabbit-flesh
should be used : first a couple boiled down for stock,
then a couple nicely fried in joints to be placed in the
liquor obtained, add various flavourings to taste, and
the result will be a good tureenful of soup. " My
servants won't eat rabbits," said to me recently a
county gentleman, " and my cook seldom sends them to
my table." Never was there a greater mistake ; the
flesh of the rabbit, the wild one, I mean, is the product of the finest vegetable foods, the most odoriferous
herbs, wild thyme, mint and marjoram, on which they
unconsciously educate themselves for the kitchen. A
young rabbit disjointed, and the pieces fried in bread-
crumbs, forms an excellent *entrée* for an every-day
dinner *en famille*, and, in the country, may even pass
muster on company days. Curried rabbits are not to
be despised, nor should we look down on the old-
fashioned mode of cooking the coney—

> " You may flavour and mingle each dish as you will,
>   Yet the rabbit with onions is best of them still."

To that most sympathetic writer on the art of cookery
and the effects of dishes, Mr. George Augustus Sala,
belongs, doubtless, the re-introduction of " Rabbit
Surprise," an invention of Mr. Patrick Lamb, the
master cook of James, William, and Anne. It must be
compounded after the following fashion :—

" Cut all the meat from the backs of two half-grown
rabbelets (that is not a bad word for young rabbit ?),
cut it in small slices, and toss it up in six spoonfuls of
cream, with a bit of butter the size of half an egg

(pullet's, not ostrich's), and a little nutmeg, pepper and salt. Thicken this with a dust of flour, boil it up and set it to cool, then take some forced-meat made of veal, bacon, suet, the crumbs of French roll, raw eggs, parsley, onion, pepper, salt, and nutmeg, toss it up like the meat aforesaid, and place it round your rabbits. Then fill up the trough in the backs of the patient creatures with the prepared minced-meat and sauce, smooth it square at both ends, brush the top with a raw egg, and sprinkle grated bread over. Place them on a mazarine or patty-pan, and bake them for three-quarters of an hour, till they are a gentle brown. The sauce required is butter, gravy, and lemon; the garnishing, orange and fried parsley."

By far the best mode of sending pheasants or grouse to table is roasted; partridges, again, are best when stewed; snipe, woodcock, and blackcock are also best to eat when done on the spit. No game bird should be baked—certainly not. As every good cook knows, or ought to know, how to prepare and roast these birds, it is unnecessary to say anything about the *modus operandi.*

The average weight of the chief birds of sport when prepared for cooking may be set down as follows :—

Pheasant	.	.	.	. a little over	2 lb.
Blackcock	.	.	.	. .	2½ „
Grouse	.	.	.	. .	14 oz.
Partridge	.	.	.	. .	12 „

An average hare, skinned and eviscerated, will weigh fully 4½ lbs., a rabbit will be a little over half that weight.

In an old book called the ' Castle of Health,' we are told that the " Fesaunt exceedeth all fowles in sweetness and fulsomeness, and is equal to capon in nourishynge."

That being so, and it is so, the pheasant being one of our best table birds, it is to be regretted that in some houses it never comes to table till it is unfit to eat, and is accompanied by several kinds of sauces and condiments in order to render it palatable. Bread sauce, fried bread-crumbs, potato chips, and red currant jelly are simply agents employed to disguise the putridity of the various dishes to which they form an accompaniment, just as in the olden time stale oysters were served with strong condiments to conceal their bad flavour. Now, when these delicious bivalves can be obtained fresh, they ought not to be " adulterated " with vinegar and pepper, but should be sucked from the deep shell in *puris naturalibus.*

Much has been written about keeping the pheasant in the larder. An eminent French sportsman laid down the law of pheasant-keeping some years ago. He said, " This bird should be the food of queens ; being brought to your larder, let it have daily your personal attention, it should not be abandoned without grave consideration being given to the act. Beware of the capricious arrangements of a cook, who may roast it two days too soon, or two days too late, according to the number and quality of your guests. A pheasant must be roasted on the day it is to be eaten ; if your friends are not with you on that day, it is their misfortune, and not, perhaps, your fault." Another writer on pheasant cookery recommends that the bird should be stuffed with a mixture of chopped oysters and mussels, and that before coming to the fire it should not be a week old, but should be used in respect of cooking " just like a barn-door fowl."

The following extract was sent to me some time ago—

it is probably from one of M. Soyer's books, the source
of it was not stated :—" When the bird is perfectly fit,
pluck it ; lard it with care, selecting the primest and
freshest bacon.   It is by no means an indifferent
question that of plucking a pheasant at the proper time.
Experience has proved that those which are kept in
their feathers are more perfumed and of better flavour
than others which have been kept plucked, inasmuch
as the air neutralises a portion of the flavour, or that
the juice intended to nourish the plumage dries up and
injures the flesh.   Your bird being plucked, it should
be stuffed in the following manner : take two woodcocks, and divide the flesh into one portion, the trail
and liver into another ; with the meat you make a
stuffing, by hashing and mixing it with some beef
marrow, a small quantity of scraped bacon, pepper, salt,
and herbs, and truffles sufficient to fill up the remaining portion of the inside of the pheasant.   Be careful
to secure that stuffing so that none of it escape, which
is difficult when the bird has been long kept.   Nevertheless, there are several ways of achieving this, and, among
others, that of placing a crust of bread over the orifice
and attaching it with a thread.   Prepare a slice of bread
an inch thick, on which the bird rests in its length.
Then take the trail and livers of the woodcocks and
mix them with truffles, an anchovy, some grated bacon,
and a morsel of fresh butter ; cover the bird with this
paste, so that it shall be soaked through with the juice
which melts while roasting.   When the pheasant is done,
serve it on the toast, surrounded with slices of orange,
and be satisfied with the work done."   A pheasant so
treated is " good enough," we are told, " for the angels."
I do not doubt it.

The hen pheasant has been supposed by many good judges to be the better for food of the two sexes, in the same way as the female turkey is more esteemed than the cock bird by some of our most cultivated *gourmets*. It has been said that forty minutes at a fairly brisk fire will " ready " a pheasant, but care should be taken to see that it is " done " ; to send to table a " bloody " fowl of any kind is, in my opinion, a great mistake, and the custom, which is somewhat prevalent, ought to be frowned down. Pheasants can be utilised for the table in many modes, which I shall not venture here to recite ; those who desire more information as to their cookery can consult the hundred-and-one cookery books that have been published during the last six or seven years.

Snipe and woodcock are familiar to us. The follow · ing is one mode of preparing snipe—it will be recognised I dare say, by epicures as the *Salmis de Bernardins :* " Four birds make a dish. Do not overdo them, but fairly well roast. Dissect and arrange the birds on a deep silver dish over a flame of spirits of wine ; divide the wings, legs, breasts, and backs ; crush the livers of the birds along with the trail, on which sprinkle the juice of four lemons, and the rind, finely grated, of one. On the dismembered birds dust a seasoning of salt, allspice, and dry mustard, or mix these spices in a glass of good sherry, which dash over the meat as arranged ; lastly, sprinkle all over with pure olive oil. Serve the dish so that it can be eaten while very hot. Be careful not to touch any of the birds with your fingers, in case you feel inclined to eat them ! "

I hope the reader will not think it necessary to treat our beasts and birds of sport in these pages in cook-book fashion, but it is really a work of some self-denial to refrain from giving formulas for their cookery ; a word or two, however, may be offered here about wood-cock : as all *gourmets* know, these are sent to table "trail" and all, the intestal part in being allowed to drip upon toasted pieces of bread laid in the pan to receive it. Some epicures like this bird made into soup, or served as a salmi ; these likes or preferences are a matter of taste ; there are those who like the trail taken out to be made into a sauce with gravy, butter, bread-crumbs, and various piquant seasonings : the place of the intestines may be filled with minced mushrooms. This bird will be done in twenty minutes. When sent to table the dish should be profusely garnished with slices of bitter orange, whilst the birds may be well sprinkled with fried bread-crumbs ; they are, of course, arranged on a bed of very "sappy" toast. It is difficult to time the keeping of this bird to every man's taste. For a party in residence the cook should study variety, giving well-kept birds one day, and others that are comparatively fresh the next day, so that all tastes may in turn be suited. A cold woodcock pie is often a feature of country house sideboards, it is made in a raised shape of paste, and forms a capital dish of the "cut-and-come-again" sort.

Of the woodcock it has been said by a competent judge, that no epicure eats the bird itself, all he wants is the trail on its bed of toast, the cock itself may be passed on to the servants' hall. "Now, look here," says this authority, "don't always cook your cock before the fire, we do so run in ruts that we fail in variety. Try this mode of doing woodcock. Stew your birds : the modus is simple. All you have to do is place a thick slice of toasted bread, not buttered, but well steeped in beef gravy, in the bottom of the pan ; wrap your bird in an envelope of well-streaked bacon, lay another slice of well-steeped toast on the top, screw down the lid tight, so as to prevent the steam from escaping, and in twenty-five minutes your bird will be food for the gods."

Another good judge of the good things of this life maintains that the woodcock is *all* for eating, and that every particle of it is precious to the palate ; he describes it as the bird of the epicure, *par excellence*, for succulence and flavour, and says its susceptibility to the arts of the cook is wonderful: " It is a bird that Lucullus himself could dwell upon."

Moral : *The woodcock lives chiefly on worms !*

The same gentleman recommends the wood pigeon for table ; it is inexpensive, and can by a good cook be prepared and be dished in such a way as to ensure for it a warm welcome, for really, in point of *goût*, it may take rank with grouse when hung for a few days. The wild pigeon as " a dish " is far before the tame doves of the home pigeon-houses ; although they are served in pies covered with dainty paste, they have not the flavour of the quest or cushat. Here is a way of stuffing wood pigeons that may be new to some of my readers: Strip off the flesh of a red herring from its bones, and mix it up as a paste, with a little flour and butter, as also seasoning to taste ; cram the bird full of this mixture, and roast and baste in the usual way over a slice of buttered toast, allowing the seasoning to drop on the bread just in the same way as if it was the trail of a woodcock. Once tried, the pigeon will seldom be eaten in other fashion. There is a foreign fowl of the pigeon kind that is much sought after by those who visit the land in which it lives, I am alluding to the nutmeg bird. I do not know if any of my readers have had the good fortune to taste it; that pigeon feeds on mace, the soft covering of the fruit referred to, which causes the flavour of the bird to be remembered by those who have eaten it. These birds are shot in thousands for table purposes; they are so fat and plump that they require to be very tenderly handled, as they burst when messed about. This bird spreads the seed of the nutmeg; it possessing a capacious appetite, it swallows the fruit quite whole, and, the mace or covering only being digested, the nutmeg itself passes safely through the bowels of the animal, prepared by nature for easier germination in consequence of its passage through the pigeon. This may appear to be a traveller's tale, but it is true, nevertheless; a friend of mine, who has been on the Pellew Islands, tells me no pigeon is more delightful when properly cooked.

The partridge must not be ignored in any remarks made about game cookery. *Perdrix aux choux* is said to be the national dish of France; whether that be the case or not, it forms when nicely cooked one of the most succulent *entrées* known in the arts of cookery. Even done by way of a plain stew, with a little white wine among the gravy, and a flavouring of lemon juice, they are excellent. The French national dish consists of stewed partridges served on a bed of cabbage and surrounded with an abundant supply of sausages cooked in the same pot as the birds. The following formula for partridge mayonnaise may come in useful, it is from the Scotch cookery book of "Jenny Wren":—"The cold partridges may be thus used. Cut off the flesh, and stew slightly with shalots and tarragon and some aspic jelly,

R

as well as other seasoning to taste. Dish tastefully, arranging the pieces neatly ; pour over them a mayonnaise mixture, and garnish neatly with little bits of aspic and some green stuff."

Partridges are, however, cooked in many modes, some of these being not a little fanciful : roasted in simple fashion, they are highly palatable ; baked in a pie, the partridge is excellent, and when braised sure to be in demand ; " larded, stewed, and served as a ragout *à la financière*, partridges will tickle and excite even the most demoralised palate." But this bird was undoubtedly made for the stewpan. Partridges stewed on a bottom of thin bacon are delicious ; a few onions chopped small ought to be placed in the pan, and the lid whilst the process of stewing is in progress must be kept firmly fixed down ; none of the steam should be allowed to escape.

There are other birds the cookery of which might be profitably discussed. Stewed wild pigeons are excellent, but it is the wild duck family I have at this moment in my mind's eye. " Only show it the fire," has been said in reference to some of these birds ; that, of course, is nonsense, only those who delight in " feasts of blood " will permit a mallard to be presented at table in the half-raw condition which it is the fashion for some epicures to say is correct. When wanted in a hurry it is a good plan to bury newly-shot wild birds in the earth for a night, wrapped up in a napkin. Then after the necessary preparations have been made in the way of evisceration, place them at the fire and partially roast them. That being done, cut the breast at intervals and place in the cuts plenty of seasoning moistened with lemon juice ; after that is done transfer the bird or birds to a stewpan and let them stew in brown gravy till they are tender. Dish on a bed of thick toast well buttered, pouring over them some of the liquor in which they have been stewed, in which has been mixed a glass of claret. The ducks should be filled with a stuffing of chopped apples and bread-crumbs. Hashed duck served with peas or turnip is excellent. The teal is described by an old writer as "a delicate fowl for the table," and widgeon are as good as teal. The pochard, too, has its epicurean admirers, some of whom seem inclined to rank it, as a table bird, with the canvas-back duck of the United States, which has of late years been elevated into an important place in the gastronomic calendar.

The following is a much-prized recipe for a sauce to the wild duck; it is copied from Dr. Kitchener, who was, perhaps, more learned in the composition of sauces and gravies than in any other branch of the culinary art. In his 'Cook's Oracle' he gives a large number of formulas for these delights of the dining man, for which see the book. The following is the recipe referred to:—" One glass of port wine, one spoonful of caviare, one ditto of catsup, one ditto of lemon-juice, one slice of lemon-peel, one large shalot sliced, four grains of *dark* cayenne pepper (not Venetian red and brickdust), and two blades of mace. Scald and strain this, and add it to the pure gravy of the bird. Serve the duck (if it be a duck) in a silver dish, with a lamp under it, and let this sauce gently simmer around the bird."

I shall say nothing about how to make a venison pasty or cook a haunch, there is nothing new in that line of cookery; and, despite the praises that have been bestowed upon it, I am sadly heretical on the subject of

R 2

its gastronomical value ; I have always disregarded the praises bestowed on it by the poet who tells us—

> " The haunch was a picture for painters to study,
> The fat was so white and the lean was so ruddy."

I must mention before concluding that rabbit-pot forms an excellent dish for a curling day ; treated much in the same manner as Irish stew, the merry curlers cannot have a better luncheon. We do not in Scotland eat our " small " birds, but of late lark pies have been seen in several country houses, much to the displeasure of sentimentalists. Thrushes are good for food in a high degree, but are very rarely sent to table in this part of Her Majesty's dominions. The ancient Romans were exceedingly fond of these birds, and prodigious quantities of them were always stored in their aviaries ready for the cook to lay hands on. Martial wrote :—

> " Of all the birds the thrush I deem the best,
> 'Mong quadrupeds the hare beats all the best."

The foregoing notes do not nearly exhaust the subject of game in larder and kitchen, as any person whom it may please to turn over the pages of a modern cookery can ascertain, and critics will please note that, although many " dishes " have been omitted from the preceding pages, it is not perhaps because of ignorance, but more likely from want of space. Some captious critics conclude that, because a thing is not mentioned, therefore the author knows nothing about it. Of partridge or pigeon puddings I have said nothing, neither shall I descant on " the best mode of currying a fresh pheasant," nor shall I give a formula for a " chartreuse of partridge," nor for Boudins of the bird of Colchis *à la Richelieu*. To make up for these " wants " in this little essay I shall conclude by giving a recipe for the concoction of Soyer's celebrated "Salade de Grouse," which I may mention is to be found in "Meg Dods'." It is as follows :—" Put a thin rim of butter round a dish, and on this stick a high border of hard-boiled eggs cut into four lengthways with a bit cut off to make them stand. Fill the centre with a nice fresh salad and tastefully ornament the egg border with fillets of anchovies ; cut beetroot or gherkins. Have three under-roasted grouse cut into neat small pieces, and prepare a sauce made of two tablespoonfuls of finely chopped eschalots, two of pounded sugar, the yolks of two eggs, two table-spoonfuls of finely chopped tarragon and chevril, a salt-spoonful of white pepper, and two of salt; with these gradually mix twelve tablespoonfuls of salad oil and three of chili vinegar ; mix all well and put the mixture on the ice. When ready to serve whip half a pint of cream rather stiff and add to the sauce, pour a little over the salad, upon which lay first the roast pieces of the grouse, on which pour more sauce, dressing them in a pyramid."

CHAPTER XVII.

SALMONIA.

I.

THE man who can wield a salmon-rod and successfully "play" an eighteen or twenty-pound fish may certainly pose as a master of the gentle craft; the trout, we know, is "game" from mouth to tail, and to secure a fourteen or fifteen-pound fighting *ferox* in Loch Awe is "a feat," the degree of merit being, of course, dependent on the means adopted to capture it, while to kill a salmon is hard work. A big, strong pike also involves the doing of some work before it can be taken off the hook: to fish for brook-trout is, however, one of our most delightful angling pastimes. Trout-fishing possesses the merit of being more come-at-able than salmon-fishing, which can only, indeed, under present arrangements, be a recreation for the "classes," as there are few in Scotland who can afford to pay for a stretch of salmon water, and still fewer who can successfully fish it when obtained.

I have read in books minute directions as to how salmon should be, or at any rate might be, captured, but none of these instructions could ever be made use of in catching any of the fish that ever came under my notice. No angler knows what may happen when he hooks a fourteen-pound salmon, or an active six-pound grilse. His first idea, unless he is an old hand at the business, is to haul the fish out of the water by sheer force, but he soon finds that plan to be a mistake. As " Peter of the Pools " said one day at Stormontfield, " That cock 'ill no fecht ; ye maun wait on your fish and humour it till you can tire it out, and then your boat-man will gaff it." Just so, and it is impossible to say, taking what may be termed an all-round view of the case, how long you may have to fight your fish ; the chances are not small, indeed, if the salmon be a large one, that it will in the end tire you out, and probably escape by the chafing or snapping of the line. To have such a fish to play means that your situation is no sinecure ; the work is engrossing while it lasts, especi-ally when the salmon is one that is newly run, fresh, strong and lively, and fond of showing his prowess by making a series of rapid rushes. Peter (of the Pools) Marshall, of the Stormontfield breeding ponds, used to relate that it once took two gentlemen, fishing on Stanley Water (river Tay), over three hours to get a salmon they had hooked into the boat, or rather on to the grass at the river-side, as they required in the end to land in order to finish their work. But the fish was worth all the trouble it gave, weighing, as it did, the nice weight of twenty-seven pounds. Peter's simple description of the work was : " She fought like a demon for her life."

I know a good deal about the salmon-angling of the period, having in my time seen a few of these fish caught both in Tay and Tweed ; but I am not an adept in describing effectively the capture of a salmon. As was said by the late Mr. Alexander " Russel, of the *Scotsman*," author of 'The Salmon,' "the most graphic description you can give of what you have done is to show your fish, *that* is the best proof of your pudding." "Brother Sandy," as Russel was sometimes jocularly called, entertained strong opinions, and was never afraid to express them, no matter what the subject might be, whether theatrical or theological. He believed that some of the paper anglers were "awful impostors." On one occasion, in speaking of a minister of the gospel, he said, "He calls himself an angler for men's souls. Poor fellow! if he be as bad a hand in the pulpit as he is on the river-side, it will be —— few souls he'll catch." Another time he said of a well-known *paper angler*, "He catch a salmon! It's far more likely that the salmon will catch him."

Although Mr. Russel's book, 'The Salmon,' was not a commercial success, it well deserved to have been so, being full of the subject, and discussing the natural history, legislation, and economy of the salmon fisheries, as well as the sport the fish affords to the angler, in a learned and loving spirit.

In a book, professing to deal with the economy of sport and the natural history of the creatures of sport, it is proper that a few paragraphs should be devoted to the "venison of the waters," which, for food and sport combined, is our foremost fish. The salmon has been written about, lectured over, and experimented upon in a way that no other fish has been; it is within my knowledge that for half a century *Salmo salar* has afforded a theme of controversy to at least a full score of naturalists and fishery economists; from the days of Humphry Davy and the Ettrick Shepherd to the time of Frank Buckland, the salmon, in river and sea, and under every condition of breeding and feeding, has given rise to hot disputation ; in every stage of its life it has been keenly wrangled over.

Beginning at the beginning of its career, when it is known as " the par," it was at one time claimed as a distinct fish, and even now, when all reasonable men admit that it is in reality the young of the salmon in what may be called its first stage, there are persons who cling to the old belief and maintain that a par is a par, and nothing but a par. It matters not to such disputants that par have been *proved* to be salmon, by being kept in confinement till they became smolts, and that these smolts, having been carefully marked before being sent to sea, have returned to the neighbourhood of their birth as grilse, and again, as has been frequently determined, grilse are young salmon. The salmon, being a fish which can be individually handled, has been captured, and being bereft of its eggs, and these having been fecundated by having the milt of the male poured over them, have been kept in boxes under a running stream of water till they have each yielded their fish, affording proof enough to settle the question. These tiny samlets have, moreover, been kept in confinement, and their growth watched day by day, till they have reached the period of smolthood, and begun to gasp for " ocean's green domain."

In connection with the transformation of the fish, from the finger-marked par to the scaled smolt, one remarkable circumstance falls to be chronicled ; it is, that half only of the brood of any one year, or about a moiety, change into smolts at the end of twelve months from the date of their being hatched, the other half of the brood remaining unchanged till a period of two years has elapsed since they quitted their fragile prison, when they, too, become coated with their scales, without which it is impossible for them to exist in the salt water of the sea.

These are the facts which inspired controversialists, and led to a series of paper wars not yet perhaps concluded. Both sides gained their inspiration from the curious fact which has just been mentioned, namely, that it requires two years to ripen par into smolts, so that, as a mere matter of course, salmon rivers contain par at all seasons ; hence the conclusion arrived at by many of the controversialists that par cannot be young salmon, and that smolts only could be young salmon, because they had scales and migrated to the sea. It would be impossible in brief space to relate all that was said or written on the subject of the " par con- troversy," or to report the various law cases which took cognisance of these fish. For a long period discussions were carried on with more or less knowledge and abundance of acrimony. It was not till a suite of salmon-breeding ponds had been constructed and brought into use at Stormontfield, on the river Tay, that it was demonstrated before all who pleased to look on that the par was the young of the salmon. Year after year, as the business of the ponds became more developed, the facts of salmon growth became more and more patent, and now, it is known to all, except those who are not willing to believe or to be convinced, that the par in time becomes a salmon. Indeed, the fact had been proved by Mr. Shaw of Drumlanrig, the Duke of Buccleuch's forester, years before the salmon nursery of Stormontfield had been planned. He gathered the spawn of these fish, and, placing them under protection, watched all the changes they underwent, and noted the much-wanted-to-be-known fact that par became smolts, and in due time salmon, able to repeat the story of their birth.

Shaw naturally thought his process could not be challenged ; in his opinion what he had done effectually settled the question, but his achievement was simply laughed at by " the scientific." " My good man," said one of the learned, " you have only proved what we all know and have long known, that salmon produce salmon. You have simply collected salmon ova, and they have in due time grown into like fish ; any person could do that." With persons who were determined not to be convinced that the eggs had first of all yielded *par*, and that the *par* had changed to salmon smolts, it was useless to argue, they still maintained that nothing of moment had been proved ; and Shaw, incited by contradiction, entered on a new series of operations which he hoped would effectually shut the mouths of " the scientific." To prevent all cavilling, he caught male and female salmon about to spawn, and, despoiling the latter of their eggs, he impregnated them with the milt of the male fish, and had the satisfaction of seeing the eggs come to life, and of witnessing the growth of the fish in their various stages and changes, and by the means he adopted was able to prove beyond all question that the *par* was the young of the salmon, and that in the fulness of time it changed into a smolt, became next a grilse, and finally *Salmo salar* in all its beauty.

Shaw conducted his experiments, of which these few lines give only the barest idea, with so much care that no objection could possibly be offered to them ; he had proved to demonstration that *par* were young salmon, and by the means adopted had rediscovered the lost art of " pisciculture."

The Ettrick Shepherd, who was a keen angler, used to say that at an early time of his life he had come to the conclusion that par were young salmon, having seen them changing into smolts " before his face." As for Shaw, he proved his case both ways in the most effectual style, by showing first of all that par grew into salmon, and that salmon produced par.

II.

Another controversy connected with salmon growth may be said to have been settled by experiments conducted by the late Duke of Athole, who, in order to settle the disputed point, whether or not grilse were young of the salmon or distinct members of the family, as several persons, both naturalists and economists, had long maintained, caused a considerable number of those fish to be captured and marked. Several of the salmon so distinguished were at various times retaken, and when weighed were found to have greatly increased in weight, as also in size, and appeared in all respects to be salmon. Many " obstinates," however, still maintain their old opinions, and assert that a grilse always remains a grilse and never becomes a salmon—pointing to the forked tale and the form of the scales with which the fish are covered as evidence of their contention. In the opinion of several who have given attention and study to the natural history of this valuable fish, there are distinct races of salmon, each of which has some distinguishing characteristic, such as a square or forked tail, a diamond or oblong-shaped scale, and other peculiarities. This may be so, indeed, nothing is more likely, and at one time much was said about the different schools of salmon and their movements.

We are still ignorant of many important data in the biography of the salmon. No one knows with any degree of correctness how the fish " fills in its time," from New Year's Day to Christmas. What purpose, it may, for instance, be asked, have the salmon in view which are ascending from the sea in March ? They cannot surely be then imbued with the instinct of reaching their spawning grounds, because neither their roes nor milts are so developed as they become at a later period of the year. Their spring visit to the rivers is a mystery which has never been solved ; it was at one time asserted that these fish spawned twice a year, but no reliable proof of the fact, if it be a fact, has been ever placed in evidence, and it is well known that on most salmon redds fish are rarely seen till late in autumn, and on some of them not even till the winter season has well advanced. Another old contention was that salmon spawned in the sea ; that might be so by accident, and, if it ever was so, then the eggs were lost, as they could not be nursed into life in the salt water.

Do salmon spawn every year ? This was a question that I think was originated by Mr. Frank Buckland, and, needless to say, it attracted attention. The present writer took some pains to investigate whether these fish spawned annually or not—the same fish, that is, for, as we all know, a large body of them is found on the spawning grounds every year engaged in that most important function of their lives. Among many others who favoured me with their opinions on this matter

were Mr. Tod Stodart, who had no doubt that the same
fish would spawn in every year, and Mr. Robert Buist,
at one time superintendent of the river Tay fisheries,
who was able to *prove* that these fish spawned annually.
That gentleman and his assistants were in the practice
of annually capturing a considerable number of gravid
salmon for the purpose of supplying the Stormontfield
nursery with eggs, and these, after being despoiled of
their ova or milt, were restored to the water, being,
however, previously marked, so that, in the event of
their again turning up, they might be identified. Their
being so identified leads to the inevitable conclusion
that individual salmon, for at least a certain period of
their lives, emit their spawn every year.

As to the rate at which salmon increase in size, there
has been much speculation. A fish hatched in the
March or April of a given year is at the end of twelve
months an animal of very small dimensions—it is
about the length of a man's middle finger, and of
infinitesimal weight, and may continue for another
year without its weight or dimensions being materially
increased. On the other hand, however, at the end of
the year it may have developed sufficiently to be considered a smolt, and make its first journey to the sea ;
and, if so, it has been proved that a young salmon
may leave the stretch of water in which it has been
hatched, as a fish of about an ounce in weight, and return in a few weeks as a grilse weighing three or four
pounds ! This is a fact regarding salmon growth which
is held to have been proved by the marking of a
number of the smolts hatched at Stormontfield, as they
were departing for the sea—an operation at which the
writer assisted. But it would be well if similar ex-

periments were tried again, so as to confirm the conclusion arrived at some years ago. The mortality
among smolts which proceed to sea is so very great,
that it has been doubted if, among the comparatively
small number of fish marked, such a large percentage
as were captured would return as smolts.

To what age and size may a salmon attain provided
it escapes the angler and net fishermen ? In other
words, what is likely to be the probable age of, say, a
salmon of the weight of fifty pounds ? Few, very few,
fish, I am aware, live to attain so great a weight ; but
every now and again a salmon which pulls down the
scale at that figure is captured, and, as no rule exists
by which the age of such a fish can be determined, I
am induced to ask the question. From information
received, I am inclined to think that a fifty-pound
salmon may have attained the age of from eight to ten
years ; curiously enough, as my readers can deduce for
themselves, from what has been said regarding par and
smolt, one fish may attain the weight named a year
before its sister or brother. But all that can be said
on these points of salmon biography is speculative ;
all that we do know is that we don't know.

The salmon is a fertile fish; one weighing about
twenty-four or twenty-five pounds will yield as many
as twenty thousand ova. Under the "piscicultural
system" more than nineteen thousand of these could
be hatched, but, when left unprotected, probably not
one-fifth the number will yield fish, and of the fish
hatched three-fourths at least will never reach the
smolt stage, so great is the average amount of mortality
connected with the growth of the salmon, although it
deposits its eggs in shallow water, and in comparative

privacy. It has been computed that not two ova of the salmon in a thousand will live to become reproductive. Other economists have estimated that only one egg out of every thousand becomes in time a fullgrown salmon. Mr. Stoddart calculated that one hundred and fifty millions of salmon ova are annually deposited in the river Tay, of which about fifty millions, or one-third only, come to life and attain the par stage; whilst twenty millions of these pars in time become smolts, that number being ultimately diminished to 100,000, of which 70,000 are caught, the other 30,000 being left for breeding purposes. In a calculation made by Sir Humphry Davy, he says that, if a salmon produce 17,000 roe, only 800 will arrive at maturity and yield a fish. It is well, therefore, that the female fish yields nearly 1000 eggs for each pound of her weight; a lesser degree of fecundity, keeping in view the enormous waste of life indicated by the above figures, would long since have resulted in the extinction of this valuable fish.

III.

The breeding-boxes at Stormontfield have been discontinued, and the Tay has now a hatching establishment of a more modern description on the estate of Dupplin, from which the salmon are almost at once transferred to the river, instead of being, as at Stormontfield, kept till they had assumed the scales of the smolt, which at one time was deemed necessary for the protection of the fish from their numerous enemies. The number of young salmon bred at Stormontfield was undoubtedly considerable, but was never, perhaps, so great as was stated. I was disappointed, at all events,

on the occasions upon which I was present at the annual
exodus of the smolts, as it appeared to me that only a
few thousands passed along the runlet from the ponds
to the river. On expressing my sense of disappointment, Mr. Buist said that many thousands had already
been sent away. There could not, however, have been
more in reality than twenty-five or, it might be, thirty-
five thousand bred at Stormontfield in the course of
the year, out of the hundreds of thousands of eggs
obtained and impregnated with the milt of the male
fish. The experiments conducted at Stormontfield were
comparatively inexpensive, the cost not being greater
than at the rate of forty smolts for a penny, so that, if
only one of the lot even became a marketable salmon of
twenty pounds weight, the profit would be enormous,
seeing that early-caught fish bring as much, on occasion, as five or six shillings per pound weight in the
London market.

Angling for salmon begins in Scotland on January
11th on the river Thurso, in the county of Caithness;
four or five rivers in Sutherlandshire open for rods on
the following day; by February 11th a large number
of salmon streams are open, including Tweed and Tay,
and in the course of fourteen days afterwards the
Scottish salmon fisheries are all open to fishermen, and,
as the Tweed is not closed to anglers till November
30th, it will be seen that we are within some six weeks
of obtaining salmon from our own streams all the year
round.

Although the salmon in Scotland is in the nature of
private property, and cannot be fished for anywhere as
a matter of course, with two or three exceptions, those
who delight in capturing the " monarch of the brook,"

S

and are able to pay for the privilege, can readily obtain
"fishing." In the North considerable portions of
various rivers are in the hands of hotel-keepers, as may
be discovered by making reference to the excellent
'Sportsman's Guide' of Mr. Watson Lyall.

It is almost needless to say that salmon angling is
an expensive pastime ; the terms for the Thurso, Loch
Tay and other streams are well known ; only rich men
can afford to pay the charges. Both of these localities
are much frequented in the season. Delightful days
on the Thurso have been chronicled before now, and
merry evenings have been passed in Brawl Castle.
The proprietor of the river (Thurso), Sir J. G. T.
Sinclair, of Ulbster, has now resumed possession from
Mrs. Dunbar, the lessee, who succeeded her husband as
tenant of the fishery. Only three of whatever number
of fish might be caught by an angler were allowed to
be kept, the remainder of the day's catch being claimed
by the lessee. But these were even liberal terms
compared to those of some others in the line, where the
angler was charged a good sum for his board and lodging,
and then had to give up all the salmon he captured to
"mine host." " To pay a guinea per diem for one's accommodation, and work hard all day long for one's landlord, is rather too much of a good thing, is it not ? " was
a remark made to the writer by an Englishman staying
for a fortnight at a northern riverside hostelry ; but in
answer the landlord says, " I never have to go seeking
for customers, they come in search of me and my house."
It is only fair, however, to say that there are salmon
fishings which go with the board and lodging charges
on some of the northern salmon streams, and at nearly
all the hotels there is abundance of trout fishing gratis.

The payments made by some lessees of angling waters to the owners of them are in many instances very heavy, amounting in some cases to hundreds per annum. In all probability, the share of the rental of the river Tay derived from the sporting stretches of that stream will probably not be less than a third of the total sum derived from the river. On the Aberdeenshire Dee the sporting rental, I have been told, can hardly be less than five thousand pounds per annum. The angling rights on Tweed are also of considerable money value. Of the Loch Tay fishery, it has been said that the nobleman to whom that sheet of water belongs could make more money out of it by netting it as a commercial fishing than by letting it to anglers.

As to the cost of living during "the season" in the hotels of the far North, I have held not a few arguments with their excellent landlords. Said one of these gentlemen to me :—" I am not like an innkeeper in a commercial town, who has a good run of business, and a steady demand every day for all the provisions he lays in ; my white fish comes a long way, and is sometimes unfit for use by the time it is asked for, and then I have to throw it away. Sometimes I prepare dinner for ten or twelve persons, but the coach may only bring five people to eat it. I have fourteen bedrooms, and for days together I won't have four persons to occupy them ; but my servants have to be paid their wages and get their food all the same. My coach goes to and fro twice each day to the station, four miles from here ; it will accommodate ten passengers, and requires a pair of horses and a steady coachman ; occasionally it will only have two passengers, and these will grumble at the fare, but my coachman has to be paid and my horses to be fed. Fill my coach at every journey, occupy my fourteen bedrooms, and I shall be happy to reduce my prices. My year only lasts about five months."

The various associations of anglers that have been formed during recent years admit of gentlemen obtaining a week or two's salmon angling in the course of the season at comparatively moderate cost. Throughout Scotland there are many fishing clubs, the members of which hold annual competitions in trout fishing; some of them, indeed, meet more frequently, and several of these associations are lessees of " pieces of water" on their own account, or meet on protected waters to hold their angling tournaments. For salmon fishing there is, or at least used to be, a " nest" of happy spirits who rented a place on the Tweed, and who fished in the daytime, and made night joyous with song and story over liberal libations of whisky toddy. The gentlemen who met in this way were professional men, men of light and leading in their sphere, who delighted in the free chaff—pungent enough sometimes it was—that went the round of the party; politics, literature, and art coming in for satire, censure, or praise as might happen. Several of the men who assembled were but poor anglers, and some of them used to come in for a good deal of smart criticism on their mode of landing a salmon, or more often their way of losing one.

The Tweed is a splendid salmon stream, and its waters are liberal to the angler in an eminent degree; that river runs for a hundred miles from source to sea, and is bountifully fed by a large number of affluents. In all probability the Tweed and its tributaries yield at least a thousand salmon and trout casts; many of those are doubtless poor enough, but others are rich in fish.

Some pools may be despoiled of half-a-dozen salmon to-day, and by to-morrow there will be another half dozen in waiting for the angler.

IV.

Having said a few necessary words about the salmon as an object of natural history, it may now be treated of as an article of commerce ; the economy of a salmon stream being interesting alike to those who capture and those who buy the fish, seeing that the public, it has been computed, pay considerably over a million sterling per annum for their salmon. Although that figure may look large, it is not, perhaps, far from the truth, but, as no official statistics are collected of the number of salmon annually caught, the value of the supply cannot be stated. An idea of the national consumption of the " venison of the waters " can only be obtained from the market returns of Billingsgate and one or two other sources of information. The salmon sold in the great " piscatorial bourse " of Lower Thames Street are chiefly fish captured in the Tay and other salmon streams of Scotland ; these are of fine shape and of excellent flavour.

England, it may be stated, derives the greatest portion of her salmon supply from Ireland, a fact not perhaps generally known. While the sum received for salmon captured in England and Wales may not be put down at more than £100,000, the value to its captors of the salmon caught in Ireland and sent to England was reckoned by the fishery inspectors of that country, in 1881, at £579,402, but in 1882 the figure was not so large, being £349,413 ; in 1883, it had risen to

£443,782; for 1884, the sum is set down at £410,856; for 1885, the figure is given as being £424,107; for 1886, £293,106; last year [1887], according to the inspectors, the amount received for Irish salmon sent to England reached £320,181. The total sum, as will be seen, received by Ireland for salmon in these seven years amounts to £2,280,847, being an average of considerably more than £400,000 per annum. What figure may denote the consumption of salmon by the Irish in Ireland I have not the means of knowing.

The salmon caught in the rivers and estuaries of Scotland, taking the average, can scarcely be estimated as producing to their captors a larger sum than £250,000. But these figures, it must be borne in mind, are in the nature of guesses. To ascertain whether the take of salmon is adequate to the extent of the feeding and breeding water to which at present they have access, it is necessary to accept such figures of production as can be found, there being no better mode of demonstrating the ratio of production in well-managed salmon waters. To make this plainer, a case may be stated :—If the River Tay, in Scotland, yields salmon of the value of £60,000 per annum, what ought to be the value of the Severn as a salmon stream? And, taking the water area of Ireland devoted to the breeding and feeding of salmon to be of the value of £400,000 per annum, what should be the return from the salmon-fishing area of England?

The Tay is the chief salmon river of Scotland; it is fed by several tributary streams, and is less subjected to pollution than the Tweed. The rental of the river may at the present time be taken as over £20,000, whilst thirty years ago it was not more than half that sum. The total amount is, of course, made up of two kinds of rental; money derived from the angling or upper waters, and the amounts paid by the lessees of the commercial fisheries. It is most probable that the rental of the commercial fisheries will be considerably over one-half of the total rental, say, as £14,000 is to £6000. It has always been a grievance of the upper proprietors that they who afford spawning ground to the fish obtain so small a portion of the income derived from the fisheries. The netting-station holders, however, are masters of the situation, being able to cream the river during the period when the salmon are running.

According to one authority on the economy of the salmon fisheries, it requires a sale of fish to the extent of twice and a half the rental to carry on the fishery with a fair profit to all concerned; but another writer on the subject thinks that estimate too low, and maintains that fish which will bring £60,000 in the market must be captured to pay a rent of £20,000, as well as taxes, wages, interest on capital, and wear and tear of fishing material. In the case of the River Tay, therefore, 120,000 salmon, grilse, and trout, each to sell on an average at 10s., would be required to produce the rent and pay the other expenses incidental to the fisheries.

This way of estimating must, in the nature of things, be rather a rough-and-ready one, but it has the merit of being probably within, rather than over, the mark. Taking the fish overhead, salmon little and big, as also grilse and trout, at 10lb. weight, and estimating the wholesale price at 1s. per pound, is one way of obtaining a formula to argue from. In the early days of the salmon season these fish sell in large cities at a much

higher price; half-a-crown per pound is then considered
a moderate charge, and at times about double that sum
is exacted, that is at times when salmon are not plentiful; in summer and autumn, when they do become
plentiful, they are at their very cheapest.

V.

The Tweed is an important salmon stream. It dis-
putes with the Spey, so judiciously managed by the
Duke of Richmond, the position of being next to the
Tay. In certain respects the Tweed is superior to both
of these rivers, more especially in having numerous
affluents easy of access to breeding fish. The Tweed,
however, flows no more as a "silvery stream;" its
waters are now "drumly and dark," not with earth
washed from the adjoining lands by rainstorms, but
with the chemical *débris* of manufactories and the
waste refuse of mills. The foul state of the river has
become a matter of consequence to the owners and
lessees of its salmon fisheries, which are valuable. At
one period the Tweed yielded a revenue from its salmon
superior to that of the Tay, and with care might,
perhaps, be made to do so again.

Tweed rises in the extreme south of the county of
Peebles, 1500 feet above the level of the sea, and in its
progress to Berwick-upon-Tweed, through the counties
of Selkirk, Roxburgh, and Berwick, it is estimated to
drain an area of nearly 2000 square miles. In its
course the river receives the Ettrick (which has previously taken tribute from the Yarrow), Teviot, and
Till, not to speak of the Gala, the Leader, the Whittader,
and other waters of minor note. The Tweed, in its

lower course, divides Berwickshire from the English borderland; but although the influence of the tide is felt at Norham, which is about ten miles from the sea, navigation does not extend above Berwick Bridge, nor, except during the herring fishery season, is there much shipping business even at the port. Tweed, it may be said, has no estuary.

Tweed salmon have long been celebrated, "pickled fish from Berwick" being at one time well known in London. After the discovery was made that salmon packed in ice would carry for long distances without deterioration, the Berwick smacks were used to convey large quantities of these fish to the great metroplis, where a ready market was found for them; but at present a very small number of Tweed salmon are sent to London—not above one-fourth of the take. Berwick is so situated as to command a choice of several excellent markets. A salmon landed at the fish-house at seven o'clock in the morning may reach a Manchester or Birmingham dinner-table before six o'clock in the evening.

The French still consume a large portion of the produce of the Tweed, especially of the bull trout, many thousands of which find their way to Paris to be dressed in those tempting ways known only to the culinary artists of the gay city. Portions of the Scotch salmon now sent to London are consigned direct to retailers, and, Tweed being 100 miles nearer London than Tay, the salmon of that river ought to be enjoyed in its perfection.

Previous to the legislation of 1857–59 the Tweed salmon fisheries were in a perilous state. The rental of the river had gone down from £20,000 a year to less

than a quarter of that sum, and even now, when the
fruits of wise legislation have long been apparent, the
rental does not all over average more, probably, than
£10,000 per annum; that is a long way better, however, than the £4046 18*s.* 10*d.*, at which the rental
stood the year before the Act of 1857 came into
operation. Happily for those who own the fisheries,
the rental may still grow, and, if those interested will
let well alone, no one can prophesy how high a figure
may in time be achieved.

Proprietors, lessees, and salmon economists all over
Scotland became much alarmed twenty-five years ago
at the then rapidly declining takes of salmon, when
some in their fright went so far as to predict the speedy
extinction of the fish. Strangely enough, a period of
apathy had existed up to about 1856; many salmon
fisheries once valuable had ceased to be productive, the
Tweed included, and during the period alluded to
English salmon rivers also greatly declined in value.
It was speedily found out, when public attention re-
awakened to the subject, that the salmon had not been
getting fair play in many of the rivers in the United
Kingdom. Rivers were remorselessly kept open till
the spawning season was far advanced, and over and
over again were the chief markets filled with spawning
fish. Occasional great battles were fought in Parliament over often-introduced salmon bills. These were
chiefly fights between upper and lower proprietors, the
latter being decidedly in possession of the field and of
the ear of the Legislature from 1828, when that Act
was obtained by Mr. Home Drummond which in-
fluenced the Scottish salmon fisheries for the long
period of thirty years. One writer, in his wrath, de-

scribed the Home Drummond legislation as "a ruinous Act," which prolonged the netting season from the 26th of August to the 14th of September, its only redeeming point being the creation of a body of river police paid by a *pro rata* assessment of the rentals.

Returning, however, from the general question of salmon legislation to a consideration of the Tweed Acts, it may be stated that these, which at the present time govern the mode of fishing and the fishing periods of that river, were passed in 1857 and in 1859 respectively, and have proved profitable to those most interested. The abolition of the still net alone was a worthy achievement. On the Tweed, at present, excepting the rod, the only legal mode of catching salmon is by means of what is called the ware-shot, better known as net and coble fishing. The stell net was in a certain sense a fixed engine, and one used to be fixed to the pier at Berwick, while a perfect crowd of them were found on the river. The difference between the stell net and the net let out from the coble was this—the one was kept floating till it was struck by a fish, the passage of which it barred, when it was at once pulled in and the salmon secured; the other, now in hourly use during the fishing season at Berwick-on-Tweed, and on other Scottish rivers as well, is shot and drawn whether there be fish or no. Net and coble fishing may during the season of capture be seen day by day from Berwick Bridge; it is the simplest possible mode of salmon capture.

Statistics of the takes of Tweed salmon used to be abundant, and even the produce of particular "shots" were occasionally made public; but, curiosity as regards the produce of particular fishing stations being now repressed, none but the lessees know the value of each fishery. " It would be wrong," says the tacksman, " to provide a stick to break our own backs, which we would be doing if we told such details of our business as is implied in knowing the number of fish taken at each of our fisheries." Besides, the statement made of one year would not be true of the next, because in consequence of floods and from other causes the run of the fish is changed, and shots once productive fall away in value, new ones, of course, being developed. Sometimes the bottom of a good shot is so hollowed out by a swift flow of water as to admit of the escape of fish which would be captured were the bottom even. Whether lessees give information or no, productive places are speedily found out and their rent increased. There are about 70 net and coble stations on the commercial portion of the Tweed generally, giving employment during the fishing season to 350 men, who earn on an average 17s. 6d. per week in fixed wages and perquisites, some of the lessees allowing their fishermen a bonus on each fish captured—a plan which is thought to insure both diligence and honesty.

Tweed anglers have the privilege of fishing from the 1st of February to the 30th of November—all the year, except the two winter months. Of course, they do not catch fish—that is, salmon—all the year round; but, like others interested, they take them when they can get them, and an expert has calculated that each of the fish of the salmon kind which they capture costs at least £2 sterling. Anglers cannot find many good clean fish in November, but, as they act as a " daur " upon the poachers, they may be tolerated, especially if they return all spawning fish which they capture to the river, which, however, is rather problematical. An enormous number are caught by anglers in some years in Tweed. The Mr. Russel already named used to value the take at about £3000 per annum.

VI.

Figures pertaining to the great Scottish salmon rivers must, of course, be taken only for what they are worth— they are simply offered as being illustrative. The Severn is a stream of still greater magnitude than the Tay, falling into the Bristol Channel after a run of 210 miles. It is fed by several large affluents; but it is open to question if the value of its salmon, all told, will at the present time much, if at all, exceed £12,000 per annum. The reason why this river is so unproductive— taking its vast water area into account, and including its numerous tributary streams, some of which ought to yield salmon in large numbers—is not far to seek, seeing the river is crowded with obstructions. More- over, the fish on their way to the spawning ground run the gauntlet of the tidal nets in a long estuary, and, being sometimes unable to pass the lower weirs, are compelled to fall back again with the tide, and so risk another chance of capture. It is obvious that, if the parent fish are not allowed a fair chance of reaching their spawning beds, the stock of a river so obstructed is bound to diminish. It has been calculated that the weirs on the river prevent the salmon of the Severn from obtaining access to about half the area of water which otherwise would be at their service. There are (or at any rate there were a few years ago) as many as seventy-three mill weirs on the river, the value of which in rent may be about £4000 per annum. If these were abolished and steam-power substituted— and, presumably, there is no practical difficulty in the way of doing so—the fish would obtain ready access to the entire feeding and breeding ground, and in all likelihood quadruple the value of the river as a salmon-producing stream. With the mill weirs removed, the main stream and its tributaries ought to produce fish of the value of a hundred thousand pounds a year; while, if the river was to be aided by the construction of ponds for the hatching of ova and the rearing of young fish, a still larger yield of mature salmon should in time result. But it cannot be too often repeated that a given expanse of water will only feed and breed a given number of fish, just as a given acreage of grass-land will only pasture a certain number of sheep or cattle.

The area of lost spawning ground in English rivers is great indeed. Leaving out of account streams which from various natural circumstances do not at the present time produce any salmon whatever, seventeen rivers might be named that only possess a salmon feeding and breeding area of one-third the extent of what it was a hundred years ago. All our salmon rivers are suffering heavily from various pollutions— " matter in the wrong place "—which poison the young fish as fast as they can be bred.

The salmon fishery rents of Scotland will probably amount to £110,000 per annum. That sum must, of course, be taken with a degree of allowance ; but that the amount named is pretty correct may be assumed, seeing that the value of our Scottish salmon supply has been estimated by more than one competent authority as being at the rate of a quarter of a million sterling per annum. In 1868, Mr. Caird estimated the yearly production of salmon in Scotland at £200,000 ; in 1877, Mr. Young, one of the Commissioners for our salmon fisheries, put the figure at £250,000, the respective values of the English and Irish salmon fisheries being placed at £100,000 and £400,000 by the same authority.

Salmon in Scotland are, as a rule, private property ; and a man's piece of water on a populous salmon stream is often more valuable than three or four of his best farms. As a general rule, the Scottish salmon fisheries are well managed : the close times are enforced, and the wise legislation which was entered upon some twenty-five years ago has borne good fruit. Some streams—notably the Tweed and its tributaries—still suffer greatly from pollution.

In the face of the increasing desire to poach, which is now manifest, it becomes important to consider how our salmon may be successfully protected, especially while on their spawning grounds. The Tweed is at present, as regards police, in a kind of transition state. Around Berwick the duty of protection is performed by bailiffs, specially appointed, but in the country districts this duty is mostly undertaken by the county constables. This has given rise to dissatisfaction and controversy ; there are those who say that the Tweed should have police of its own, and there are others much enamoured of the present system. To a river which passes through four counties, a portion of which may be said to be in England, and having numerous affluents suitable for the breeding of fish, a practical system of police is of vital consequence, but there is a difficulty in finding honest watchmen and in separating the policeman from the poacher. Of course,

it is impossible that any real protection can be given
so long as the people think they have a right to as
many fish as they can capture, and Lord Minto tells us
" that not one man in a hundred believes himself
violating any moral law when he offends against the
Tweed Acts."

The natural enemies of the salmon (man being excluded) are so very numerous that poachers may well
be dispensed with. Nature provides so ingeniously for
the keeping down of superfluous stock, that when man
steps forward and ruthlessly captures the fish, at a
period when they are unfit for food and before they
have had time to repeat the story of their birth, the
balance of nature is sure to be disturbed, if not over-
thrown. Nothing has been better proved than that a
given expanse of water will only breed and feed a given
number of fish. Hard names have been bestowed on
the Tweed Commissioners for carrying out the Acts of
Parliament against the poachers, and the Acts, by some
complaining spirits, have been called " a disgrace to our
legislation."

The Tay proprietors have been more fortunate; that
river flows through a land where for the most part there
is no population to disturb its finny treasures. On the
Tweed and its many tributaries there is a considerable
population, many of whom have but slight knowledge
of " mine and thine," and all of whom have a taste for
salmon and a strong desire for gain. The cost of pro-
tecting the Tay salmon fisheries is only about a fourth
of what it costs the Commissioners to protect the river
Tweed.

The public have well-nigh become impatient of
salmon legislation, and of inquiries into the fisheries of

particular rivers. In Scotland there are about twenty
Acts still in existence, and a new one about to be introduced to Parliament. The general public, too, have
begun to grow a little jealous of the favour bestowed on
the venison of the waters; but, knowing what befell
the fish in the days when the economy of a salmon
river was less understood than it is now, and when the
fish was not so well protected as it is at present, the
public must see that more or less legislation is still
necessary for the thorough protection of a valuable
article of food. What would become of our salmon if
they were left to the tender mercies of the poacher? In
a few years' time there would not be a fish of the
salmon kind left in our streams. That may appear a
bold prophecy, but coming events cast their shadows
before, and its utterance is based on experience.

It is certain that at one period the salmon waters
of Great Britain were, through greed and false economy,
in imminent danger of being fished to death. It is
equally certain that the persistent inquiry and wise
legislation of recent years is tending to restore them,
and if further blunders are not perpetrated they have a
chance of being restored to their pristine condition, and
the people may yet hope to see salmon in the market-
place at a reasonable price. Those who complain most
loudly against salmon inquiry and salmon legislation
are those who have no right to complain at all. The
philosophy of the whole question lies in a nutshell. If
the man who causes two blades of grass to grow where
only one grew before is a benefactor to his race and his
country, the same may be emphatically said of the
man who rears two salmon to-day for the one he reared
twenty years ago. Much, however, remains to be yet

T

learnt about the economy of a salmon river, notwithstanding the great amount of knowledge which salmon
lairds have been enabled to acquire during the last
thirty years.

It is not now so difficult as it was once to divine the
future of salmon fisheries. Such a valuable product as
Salmo salar will be cherished, and wise counsels will
undoubtedly prevail among those who own the fisheries.
Salmon fishery proprietors have acquired wisdom ; they
are the persons most interested, and surely now they
know what is best for their interests. The best
guardians of a Tweed or a Tay ought to be those who
own it ; the salmon proprietors of Great Britain have
long ago discovered that fact, and are now acting
accordingly. It is difficult to see how Scottish salmon
rivers can be rendered more productive than they are ;
being private property, they are well looked after,
and in many of them there must be a large stock of
breeding fish, though in others the weight of the salmon
caught shows there is room for more. But, taking
weight as a criterion, does it matter much whether a
thousand fish are caught each of the weight of thirty
pounds, or double the number at half the weight ?

VII.

Thirty years ago salmon were decreasing in weight ;
now they are increasing. It has been suggested that
the river Tay, and indeed all Scottish rivers, should be
formed into joint-stock companies for the benefit of the
united proprietary, including those who so handsomely
give breeding room to the fish. There are at the
present time over 130 fishing stations on the river

Tay, and some 850 persons are engaged in their working for seven months in the year; in all probability, this involves the annual expenditure of a sum of £15,000 in wages. Were the fisheries of the river Tay to be formed into a joint-stock company, this amount of expenditure would in all probability be reduced to less than a fourth of the sum now paid; for in that case the capture of the fish could probably be efficiently secured at half-a-dozen instead of 130 stations. The saving to the united proprietary in wages and fishing gear would be large; and a still greater benefit might accrue from the better-regulated capture of the salmon. No fish, by such a plan of conducting operations, need be taken till it is certain it would be wanted; in other words, the pulse of the market could be felt by means of a telegram or two, and if salmon were over-plentiful fishing for a time might cease. The weight of the fish to be taken could also be regulated, as well as the number necessary to pay a good dividend.

Salmon fishing partakes of the nature of a lottery. On the river Tay, for instance, the various stations are annually put up to auction, and let on behalf of the proprietor to the highest bidder, neither party at the time of the transaction knowing whether, when the fishing season arrives, there will be any salmon to capture, so that a man may have a comparatively small rent to pay in a year when fish may be caught in abundance, and be fixed at another time with a much bigger rent when fish are far less plentiful. In the productive salmon years of 1883 and 1885, the fishery rental of the river Tay was £17,773 and £20,417 respectively, but in 1887, when the take was greatly less than it was either in 1883 or 1885, the Tay rents reached a total sum of £22,143. In 1886 the figure was still higher, being £22,542. Although the non-extension of the close period, which was asked for in 1888, proved a disappointment to the commercial fishermen, the upper proprietors, the men who afford a breeding place to the fish, must have been pleased, seeing that under the close time as now fixed they do not obtain very many salmon as a reward for what may be termed their patriotism. If the supplies are to be kept up, it is essential that a large percentage of the breeding fish should reach the upper waters in time to " repeat the story of their birth." Some of the valuable stretches of breeding ground on the higher tributaries, where the fish which perpetuate the stock of the stream make their nesting-places, are of no money value; the owners of them not having in some instances the pleasure of taking a few fish even by means of the rod, in consequence, perhaps, of the close time having come in before the fish arrive on the breeding " redd." As Sir Walter Scott pithily said, " The upper proprietors are simply clocking [brooding] hens for the benefit of the lower lairds ; " and if they were disposed to act in a " dog in the manger " spirit they might greatly hurt the commercial fisheries.

It is affirmed by some persons that there are at present more salmon in the Tay than it can well feed, but such a statement must be accepted with some degree of reserve ; and, whether it be so or no, the great competition amongst fishery lessees and the annual mortality incident to salmon life under natural circumstances forbids the hope of any stream ever becoming " too crowded with fish." In the productive years alluded to (1883 and 1885), it may be taken for granted that a larger than usual number of gravid salmon reached their breeding waters. But, if that be so, what has become of their progeny ? Eggs deposited in these years have long been due as edible table salmon, ranging in weight from, perhaps, twenty to thirty-four pounds. In the face of that, we have just experienced throughout 1888 a rather non-productive year of salmon fishing in Scottish rivers, with perhaps three or four exceptions. The best men are unable to account for the falling off in the takes which has characterised the fishing of " 88." The old excuses have been trotted out to do duty, the coldness of the season having in particular been loudly advanced as one reason for the shortcoming.

The chief obstacle which as yet remains to hinder the growth of an almost unlimited supply of salmon is that the rivers are polluted; clear, clean, wholesome water is as the breath of life to all fish. There can be no perfect development of the salmon fisheries, therefore, so long as our rivers continue to be used as gigantic common sewers. It has again and again been given in evidence that the poisonous stuffs sent into the water from manufactories which abut on the river kill or cripple the growth of the fish. It has also been said that the chemical manures now so much used by farmers have, so far as they have been washed into salmon-breeding streams, proved most deleterious to the young and tender fish. So are also preparations used in sheep washing, although the latter do not cause much harm in a large stream. Healthy water in great rivers means, without doubt, a larger supply of salmon. Let us have a clean stream for our fish, and salmon will become as plentiful as ever they were.

The system of drainage now in use is inimical to fish life; the water comes down full spate at a moment's notice, flushes the bed of the river for a time, and then leaves it empty. Is it to be expected that fish can keep healthy in waters which for weeks may run so low that they are little better than common sewers? I was on Tweed recently, and saw numerous instances of pollution. On this matter I go " the whole hog." I want— not only for the sake of the fish, and for those who capture them, but for humanity in general—clean and clear flowing water. There can be no doubt that the flow of liquid stuffs from manufactories is so much matter wasted; in a river it is in the wrong place.

Of the salmon disease (*Saprolegnia ferax*), which has played such havoc in the more important Scottish rivers, it is difficult for a non-scientific man to say very much; indeed, the outbreak has greatly puzzled the " learned " in such matters. Tens of thousands of fine salmon have fallen victims to the " fungus " during the last seven or eight years, and, although fewer fish have in some seasons been attacked than in others, the disease still prevails, and upon a rough calculation the loss to the owners or lessees of fisheries for salmon in Scotland will not have been less in the time indicated than £100,000. Many opinions have been elicited as to the cause of the disease, and cures have industriously been sought for without as yet having been discovered. Cross breeding is now being thought of as a remedy, and there is no practical difficulty, in these days of piscicultural progress, to stand in the way of a trial being made. Impregnated salmon ova can be forwarded with facility and safety for hundreds, nay, thousands of miles, so that there is nothing to prevent the introduction to the Tay or the Deveron of the salmon of the Severn, the Tyne, the Dee, or any other English stream. It is somewhat surprising that the salmon fishery owners of the River Tay, who possess a splendid hatchery on the estate of Dupplin, and who in such a matter would be working for themselves, have not attempted the introduction of new blood in the way indicated. Crossing, as has been stated in a previous page, has been tried in the Scottish deer forests with a considerable degree of success, and, in one or two experiments made on the grouse moors in the way of crossing, the birds are said to have been much improved. Why, then, should a trial of the same sort not be made with the salmon?

CHAPTER XVIII.

TROUTIANA.

I.

SCOTLAND is the land of the trout. Nothwithstanding that its waters have been remorselessly fished during the last twenty years, there are still trout in its burns and streams, and in its lakelets and lochs; the original home of the far-famed and now widely spread *Salmo Levenensis* is yet full of fish and open to anglers for a consideration. More than that, Loch Awe, with its "great lake trout," is accessible to all and much frequented. But, to get trout in plenty, an angler must hie him away to distant glens and lonely streams of water, to the solitudes of the highlands and islands. Streams within walking distance of a town or city are barren; if a fish should perchance show itself, there are a dozen anglers eager to capture it. From any river which is open to fishermen without let or hindrance trout soon vanish, and, even in localities which have become easy of access by means of railways, fish soon become scarce. Twenty miles from Aberdeen, I asked an angler one day to allow me to peep into his basket; there was not a trout in it that ought to have been captured, they were so small.

About three years ago the *Dundee Advertiser* collected

a vast amount of information for anglers regarding the condition of our rivers and lochs, and their stocks of fish. The news obtained was to the effect that in four-fifths of the waters reported upon the supply of trout and salmon was steadily falling off, but as to the cause of the decrease correspondents differed; many reasons indeed, were offered, but most of those who gave their opinion seemed to think that " pollution " of the water in some of its many shapes had most to do with the scarcity of these much-prized fish—the trout. The chemical manures now placed on the land are largely drained into the waters, whilst manufacturing *débris* of all sorts is permitted to flow into our streams. But, while believing that mischief results from these sources, it is as well not to forget the fact, that trout have become scarce because they are over-fished; for every two or three men who handled the rod thirty or forty years since, a round dozen are doing so to-day, with this result, that trout are being caught which have never been given time to multiply their kind. It must not be forgotten that a river which contains a finny popula- tion sufficient for forty anglers would soon become exhausted were it frequented by four times the number. A given expanse of water will only provide a given number of fish.

Angling of late has been much written about, and its incidents have been discussed by the press and in Parlia- ment. Fishing as a pastime is now, as one may say, a well-worn theme of literary effort, so that almost nothing new can be said about it. No eye-witness of the sport of trout fishing could believe from what he sees that any man could spin a long and lively yarn about such a simple matter as the hooking, playing, and landing of a trout weighing some five or seven ounces. Yet such literary feats have become common. " I can fish a little," said one day a well-known Scottish *littérateur*, but I'm blessed if I can write about what I do; I caught five trout yesterday in the Whittader, and one of them was a big one." That was usually the story he told. But other writers have been more prolix whilst describing their feats on lake and river, taking those who read their lucubrations into their confidence in no unmeasured way. One writer, who three years ago went grayling fishing, began his narrative by telling what he said to his wife on leaving home, how much tobacco he took with him, and how many pairs of socks he placed in his valise. In describing his angling he burst into a canticle in praise of the pipe, told a little anecdote about some trout fishing he enjoyed once upon a time somewhere in Devonshire, and, after stating how people should behave on the water, concluded by stating what he had ordered for dinner! The writer having so much to say about himself and his personal tastes, what kind of bacon he likes for breakfast, and the beer that should be drunk at dinner, has, as is usual in such cases, very little indeed to say about the fish he is after or the best modes of capturing it. Yet the article found a place in the columns of a popular periodical, and was described by a critic as being " not only interesting in respect of the information given, but brilliantly written."

Trout fishing is an exceedingly popular pastime, and eagerly indulged in by men who can obtain access to a stretch of well-stocked water, which, as has been indicated, is ill to find, a difficulty that has driven anglers to organise clubs and become lessees of lochs and rivers in many parts of Scotland, or, failing to obtain water of their own, to take refuge on such protected lochs or rivers as by payment of a fee are open to them, trout fishing being much sought after. The trout is a game fish, and fights his foe with a dash and determination which gives zest to the battle. I am well acquainted with the trout of Loch Leven (at Kinross), and can recommend a day on that fine sheet of water to those who have never tried it. A day there, however, cannot be got through under a good few shillings. A friend of mine, who pays about four visits to the loch in each year calculates that each fish he brings home costs him a crown. A basket of twenty has often been made in quick time, none of them being much under the regulation weight of one pound ; but, of course, as on other lochs, sport is unequal ; a man may expend his pound note, and be rewarded by taking an accidental perch only, a fish as plentiful in Loch Leven as pike.

Loch Leven trout weigh from twelve to about twenty ounces, but trout of two pounds are far from being rare, and "pounders" are the rule. As many who have tried their hand know, it needs a smart angler to make sure of landing them. Many a clever disciple of good old Isaak Walton has failed in the attempt ; and upon one occasion, when assisting at a little competition held there, I soon found out that the Loch Leven fish have a will of their own, and do not allow themselves to be caught as a mere matter of course, not even by anglers provided with all the wonderful upholstery of fish-catching which tackle-merchants are so industrious in providing.

The classic water of Loch Leven has so often furnished a theme to angling writers, that I dare say I would be excused were I to pass on at once to other scenes, but I desire to say just a few words about these trout, which are now found in so many lakes and rivers, having been distributed far and near by the authorities of the Howietoun fishery established by Sir James Gibson Maitland, of Sauchie.

My knowledge of Loch Leven began in early life, and my acquaintance with its boatmen has been often renewed. In those days—I am harking back to the tune of half a century ago—fly-fishing was rarely tried, and as a matter of fact there were few to try it; the lessee, however, allowed a friend or two to " fish " any way they liked. I cannot remember a time within fifty years when its fish were free to anglers. It has always in my days been a property loch, inasmuch as there was a lessee of its fisheries ; when first I used to fish in its waters, it was let to a person who netted the trout and distributed them by means of the stage coaches that carried them to Edinburgh, and thence to London, packed in ice. At present Loch Leven is farmed by a joint-stock company, who hold it on lease from its owner, Sir Graham Montgomery, and the fishing is free to all who can pay hire of boats and wages of boatmen ; a few hours on the loch soon breaks the back of a sovereign, as the charge for the boat is half-a-crown an hour, and three shillings for one man, the association paying the other. On this classic sheet of water we can see modern angling in its most pronounced fashion.

In all the ways open to honest anglers Loch Leven trout may be captured. Some big examples have been got by trolling, but the majority of the fish taken now are caught by means of the fly. In the course of the season the loch is the scene of many competitions, numerous

clubs having selected its waters as an arena on which
to fight their battles. On these occasions quite a fleet
of boats may be seen on the water, each containing a
couple of anxious anglers intent on their work. On
such days hundreds of trout are sometimes obtained.
Loch Leven being a large sheet of water, there is room
for a score or two of boats, and at these tournaments as
many as two thousand pounds' weight of trout will be
captured in the course of the season by the clubs
engaged in the competition, whilst other anglers, fishing
on their own account, will probably basket four or five
times that weight. The supply in the loch is kept up,
or at least aided, by means of the piscicultural plan of
breeding, thousands of ova being annually hatched
under proper protection; the baby fish obtained in that
manner are, of course, added to the general stock, being
first of all placed in the tributary streams.

As these trout gain strength they gradually work
their way into the loch, and in time afford sport to
anglers. How these fish came by their beautiful colour
—their flesh is pink like the flesh of the salmon—still
affords matter for surmise, although the subject has
been frequently discussed by such learned naturalists
as Jardine, Yarrell, and Couch. One reason given is
difficult to get over ; it is in plain language that " it has
been always so," and so it undoubtedly has, but, as no
fresh-water trout other than that of Loch Leven is known
to be of the same colour, the controversy required, of
course, to be fought on a wider basis, and the conclusion
arrived at by those who gave attention to the subject
was that the cause of the peculiar colour lay in the food
to which these fishes have access. Others, who also
gave time to the investigation, asserted that in all like-

lihood the so-called trout is a descendant of land-locked
salmon. There are, doubtless, many who will smile at
such a " theory," but, as has been asked, " Who knows
what took place in the beginning ? " We hear now and
again of some fish that are described as fresh-water
herrings, and among them the vendace. There are
land-locked salmon in America, and there is no im-
probability in the theory that the Loch Leven trout may
be the descendants of salmon shut out from the sea by
a sudden convulsion of nature. *Salmo salar*, as is well
known, can live in either salt or fresh water, in the
latter of which it is born ; and, therefore, it is not
difficult to conceive that if shut in Loch Leven it has
become reconciled, and is able to feed and breed in
such a sheet of water. It is an old saying of folks who
live in the vicinity of the loch that it was at one time
inhabited by eleven different kinds of fish, although it
would, we think, be somewhat difficult to name them.
It is quite certain, however, that in addition to the
salmon-coloured trout a common sort is also to be found
in that vast expanse of water, of which examples are
frequently caught. The perch, too, used to be taken in
the loch in large numbers, as also that " fell tyrant of
the liquid plain," the pike. Loch Leven is likewise
famous for its eels, which are " large, fat, and luscious,"
and find their way every year in considerable quantities
to London, and to other parts of England as well. It
is a matter of tradition that fine char were at one time
found in this famous sheet of water, which the late Mr.
Frank Buckland used to say was the biggest and finest
trout-pond he had ever seen.

There are anglers who, never having visited the
loch and acquired personal knowledge of its fish, are of

opinion that they are easy to catch. A visit to the water will very speedily dispel that illusion. The trout of Loch Leven, although abundant, are anything but tame, and are not to be taken without much pains and trouble : as has been said of some other animals, " they are game to the backbone," and fight like warriors for their lives.

Anglers on Loch Leven, it may be stated, are entitled to keep all the trout they can capture, and that every effort is made to keep up the supply is evidenced by the fact of 300,000 fry having been added to the stock a few months ago, namely, in March 1889.

II.

At present there is no close time for trout in Scotland ; it is to be hoped, however, that these fish will have attention bestowed on them in any future legislation, and be afforded a period of protection during their breeding seasons. Just now Loch Leven may be looked upon as the starting-point of the trout angler's round. It can be easily reached in two or three hours from three of the most populous towns of Scotland, while one can generally make sure of a fair day's angling on that classic sheet of water, the fish caught being sure to be worth the trouble of carrying home. Loch Tay, again, is the usual starting-point with more ambitious fishers, men who think only of catching the salmon. Later in the season some of the same men will be found on Loch Awe seeking the great lake trout, which are ill to find, and not easy to capture.

It would serve no purpose of utility to carry the reader to every seat of trout fishing in the lonely glens and mountain lochs of Scotland, nor is it necessary to descant on the style and appearance of the " burn trout " of that country—which, as has been said, are still abundant in those places that can be readily found by earnest inquirers. Trout are to be got everywhere throughout Scotland, and in the northern counties can still be taken in quantity, streams and lochs abounding all the way from the counties of Fife and Forfar to those of Sutherland and Inverness. In Ross and Cromarty shires too, as Lyall and other guides make known, there is plenty of fishing. And there and in other parts of the North may be seen some of the grandest scenery of Scotland, an ever-varying panorama of hill and glen of the most picturesque kind, a true land, in fact, of mountain and flood from Aberdeen to Cape Wrath, from the falls of Glornach to the banks of Loch Altna-harrow. The angling resources of the North have been described as inexhaustible : take, for instance, the trout stream which flows through Strathbogie in Aber-deenshire, in which there are " pucklies of fish," as a taciturn farmer's wife admitted to me when I inquired if there was any use of trying the Bogie.

Anglers who despise small fry, and must be " at the salmon," try the Dee, which is an early and some-what productive stream. Mr. McNab, of the Fife Arms, has a long stretch of the Dee on lease, and the guests of " mine host " are made welcome to try any part of it without charge. The landlord of the Inver-cauld Arms, Ballater, holds a lease of a good stretch of water, which, if he fails to let as a whole, he will then arrange for a rod or two at figures varying from, I think, £20 to £35 per month, according to season. April being esteemed the best month, his charge for the whole stretch of water for that month is, I believe, £100. Trout are plentiful in the Dee, and dwellers in the hotels are allowed to capture them free of charge. The Ythan, an Aberdeenshire stream, has a run of some forty miles, and is famous both for its yellow and its sea trout. Anglers residing at Ellon New Inn, and at the hotel in Newburgh, can have access to its waters free of charge. It is a late river, the Ythan, and is about its best in August and September.

Sea trout are plentiful, and provide quite a plethora of sport in two or three Scottish rivers : they can be taken by minnows or sand eels, or a strip of herring; but the largest ones are got in the salt water, particularly in places where streams of fresh water flow in. In sea-fishing care must be taken, a steady guide well able to handle the boat being indispensable; the good strong ones among the sea trout cannot be taken without a deal of trouble.

" It's a far cry to Loch Awe " from some places, but once there and snugly established at one of the water-side inns an enjoyable time may be put in by ardent anglers, there being " a wealth of water in Argyllshire," much of it within easy distance of their temporary home. A month's hard work will not exhaust the fishing of any district of that well-watered county ; it is necessary however, to offer this word of warning not only as regards Argyllshire, but all other northern counties, namely, that most of the rivers and lochs, being let with the shootings, are strictly looked after, still there are plenty of open spaces, and a few where permission to fish can be obtained. The major proposition with High-land lairds is, of course, to make money out of the gift with which Providence has so largely endowed them in

U

the shape of moor and loch. Numerous angling associations are lessees of water in Argyllshire, and the members are always ready to advise a 'prentice hand as to the proper bait for a given cast. That I make no pretence of doing myself, because I am a little "touched" in this matter, and do not hold very orthodox opinions, my idea being to get my fish out of the water with whatever fly will lure it from its liquid home. Trolling is the mode of fishing usually tried on the biggish lochs of Argyll and Inverness shires, in which pretty sizeable fish are found, "thumpers" of from two to four and a half pounds. And for angling homes there are nowadays many tolerably comfortable inns, where they can do almost everything for the table but properly cook the fish which have been caught at their doors. Very few people, I believe, notice the changing flavours of fresh-water fish, but their flavours are as varied as the places where they are caught—often enough spoiled, however, in the cooking, *frying* at country places being the fashion, and, as I maintain, no mode of cooking, as a rule, kills flavour faster than frying. That process reduces all fresh-water fish of the trout kind to a dead level of taste. Very large trout should be boiled, taking care to put plenty of salt in the water in which they are cooked. Trout are excellent when roasted before the fire in a Dutch oven. Middling-sized trout make a good stew or *souchet, à la Hollandaise,* so do perch.

The speciality of Loch Awe, so far as anglers are concerned, lies in the fact of that sheet of water being inhabited by the *Salmo ferox,* or "great lake trout." "But where is Loch Awe?" methinks I hear some reader ask. "It is in Scotland, I know, but in what part, and how am I to reach it?" Yes, Loch Awe is

in Scotland, in the picturesque county of Argyll. Scan
your map and you will see, running parallel with Loch
Fyne, beginning as I may say at the end of the Sound
of Jura, a long and sinuous strip of blue—that is the
home of the great lake trout. The loch is much
bigger in reality than when measured by the scale, it is
over thirty miles long and two in breadth. Travellers
have no difficult task to encounter in finding the liquid
home of these trout. The only danger is that, fascinated
with the scenery *en route,* the angler may pause by the
way. There are many beautiful spots that lovers of
scenery might fall in love with before they take up
their quarters under the shadow of Mighty Ben
Cruachan.

Arrived at Dalmally, a fisherman will find all he
can desire in the way of creature comforts so far as
the commissariat is concerned. Were it not for the
outlook, he might fancy he was not very far from the
markets of Leadenhall and Covent Garden. To-day,
"all the comforts of the Saltmarket"—all the delica-
cies of the season—are vouchsafed to tourists in even
remote parts of the Highlands. Could Johnson and
Boswell rise from their graves and once more gaze upon
the scenes of their travels, how great would be their
astonishment! Three seasons ago, I counted seven
different brands of champagne on the wine card of a
Highland inn. Communication with lowland cities is
now so frequent, and so easy, that all sorts of luxuries
are looked for both at Oban and Dalmally. Good
Scottish fare—cockie-leekie and haggis to wit—may be
obtained everywhere ; and the ubiquitous restaurateurs
of Glasgow would undertake, on receiving twenty-four
hours' notice, to serve a veritable banquet on any of

the twenty-four islands of Loch Awe, sending on a couple of their French *chefs* for the occasion, nor would the *menu* be wanting in the choicest essentials of a dinner of the period. There is choice of houses of entertainment on Loch Awe, in all of which may be found well-ventilated rooms, soft beds, and wholesome fare, with moderate charges to boot; however, I refrain from mentioning names as being invidious.

Hotel accommodation for anglers and other sportsmen throughout the Highlands of Scotland is, at the present time, plentiful and excellent—a great contrast to what it was about fifty years ago. Even in the far North, elegant and commodious structures have taken the place of the miserable inns of long ago ; and so far as lodging, liquor, and food come under review, nothing is left to be desired by wearied and hungry travellers. The days when satirical tourists found so much to sneer at are past, and if the person who wrote the following severe lines were again to visit the little town where he was so badly entertained he would doubtless be gratified by the change :—

> " Your salmon are so fat and red,
>   Your fowls so thin and blue,
>   'Tis seen which Providence has fed,
>   And which were reared by you."

As my readers have been made aware, Loch Awe is famous as the dwelling of the *Salmo ferox*, which, however, is found also in some other sheets of water in Scotland. The loch is open to anglers; for the " right of fishing " there is nothing to pay, any person may fish, trolling is the usual mode of capture, and five shillings a day is the usual cost of the boatman and his boat. When at Loch Awe we are still in Argyllshire, and there are, as I have hinted, many other lochs in the county, perhaps a hundred and fifty, all of which yield handsome tribute to the industrious fisherman, some of the trout being very heavy. Loch Shiel I cannot speak about from personal knowledge, but a friend, who has fished it, tells me it is an enjoyable locality. Anglers who can obtain permission from the lessee of the Black Forest should try Loch-na-Braw, where a basket may in brief space be filled with sizeable trout, weighing about three to the pound. On the islands, which are included in Argyllshire, are to be found innumerable sheets of water, many of which are abundantly stocked with trout. The islands of Islay and Jura, as also those of Mull and Colonsay, are worthy of being visited, and sport on all of them is plentiful and lasting. The scenery in most parts is more than picturesque, it is enchanting, and the days and nights, as a rule, are mild all the year round; there is no spot "throughout Scotland" on which an angler could dream away a summer so pleasantly as on these beautiful isles of the Western Sea.

Coming now to "the fish" of Loch Awe, I may state that on my first visit to that famous sheet of water, since which day many years have elapsed, things were homelier than they are to-day. A friend and myself lived at a farmhouse *near* (*i.e.* three miles from) the water. We were able, however, to obtain a boat in order to fish, but our up-putting during our few days' stay was nothing to boast of—very primitive indeed. It is close on a hundred years (it was in 1790) that the discovery of *Salmo ferox* took place by a Glasgow gentleman of the name of Morrison, who was in the habit of visiting the neighbourhood. These fishes were

first of all submitted to Sir William Jardine, and it was
that eminent Scottish naturalist who first scientifically
described them and wrote of them as *ferox*, a name
which he thought suitable to their habits and prowess.
Although thought to be unique when discovered in
Loch Awe and described by Agassiz as differing somewhat from the Continental species, it is now known to
inhabit various other sheets of water. It has been
found in Loch Laggan, Loch Shin, and Loch Loyal and
Assynt, as well as Loch Awe, roving at will and exact-
ing tribute with dashing rapidity and powerful jaws
from the smaller fish. Those who reside near these
lochs capture the big trout with night lines. They are
occasionally tempted to rise to a small fly during
the day, but the surest method is the trolling tackle,
baited either with a small trout or an artificial minnow.
They are extremely voracious, and having seized the
bait will allow themselves to be dragged by the teeth
for forty or fifty yards, and when accidentally freed will
seize it again with renewed vigour. Specimens of this
ferox are found in Lough Nenagh in Ireland, and in
Ullswater Lake in Cumberland; in Ireland it is known
as the Buddagh. This great trout has also been found
in Lough Corrib and in other places in Ireland. These
giant fish need elbow-room, space in which to feed and
grow; they must also have a varied bottom, and these
conditions they obtain in Loch Awe. One may try for
many days but not get a specimen; they are so
mysterious that for weeks not one will be seen; that
there is more than one kind is certain, the red-fleshed
fish being vastly different from the white-fleshed ones.
A good red trout of Loch Awe is a fish any gentleman may be proud to offer his guests, but the white-

fleshed trout are poor in flavour and coarse in texture, and not worth powder and shot. The *ferox* is game to the back-bone, it "submits to be killed rather than surrender," and it has been said of Loch Awe and its surroundings that, while the scenery is fine, the sport is finer.

III.

We have now two "fisheries" in Scotland in which trout are bred in tens of thousands—especially Loch Leven trout. It was thought at one time that these fish would not thrive in any other sheet of water, but that has long since been proved to be a vulgar error. By means of their eggs these trout have been sent far and near—even to the United States of America. The manager of the Howietoun Fishery has announced that he is in a position to supply eggs of the Loch Leven trout in millions; the proprietor of the Solway Fishery also professes to be able to supply large quantities of eyed ova of these fish; and, as a thousand only cost a few shillings, there is nothing to prevent gentlemen who are stocking their waters, old or new, useful or ornamental, from selecting these or other fish, which they can also obtain as yearlings and two-year-olds. The ova or young of American brook trout are likewise dealt in at these fisheries, as also the ova and young of several other fishes. For gentlemen who let their lakes and streams along with their grouse moors or deer forests, these fisheries are doubtless a great convenience, seeing that it is possible for them to stock their waters with an abundant supply of the best kinds of sporting fish, which admits, in some instances, of their being let in consequence at higher rents than might otherwise be obtained.

By means of the two fisheries alluded to, "pisciculture" is now established as an art in Scotland. I have already spoken of the Stormontfield Salmon Nurseries and the experiments conducted by Shaw in salmon breeding. The proprietors of the Tay have continued for the benefit of that river the system of artificial spawning and protected egg nursing which were begun at Stormontfield; on some of the other Scottish salmon streams pisciculture has also, I believe, been tried, likewise at Loch Leven. There is nothing, however, to prevent every stream in Scotland from being provided with an establishment of the kind indicated; it has been again and again proved that it is possible to breed salmon from the egg stage till they become the size of smolts and have attained probably the second year of their age, at an almost nominal figure per fish. Let us take it for granted that some good stream with plenty of pure water not hitherto occupied by such fish is to be converted into a well-stocked salmon river; in the first instance, large numbers of eggs would have perhaps to be purchased, if they could not be obtained by agreement from some neighbouring stream. In due time, however, when the new salmon river became able to supply gravid fish, £120 per annum would be sufficient to pay fair interest on outlay for construction of ponds and for the work of providing an annual supply of eggs. Say that about thirty pairs of fish were spawned, each pair yielding 8000 ova, and the necessary stock of milt, 240,000 eggs would be the result, and of these, if well looked after, only a small percentage would fail to yield fish;

but taking it that only 220,000 did so, and that such a number of smolts were sent to the sea, the return would be prodigious if, in the course of three years, the odd 20,000 were to reach consumers as table fish, of the value of 10s. each.

It has already been stated in these pages that the mortality to which these fish are subject is enormous, especially when left to nature. Bred and fed for a year or two, the young salmon when sent out to seek their fortune in the sea are better able to take care of themselves than when by the natural hatching system they are left defenceless to the tender mercies of their enemies. So soon as Stormontfield was opened, the rental of the river Tay began to increase, and to rise from, say, £10,000 to £20,000 per annum.

No practical difficulty stands in the way of pisciculture, which can be accomplished either on a small or large scale. I assisted a few years ago at the stocking of a little pond on a gentleman's estate, on which occasion a stock of 1000 American brook trout were brought in safety from a distance of over 120 miles. They were contained in a glass carboy and were none the worse for their long journey, the whole stock being alive and lively. A large tub having been filled with water from the pond which they were to occupy, they were very gradually acclimatised, so to say, and ultimately turned into their future dwelling-place. At first they all huddled together in a black mass, but, quickly gaining courage, they began to look about them, and finally were seen in a few days darting about in search of food. Where larger quantities are required they can be similarly dealt with. Food must be supplied; liver boiled hard and grated is good, and a dead bird or two

or a few rabbits may be hung over the water so that
the troutlets may obtain a plentiful supply of maggots.
In streams where eggs are laid down care should be
taken to protect them as much as possible, as fish ova
form a welcome tit-bit to numerous birds. In all cases
it is as well to imitate nature as nearly as circumstances
will admit. On the other hand, the example of the
gentleman who laid down 2000 eyed ova in his newly-
made pond and then threw into it 300 two-year-old
trout must not be followed. In the " fisheries," crossing
or inter-breeding is being carried on experimentally,
and may in time result in practical benefits of some
kind to all interested.

From a price list in my possession, I note that eyed
ova per 1000, carriage paid, can be purchased for 30*s.*
in the case of Loch Leven trout; American trout ova
cost 10*s.* more than that sum per 1000; for eggs from
very superior fish of the same kind £4 is wanted.
Salmon ova and the eggs of the char range in price
from 30*s.* to double that amount. Fry of these fishes
can be obtained at prices ranging from £1 to £5.

Angling as now practised is greatly dependent on the
protected waters being well stocked with fish, and by
the modes mentioned above these rivers and lochs can
be rendered populous with trout at comparatively small
cost; a quantity of 10,000 trout ova can be purchased
for the sum of £6, and if that number were to be successfully hatched, it would, of course, add largely to the
chances of sport on even a pretty large loch. At the
" fisheries " in Scotland a very large trade is carried on
both in eggs and fry as well as in larger fish. The establishment at Howietoun cannot have cost less in its
construction than £12,000 or £14,000. It is a sight

that is worth seeing, especially at feeding time. It is an open secret that the fish at Howietoun are hippophogists ; they feed on the flesh of horses, some four or five of which are killed every week by the attendants and duly devoured by the denizens of the various ponds ; only healthy animals are received for this purpose, and, before being despatched by means of the poleaxe, they are allowed for a period of three weeks or a month to roam over the juicy grasses of the neighbouring fields. Other food-stuffs are also in use, particularly clams, which are brought to the ponds in enormous quantities from the fishing port of Newhaven' near Edinburgh ; snails are likewise in request, and a particular snail which is found in Loch Leven has now been acclimatised at Howietoun, and will in future years play a prominent part in the feeding department, as the fish eat that particular snail with great avidity, and thrive and grow fat upon it apace. As one of the labourers at the place says, " The meat for the fish is a great *eatem* in the expense," and the feeding arrangements of all kinds at the fishery have been carefully devised, and are systematically carried out. This fishery is half-an-hour's drive from the railway station at Stirling and is well worthy of a visit. The other Scottish fishery, which is also a sight worth seeing, may be reached from Dumfries ; it is called the " Solway Fishery."

CHAPTER XIX.

Trout and Sport in the Borders.

Following the trout to those streams that run in the
south of Scotland the angler is sure to find sport, not,
perhaps, in the same abundant measure as in days long
vanished, when there were no fast-speeding railway
trains to bear fishermen away from the big seats of
population to the rivers and lakes of rural places, but
quite sufficient to prove satisfactory, if the ambition of
the angler is modest enough not to covet fish for the
mere desire of being able to return home carrying a
creel crowded to its lid with the speckled beauties of
our border streams. Many anglers are now so bent on
what Mr. Ruskin has called "the lewd sensation of
slaughter" that nothing will stay their hand but the
want of fish; there are men who only think of their
present work, and give no heed to the years that are
coming, hence they do not blush when they are caught
with a dozen or two of baby fish in their possession—
trout of the future, in fact, which next year, or next
again, would have afforded something like real sport.
As to what may be called the streams of "the borders,"
their waters flow in a wide range if we interpret the
phrase in a wide sense. It is somewhat difficult, how-

ever, to say where the borders begin or end, but the counties of Berwick, Roxburgh, Selkirk and Dumfries, as well as Galloway (Kirkcudbright and Wigtown), may all be laid under contribution by the border angler.

Some of my earliest angling reminiscences are connected with the river Till, a tributary of the Tweed. At the time indicated, many fine trout were captured in that stream by means of salmon roe—a very killing bait, with which it is now illegal to fish. Several persons throughout Scotland at one period supplied this substance, and one or two of the "muggers" residing at Yetholm were famed for their preparation of roe; but the chief provider of this bait for the use of anglers in Scotland was a person named Easton, who carried on the business of a hairdresser in the town of Hawick, and was himself no mean angler; his roe commanded a higher price than that supplied by any other dealer, and ultimately became a means of his "making money," as the saying goes. In the days referred to, some fine large trout could occasionally be taken in Till water by means of several kinds of bait, but chiefly by worm and salmon roe. The "muggers," as the gipsies of Yetholm are called, are keen fishers, and good at the work—a band of gipsies never want for fish. In the old coaching days, I remember upon one occasion, while travelling to Edinburgh, of the coachman of the Moffat coach being offered as many trout as would have filled a small washing-tub for half-a-crown; they had been captured by two muggers who were travelling in the district, their angling upholstery being of the rudest description; but all gipsies seem as if they had been sent into the world to fish for trout or salmon, holding it to be no sin to take a "fish" when it offers—"fish" in the borders usually means a salmon.

Much has already been written in these pages about the Tweed, more particularly with reference to its salmon, for which it has always been famous, while the men who have fished it have never lacked notoriety, especially the professional fishermen who found work and wages on its waters. One of my pleasant memories goes back to John Younger, the shoemaker poet of St. Boswells, who wrote in his time a remarkably good book on angling, so good that it really ought to be reprinted—indeed no more reliable guide as to baits and casts of water in his own countryside has ever been, or is ever likely to be, published. John Younger used to "let out" bitterly when he was provoked about Mr. Scrope, the deer-stalker and salmon angler, "who stole my *flees* and published them as his ain." No doubt Younger was ill-used in this matter. In his work on salmon angling, Mr. Scrope gave drawings of a number of flies which the shoemaker of St. Boswells had "invented" for his own use, and which he "busked" and sold to his friends and patrons, who were numerous, for in the course of his lifetime he had acquired the good opinion of many men. Dukes and other nobles, poets, play-actors, journalists and weavers, cotton lords from Manchester, and merchants from Glasgow, together with "writers" from Edinburgh, delighted to call on the village shoemaker, to talk over the agreeable art in which they were all interested.

As Younger had previously published plates of his "ain flees" in a book he had written, he was able to claim his own handiwork. The shoemaker, who was an ardent Radical, wrote pretty severely of the man

he used to call the "aristocratic salmon catcher." A
portion of what he said may be transferred to this page.
" Mr. Scrope, some year or two thereafter, published a
splendid book on fishing, under a show of plates and
price as great in proportion to mine as the amount of
his original fortune in life was above mine, not as he
stood higher in knowledge of his subject or in manual
ability, but in worldly circumstances, and consequently
in the world's eye. Thus the world goes generally—
while I am valued at eighteenpence, Scrope sells at two
guineas! God help me and the world both; we are a
farce to think on, a sorry farce indeed. It is puzzling
to suppose which is the most to be pitied. Scrope's
six flies are mine, of course, to a shade; they could
indeed be properly no other, only that he has described
them in other words (even figured them in painted
plates), with perhaps more quaint formality in tufts
and toppings, and under fanciful local names, such as
' Meg in her braws,' ' Kinmont Willie,' ' The Lady of
Mertoun,' and so on."

Younger was able to give all who visited him good
counsel as to border angling, and the best baits with
which to catch trout. And, if his opinion about the
bigger fish was asked, he used to say in his forcible
way: " It takes a man to catch and play a salmon.
There's a gentleman living here on Tweedside that sits
in his boat and sends his man on to the bank to land
his fish, in the mean time hooking another one when he
can with his second rod. Now, any fool may hook a
salmon, but it needs a wise man to get the fish out of
the water—in my opinion to play and land the salmon
is the test of the true angler." The gentleman alluded
to was Mr. Scrope, whom the men of Tweedside, he

used to say, looked upon with contempt as an angler.

Thomas Tod Stoddart, with whom I had once some correspondence, was another of the "Angling Spirits of Tweedside"; as poet and fisherman he was well known, and one or two of his works, I gladly notice, have been recently reprinted. Stoddart in his day was "hail fellow well met" with such men as "Christopher North," the Ettrick Shepherd, Professor Aytoun, Robert Chambers, Thomas De Quincy, "Russel of the *Scotsman*," and in his lifetime with Sir Walter Scott, the great "Wizard of the North," himself, and was appreciated by them all. Get leave to go a-fishing with Mr. Stoddart and you were sure of having an enjoyable time of it; if, perchance, you were a poor hand at the business yourself, you had the advantage of seeing your companion "luring the speckled trout from the brook" with all his might and with the trained skill of an adept at the business. And you had in addition at intervals, that is, in the pauses of fishing, a flood of talk—and such talk! It was as good as a liberal education to spend a couple of days with this well-known Tweed celebrity of the fishing-rod. With the Tweed and all its tributaries he was minutely acquainted; he knew the whimpling burnies, and was familiar with the pools where lay ensconced "the monarch of the brook"; he could tell the exact spot of water where you might find that "fell tyrant of the liquid plain," "Mr. Pike." Then he could say words of wisdom about the botany of the river-side; he knew much of the natural history of Tweeddale, and had been familiar all his days with the "tales of the borders,"—the legends and the lyrics of the troublous times which had set their marks of tragedy and romance on the glens and on the towers and castles of the district in which it was his fate to reside. But here there is not space to chronicle all that might be said about Stoddart; he has, however, in some degree chronicled his own life in the autobiography prefixed to his ' Songs of the Seasons.'

Of Hogg, the Ettrick Shepherd, who was a " natural sportsman," much might be said in these pages, but I cannot write much about his sporting proclivities from personal knowledge, not having seen him " to speak to " more than perhaps three times. The late Dr. Robert Chambers told me that " James " was one of the keenest and cleverest trout-catchers he had ever known, and if I am not mistaken Professor Wilson (" Christopher North ") has spoken of his prowess with the fishing-rod on the border streams, especially those in the neighbourhood of his residence, not far from St. Mary's Loch and " Yarrow stream," where well-filled baskets of fair-sized trout, running from three-quarters of a pound to double that weight, can still be captured without great exertion. Speaking of St. Mary's Loch reminds one of Tibbie Shiels and her well-known cottage, the " howff " of two or three generations of anglers from Edinburgh and other places who used to frequent the border districts. " Tibbie's " has been immortalised by several writers as the rendezvous of some of the cleverest men of the country; ministers of the Gospel, professors from Edinburgh and Glasgow, publishers, advocates, writers to the signet, authors, actors, and artists have often held " high jinks " in St. Mary's Cottage, where many words of wit and wisdom have been heard over the toddy which used to grace the board at night, and in the mornings the " Loch o' the Lowes " was handy for

x

a bracing bath and a long swim. Most of the rivers in Selkirkshire yield sport, there being in some of them abundance of half-pound trout, which fight boldly for their lives and give work to the angler.

The writer has now in his mind's eye another sportsman who delighted to roam by the border waters, namely John Wilson, Professor of Moral Philosophy in the University of Edinburgh, best known as the " Christopher North " of *Blackwood's Magazine.* The professor used at divers times and in many places to speak of James Hogg, not as a poet, but as a good shot and an excellent fisher. The Shepherd of Ettrick could always seduce the philosopher from his work in town by inviting him to come and kill a blackcock, or take part in a gathering of coursers. Many a joyous day they passed in each other's company, and often the pair would merrily chaff each other. The professor on one occasion invited Hogg to visit him in Cumberland about the 12th, but the Shepherd could not see it : " My dear and honoured John," he writes back, " I never thought you had been so unconscionable as to desire a sportsman on the 11th or even the 13th of August to leave Ettrick Forest for the bare, scraggy hills of Westmoreland ! Ettrick Forest, where the black cocks and white cocks, brown cocks and grey cocks, ducks, plovers and peaseweeps and whilly whaups are as thick as the flocks that cover her mountains, and come to the hills of Westmoreland that can nourish nothing better than a castrel or stonechat ! To leave the great yellow fin of yarrow, or the still larger grey locher, for the degenerate fry of trout-beck, esthwaite, or even wastwater ! No, no, the request will not do ; it is an unreasonable one, and not like yourself."

Wilson was a fair all-round sportsman, and in his day many and many a bird fell to his gun, and many a salmon felt the power of his handling, but it was in trout-fishing that Wilson excelled, and " the contemplative man's recreation " was his great delight. With his trout-rod in his hand he could count not on single fish, not even on dozens, but on dozens of dozens! There lived once, as has been often told, an American who was such a splendid shot that whenever a bird saw him approaching it saved him the trouble of shooting by at once falling dead at his feet. Wilson with his angle possessed a similar gift; it looked as if there was a competition among the trouts as to which should first have the honour of swallowing his bait; they came to him not in single spies, but in battalions. Here is what Hogg said, upon an occasion when Wilson contributed an extemporised supper to a famished party who had eaten up a small country inn; he asked them if they liked trout, and, lo! when an affirmation was given, he produced the result of his day's work in such numbers that all present were literally astonished : " Your creel was fu', your shooting-bag fu', your jacket pouches fu', the pouches o' your verra breeks fu', half-a-dizzen wee anes in your waistcoat, no' to forget them in the croon o' yer hat, and last o' a', when there was nae place to stow awa ony mair, a willow wand drawn through the gills o' some dizzen great big anes."

To chronicle Wilson's feats would undoubtedly astonish the reader : at one place he takes six dozen, at another ten dozen, at another eighteen dozen. One day, whilst limping about, having wounded his heel leaping with a band of tinkers, he tried to ease the pain by fishing in Loch Awe ; he hooked a *ferox*. " His line was weak, and, afraid to lose it, he cast himself into the loch, yielding to the motions of the strong creature until it became fatigued and manageable. Then he swam ashore with his victim in subjection, and brought it home, but he was without the bandage, and his heel bleeding copiously."

My readers do not grow weary, I hope, of such reminiscences, they crowd the chambers of my memory, and along with other recollections of the kind might be greatly extended. Notices in particular might well be given of the Richardsons and Kerrses, one of whom told a gentleman who had engaged his boat, but never offered him a pull at his flask, that " them that drink by themselves should fish by themselves," and so pulled ashore. The Purdies, too, deserve brief record ; all who have read the charming life of Sir Walter Scott written by his son-in-law, John Gibson Lockhart, are already familiar with " Tom," the great novelist's out-of-doors attendant and forester. A brother of Tom's, Charlie Purdie, was the Abbotsford fisherman. One of " the Purdies "—John—born in the first year of the century, died about three years ago, having attained the good old age of eighty-six years. Old John, at one time fisherman attendant to Mr. Broadwood, lessee of the Pavilion water, was an angler of the old school, and would not countenance any but ·the old-fashioned ways of fly-busking and fishing ; " new-fangled " modes of doing things on Tweed were his aversion. John was much respected, and often visited by anglers and patrons in his cottage close by the Bridge at Darnick.

In his 'Lay of the Last Angler,' the Rev. Robert

Liddell has, as the following lines demonstrate, something to say about this Tweedside celebrity :—

> " John and I are oldish friends.
>   O'er forty years our time extends,
>   He's been with me for many a spurt on
>   The streams and pools of bonny Merton ;
>   He's given me many a useful lesson,
>   How to be ' canny,' or to press on
>   A heavier strain against one's fish,
>   And tire it out as he would wish.
>   He could get out a splendid line
>   Into the wind, or ' fishing fine ' ;
>   In heavy water, when afloat,
>   No one could beat him with the boat ;
>   In short he's master of the art
>   In all details and every part ;
>   If Cambridge gave degrees to anglers,
>   John would be first of Senior Wranglers."

Sir Walter Scott was not himself a disciple of good old Walton, but his friends were made free of whatever water he possessed, and with the view of being shown plenty of sport were handed over to Charlie Purdie, who was probably lessee of the Abbotsford water ; but,. whether or not, there was salmon fishing for such of Sir Walter's visitors as could handle a rod, whilst many a merry party was made up at the Abbotsford dinner-table to burn the water.

" Burning the water " was forty and fifty years since one of the most enjoyable of all the sports of all the broad borders. True it was a pastime of a rough-and-ready sort; being, however, an open-air function of an unusually hilarious kind, many liked well to participate in the excitement to which it gave rise, and often even at the risk of being half drowned some green hands would insist on taking part in the business. It is almost unnecessary to say that " burning " was a winter evening's recreation, and I regret to add that most of the fish killed were big with spawn, "bagots" we called them, or salmon, perhaps, which had just performed that important duty—these were known on Tweedside as " kelts." Burning the waters, once so frequent on the Tweed and some of its tributaries, is now an illegal mode of fishing, although, as old customs die out slowly, it may still be occasionally heard of as being in vogue in one or two out-of-the-way places seldom visited by " the bailiffs." The burning may, when the water is suitable, be accomplished from the banks of a stream, or by means of one or more boats, according to the size of the party taking a share in the work. No sport (hare-hunting excepted) gave more delight to the master of Abbotsford than the leistering of a salmon by the light of a pine-wood torch in the early part of a long winter's night, when a feast on some occasions would be improvised, a fire would be kindled, and a kettle* would be

* Salmon is never better cooked than when prepared as a "kettle." The Tweed kettle, it has been written, was invented by the monks of Melrose, who were famous in their day and generation for good living. It was said of them that they

> " Made gude kail
> On Fridays when they fasted,
> Nor wanted they gude beef and ale
> As lang's their neighbours' lasted."

Sir Humphry Davy's mode of cooking a Tweed fish was the same as in the case of the kettle : " First catch your salmon," he says, " then kill him by dealing him a quick blow on the head, cut the fish through the bone at inch distances (having first taken out all the intestinal matter), hold him up after this that the blood may flow got ready ; meantime a bowl of whisky punch would be brewed, flour scones and oat cakes would be handed round, accompanied with sundry glasses of prime Edinburgh ale, or, as it was called in fun, fine Scottish Burgundy, so that the ladies and gentlemen who formed the good company were well feasted.

The leistering would proceed, and on occasion not without mishap: some unlucky but eager wight, anxious to display his skill in handling the salmon-killing spear, would overbalance himself and fall into the water, but no fatal result ensued ; quickly rescued by his companions, he would be at work again after having a quaich well filled with Abbotsford whisky administered to him by Sir Walter's butler, who was in attendance, having first visited a neighbouring cottage and obtained a change of clothes. Burning the waters has always been accompanied by just a spice of danger. I have myself seen men at the work who on occasion made narrow escapes from death by drowning. Poachers were exceedingly partial to this mode of salmon catching, which, as has been stated, is now illegal, and cannot be practised even by the owner of a fishing. Formerly the salmon lairds themselves used to be fond of the pastime, and were not slow to take a share in it. Oftentimes the scene at a burning was exceedingly

---

out of the body, then place him in a bath of cold water for ten minutes. Next take him to the pot, in which the pickle must be boiling previously, and then slice him down, throwing the biggest cuts into the pot first, and letting the water come to the boiling point after each slice has been thrown in." That formula was characterised by "Meg Dods" as being after the old fashion of the pickled salmon prepared at the Scottish fisheries for the London market, than which nothing was at the time thought better.

picturesque on a dark night ; as the glare of the torches flashed out a light on bank or water, and as fish after fish was transfixed on the prongs of the leister, the excitement, helped by various appeals to the bottle, would wax fast and furious, till the last salmon was leistered for the night, and the last man had taken his departure, homeward bound having a walk of five or six miles in prospect, lightened, however, by the knowledge that he would obtain a warm welcome, seeing that he carried in the pocket of his maud [plaid] a couple of sixteen-pound fish.

Sir Walter Scott, as has been already stated, was no hand with the fishing-rod himself, but he exhibited keen sympathy for all out-of-door sports, and, in his capacity of sheriff of the county in which he lived, he was even lenient in dealing with the poachers of his neighbourhood, much to the chagrin sometimes of his brother lairds, who were desirous of putting down poaching by means of the strong hand of the law, and without consideration of circumstances ; but the great novelist used to say: "No, no; all the cases are not alike, and I'm disposed to wink at the offence of a man who kills a hare for his own pot." Tom Purdie,* Sir

---

* Tom deserves a passing word in this brief chronicle of Border Sports, seeing that, next to Sir Walter, he was "the great man" of Abbotsford. The sheriff *discovered* him at the bar of his court, and, from being a sort of "ne'er-do-well," converted him into a useful member of society and faithful and affectionate out-of-doors servant—a sort of hybrid, between a farm grieve and a forester. Having in his early days been himself a bit of a poacher, Tom was ill to cheat, and was as honest as steel. Here is a little scene from Lockhart's 'Life of Scott,' which will better show the status of Tom Purdie than a page or two of elaborate writing: "Scott, being a little fatigued, laid his hand on Tom's shoulder and

Walter's well-known henchman, was reputed to have been himself at one time a border poacher.

The "Abbotsford Hunt," in the opinion of all who were privileged to enjoy the fun and excitement which attended it, was the finest meeting of the kind in all the borders. A farmer of the Dandie Dinmont type, who used to take part in the sports of the day, coming home late at night, after having liberally partaken of the hospitalities of the occasion, with just a " wee drap " of the contents of the far-famed Abbotsford punch-bowl " in his 'ee," exclaimed to his better half, " Losh, woman, what a day we've had ! I wish I could sleep till this time next year : the Hunt is the only thing that's worth living for."

That farmer's opinion would, no doubt, have been endorsed at the time by the opinions of a hundred people who had been equally delighted. But, although the Hunt was a popular gathering, the lord of Abbotsford took care that it should be as select as possible—the right people only were asked to take part. Sir Walter knew that it would not do to let the affair be common to all, and his conservative instincts insured that the company should be tolerably select. There were many who would have been proud to have been asked that

---

leaned heavily for support, chattering to his ' Sunday pony,' as he called the affectionate fellow, just as freely as with the rest of the party ; and Tom put in his word shrewdly and manfully, and grinned and grunted whenever the joke chanced to be within his apprehension. It was easy to see that his heart swelled within him from the moment that the sheriff got his collar in his gripe. Whoever might be at Abbotsford, Tom always appeared at his master's elbow on Sunday when dinner was over, and drank long life to the laird and the lady, and all the good company, in a quaich of whisky, or a tumbler of wine, according to his fancy."

received no invitation. I am not too much exciting the expectation of the reader, I trust, for the Abbotsford Hunt was not a chase after the fox, it was simply a coursing meeting! As it went on, the fun grew fast and furious, host and guests enjoying themselves as if they had been so many children out for a romp.

Sir Walter was a very good horseman, having in his day been adjutant to a corps of yeomanry. Behold him, then, mounted on Sibyl Grey, a kind of big pony, surrounded by friends and attended by his retainers. Lairds and farmers, of the true Dandie Dinmont cut, were present from distant border farms—from Liddesdale and Teviotdale; and philosophers from London, as well as lawyers from Edinburgh, formed part of the concourse. Guests who were inmates of the house, whether they were members of the peerage or partners in his printing-office, must to the hunt. Lady Scott and her daughters in their comfortable "sociable" made all who came welcome; other ladies in other carriages; old men in dog-carts, and young men on foot; good walkers, able, by taking a short cut across the field and plantations, to be at the scene of action as quickly as those who rode on horseback or were carried in a trap were all there.

The scene of the hunt was usually selected, not only for its plenitude of hares, but for its surroundings. About Newark Castle the sportsman stood on classic ground. "The dowie dens of Yarrow" were not far distant, and full oft some of the visitors would recur to the conclusion of "the lay":—

> "When summer smiled on sweet Bowhill,
> And July's eve with balmy breath
> Waved the blue-bells on Newark heath."

This kind of sport having been often described, it would be only tiring my readers to say much more about it. The place usually selected for the hunt was a stretch of low mountain-side, where were watery gulfs to be feared, and dangerous bogs to be circumnavigated; men and horses, too, full often going splash into some treacherous morass, covered with a bright green carpet, and looking anything but a trap. Crowds on foot and on horseback would push after the dogs, and while doing so many a man would measure the ground. The great author himself, on more than one occasion, while cautiously jogging along on Sibyl Grey, has been made to kiss the grass which bordered some hidden ditch or drain; and once, when Sir Humphry Davy was in full enjoyment of the sport, he plunged neck-deep into a well, from which he came forth a pitiable spectacle. Mackenzie, the venerable author of the ' Man of Feeling,' had a quick eye, and would observe a hare before any one else : the old gentleman was a frequent attendant of the hunt, and was always, old as he was, the brightest of the bright company, active and *débonnair*, full of spirit. Sir Walter himself was wondrous active, riding along the line, directing, inspiring the day's work with many a joke for those who could take it, and with kind words and a winning smile for all, feeling more at home even than he did in his library, when busily preparing a bundle of manuscript for Ballantyne's devouring printing-presses in " Paul's Work."

Hospitality was plentifully dispensed in the course of the day to all around, cakes and ale being liberally handed about, with tastings of stronger liquors for those who liked to partake of them; the Abbotsford stock cask of whisky having a wide reputation, drams were in demand, the quaichs being frequently requisitioned by the stalwart border farmers, who were on the ground early and remained to the last. The day's work, as was fitting, was brought to a termination in the dining-room with the customary banquet—a jovial dinner of good things ; of fragrant and palatable soup, made from hares killed in the battle ; of trout caught and salmon speared in the waters of the classic Tweed ; of Cheviot mutton, bred and fed by the laird ; of moorcock shot on the estate ; of fruits grown in the garden, and wine stored in the cellars of Abbotsford. "The dinner" was usually a joyous affair, and for those of the coursing company who were, as the saying goes, "too blate" to join Sir Walter and his guests, there was spread a second table, at which as much good cheer was served as was set out in the chief dining-room. Sir Walter was kind to all, and, although he feasted the great on fitting occasions, he never forgot the small ; even when surrounded by the greatest of the land, the brightest in intellect or the richest in purse, he never forgot his humbler friends and neighbours, the yeomen of the district, among whom his popularity was un-bounded. There was not a farmhouse or cottage within many miles of Abbotsford in which the great novelist was not a welcome guest. "Hail-fellow-well-met" with the farmer, and always in favour with the farmer's wife, he was dignified withal, and never forgot himself, or allowed those with whom he spoke to forget that he was not only the lord of Abbotsford, but sheriff of the county as well.

Enough, perhaps, has now been said about the Abbotsford Hunt, at which I never was present ; whatever claim I may possess to reproduce the scene arises from the fact of a note-taking relative having more than once been among the company.

In glancing over what I have written, I find I have forgotten to chronicle the brewing of the punch, which was a speciality of all Abbotsford dinners when there was company.

This compound was explicitly made after the following manner: First of all—and it is important— see that you have by you a few bottles of fine old Jamaica rum; if you have, then proceed as follows to make up a syrup of cold spring water, lime juice, and the finest lump sugar; begin by melting your sugar little by little, then squeeze your lemons, from six to fourteen, through a drainer into a bowl—see how this tastes—it should neither be too sweet nor too sour; if you approve of the foundation, begin to add the rum; there is no rule as to the quantity, but take care to leave room for the water, which should be pure and cold, and when the bowl is five-sixths full squeeze in the juice of a couple of limes by dipping them in the contents, and running them round the inside of the punch-bowl. Take care, in confectioning this delicious liquor, not to have too much water for the quantity of rum, nor too much rum for the bulk of water; study the blend; one of spirit to five of water should about hit the mark—*chacun à son goût.*

All the sports of Scotland are, of course, common to the borders, and the men of the district are keen sportsmen; steeple-chasing, hunting and horse-racing they take an active share in when opportunity offers. The well-known "burr" of the border is often heard at Doncaster, and there are men in the south of Scotland who have not missed seeing "the St. Leger" for the last quarter of a century. There are, or at least there used to be, societies for the encouragement of manly sports all over the border.

If I am not mistaken, the first properly constituted society for the carrying out of border sports was "St. Ronan's," at Innerleithen, where, for many years, the Ettrick Shepherd was in his glory as the presiding genius of the scene.

"The St. Ronan's border games" were, I think, originated just after the publication of Sir Walter Scott's novel of 'St. Ronan's Well.' They were conducted by a body of border archers arrayed in doublets of Lincoln green, and wearing on their heads broad Tam-o'-Shanter "bonnets of blue." For many years this meeting was a great success, and was often honoured by the presence of Sir Walter. The Shepherd was captain and general manager of the games, and took part in several of the pastimes incidental to the joyous meeting, many a time and oft taking a prize from out the grasp of younger men. At the dinner with which the sports wound up Hogg took the chair, which he filled to the admiration of all who graced the board.

Bordermen are fond of their fishing-rod and gun, and their character for loyalty and patriotism has found scope in the Volunteer movement. Foxhunting has always held its own. A pack of foxhounds is kept up with all requirements by that most popular border nobleman, his Grace the Duke of Buccleuch. Greyhound coursing is, however, *the* sport of the borders, the Earl of Haddington being a most princely supporter of the leash on the borders, or, indeed, in all broad Scotland. His lordship has in his service the well-known Sandy Grant, one of the best of trainers. Many southern farmers breed their own dogs, and strains of blood may be found at local meetings which might prove victorious further afield. Bowling is also a border institution; wherever you find a curling pond you are never far from a bowling green. At Abbotsford Sir Walter had his bowling green erected near the house of his coachman, in order that he might sit there at night and listen to the evening psalm of Peter Mathison, his faithful master of the horse. A feature of the bowling season of the present day is the great border bowling tournament, which generally takes place at either Hawick or Galashiels, and lasts two or three days, the sport being generally presided over by that most genial sportsman and gentleman, Admiral Bailie, of Dryburgh. Such friendly trials of skill present to us a happier state of affairs than the border fights and feuds of two hundred years ago.

At certain seasons—on Fastern E'en in particular—there take place in several of the border towns spirited and keenly-contested games at handball, in which one division of a place will be pitted against another division. I do not know the origin of the practice, but it has been a custom, I am told, of centuries, and even the women take a part in the pastime. Handball is also played in other parts of Scotland, especially in the parish of Scone, in Perthshire, at the same date, the bachelors playing against the married men, or in such other fashion as may be agreed upon. In his ' Book of Days,' Dr. Robert Chambers chronicles this popular Scottish custom as " Candlema' Ba'," but falls into the mistake of calling it *football*. " On one occasion, not long ago," says the Doctor, " when the sport took place in Jedburgh, the contending parties, after a struggle of two hours in the streets, transferred the contention to the bed of the river Jed, and then fought it out amidst a scene of fearful splash and dabblement, to the infinite amusement of a multitude looking on from the bridge."

These desultory and, I fear, rather bald notes of border doings in the way of sports and pastimes may be appropriately brought to a conclusion with a note of an old border practice, still kept up with care in the south of Scotland—I allude to "the common riding," or riding of the marches. This ancient custom is loyally and merrily kept up in the towns of Selkirk, Hawick, and Langholm ; indeed at Hawick this annual festival has almost the character of a carnival, and is carried on for days, and *nights* as well, for on such festive occasions he would be a bold policeman who would dare to enforce the hours of the Forbes McKenzie Act. At Hawick on these occasions may be heard the old war song, or at least a version of it :—

> " Sons of heroes slain at Flodden !
>   Met to ride and trace our common ;
>   Oral fame tells how we got it ;
>   Here a native muse relates it—
>
>   Tyr hœbbe us, Ye Tyr ye Odin !
>   Sons of heroes slain at Flodden,
>   Imitating Border Bowmen—
>   Aye defend your rights and Common ! "

CHAPTER XX.

VERMIN OF THE MOORS AND MANORS.

I.

I REGRET to say that, in the name of sport, I have during my lifetime looked on or taken part in a good deal of brutality, and it is certain there are many men who might, were it their cue to do so, make a similar confession. Some animals are not hunted in any fair meaning of that word, but are doomed at once to death, and the death to which they are doomed is often one of extreme cruelty. Cock-fighting, which I have seen, as also rat-killing, were often enough shocking exhibitions, as must have been bull-baiting and two or three others of our vanished sports. Half-a-century since, cock-fighting was pretty common in the rural districts of Scotland, and was even at one time a pastime in vogue at parochial schools, the vanquished fowls being accepted by the master as a perquisite. At an even later time there were in Glasgow at least a couple of well-frequented rat-pits, the doings in which afforded gratification to many lookers-on; but such pastimes have happily gone out of fashion; it is long since cock-fighting came to be looked upon with a cold eye both by scholars and their parents, and now one never hears

Y

of that kind of sport in Scotland except, perhaps as a reminiscence.

Another so-called sport which has in Scotland been pretty well frowned down is badger-baiting, which at one time was common enough. I am bound to confess that upon the occasion of my first witnessing a fight between a badger and dogs no sense of fair play was evinced, dog after dog being set on the animal till he succumbed, his death, as a matter of course, being a foregone conclusion. For my appearance at one of these sickening spectacles I was indebted to Jamie Skinners, with whom I have already made my readers acquainted. That poor waif took me with him to a farm about three miles west from Edinburgh, occupied by the Laings of the Royal Horse Bazaar, where two or three of the animals in question were usually to be found. The " ploy," as Jamie called the affair, had been arranged to gratify the officers of the Army then quartered in Edinburgh Castle and at the cavalry barracks of Jock's Lodge. The affair was altogether revolting, the brock being ill to draw had to be smoked before he would leave his earth. On coming out he was promptly seized by a dog, when there ensued a terrific struggle between the two animals, the dog speedily getting the worst of it ; but, a fresh terrier being set on the exhausted badger, the struggle was re-newed, the services of a third dog being required before the wretched beast was killed. There was really no element of sport in the affair, and it certainly left on my mind a most disagreeable impression.

At the next fight of the kind at which I was present (under the same auspices), the badgers—there were two—had the best of it, as after a prolonged struggle the dogs were worsted, two of them being killed. The affair was simply a "worry" from beginning to end, the animals of both kinds being terribly vicious, and evidently determined neither to take nor to give quarter: one of the badgers, indeed, became particularly savage in the course of the fight; but both, it may be mentioned, made their escape for the time. The comment made on the battle by poor Jamie I have not yet forgotten; "And so," he said, "those fellows ca' themselves gentlemen, an' what they are doin' sport; puir sport, it's surely a nickname."

The poor waif was right in the expression of his sentiments; badger-killing is a kind of pastime which no true sportsman ought to have any sympathy with, far less take part in it. It is of the essence of all sport that the beast or bird to be hunted shall be allowed a fair chance to escape—shall, in fact, have *law*.

Why the badger should be selected to be baited and killed I have never been able to understand. These animals are frequently found in the Highlands, and are perfectly harmless, if left undisturbed. Badgers, bar their paws, are not unlike small pigs; like foxes, they live about rocky places or tree roots, feeding chiefly on snails, worms, and frogs, and on such dead animals as they happen to fall in with, and are exceedingly particular about the furnishing with soft moss of their holes; they are frugal and careful animals, the badgers, and why they have been selected for persecution is not easy to understand.

So far as I have been able to ascertain, a badger has not the game qualities nor the staying powers of the fox, nor is it endowed with the cunning of that animal. On the contrary, it is choleric in the extreme, and flies

Y 2

into a paroxysm of passion when it is interfered with, and then becomes exceedingly vicious and determined. There has been much controversy as to one or two points connected with the natural history of this animal, and in particular as to its period of gestation. Many believe that it carries for a period of thirteen months, and there is evidence to attest that many months have elapsed before the female has dropped her young, the litter usually being six or seven. This is a matter on which I am unable to give my personal opinion. The old writers about badgers whose works I have consulted do not say a single word about the period of gestation of the animal, or the number of its young. One author tells his readers to " beware of the badger's teeth," they are so sharp and venomous as to bring certain death to those whom they bite. Dogs seem instinctively to fear this animal. On the occasion referred to, three of these animals, "gamesome" terriers as a rule, fairly turned tail when they saw the brock.

The badger should, I have heard it said, be waited for of nights, when he can be better hunted ; the animal is not often seen during the day, and if an interview is wanted he must then be dug out : when in his earth he is in a place that might have been designed by some military engineer. An old relative of the writer told him that on one occasion he saw a badger keep at bay all the dogs on a farm, some nine in number. Almost no dog will taste the flesh of a badger, but I remember seeing in the West Highlands badger hams, that were excellent, certainly not inferior to hams cut from a well-fed porker. Highlanders, too, were at one time, and may still be for anything I know, great believers in the efficacy of badger's grease ; in some Highland places it formed the universal cure for all kinds of cuts and wounds. Belief in its efficacy no doubt helps the cure. The skins of badgers are made use of by the Highlanders as pistol furniture; they make their philibegs of them.

II.

I am pretty well acquainted with the otter, an animal much fancied in some districts as a medium of sport, and which is regularly hunted at certain seasons of the year. In one or two rivers that I know, the otter plays havoc with the fish; moreover, he is somewhat dainty in his tastes, and must have, if possible, for his nightly meal a portion of a fine new-run salmon. Old Sandy Mackenzie, ferry boatman on a Scottish salmon stream, told me that he gets about thirty fish in the course of the year "on the rocks yonder," with only a big bite taken out of their shoulder; they are not *hashed* in any way, but are perfectly good to eat, and have been eaten by himself and family for eleven years, the flesh being carefully cut at the bitten part so as to avoid any impurity left by the animal's teeth. Sandy watched the rocks for a season without ever seeing the otter or otters that did the mischief, but his wife every now and again found the fish early in the morning.

A day with an otter (I was present on two occasions at a hunt) yields exciting sport—sport not free from danger on some rivers. Description in print seldom does justice to an otter hunt, during which so many things occur, that it would take pages to record them. The sport being on the water adds largely, of course, to the interest of the struggle. It is not, I think, generally known that water is not the "native element" of this animal, of which, indeed, it is not particularly fond, and in places, for example, where there is a crook in the stream in which it may be fishing, it will assuredly leave the river and cross the land in order to regain the water. The otter prefers life in dry quarters. The period of gestation of the female otter, I have been told by persons who have studied their habits, is close on two months; they breed all the year round and are fond of their young. Otters have bred in captivity. They have a mission, these animals—it is to devour all the eels they can find; they eat trout, of course, and they disfigure the salmon in the mode I have stated, but from information received, I think they prefer the eel as food; they are adepts in finding these slippery customers and are known to " remove " a large number of them in the course of the year; in several parts of Scotland the otter is not molested because of its penchant for the eel, which is held in detestation by many Scotch people.

So long a time has elapsed since I saw the otter hunt I have referred to, which took place on the river Tyne under the auspices of the young Dunlops (the sons of the distiller), that I am unable to say where the pack came from, but my impression is that it was from some place on the borders—probably it was a scratch pack got up for the purpose. The affair lasted for three days, at intervals, and caused quite a sensation, gentlemen on the concluding day coming from Edinburgh to see the sport. I remember pretty distinctly the kill, which occurred on the dam just below the bridge at Fairbairn's Wauk Mill. All were on foot, and the crowd was so great that a little boy was knocked into the water and nearly drowned; those present were so busy watching the otter, which was at close quarters with the dogs, that the accident was unnoticed except by one of Mr. Dunlop's grooms, who jumped into the dam at the wooden bridge and intercepted the child as he was being carried away by the current. So far as I know, there never has been in Scotland any regularly organised hunt of the otter; in various places the young men, where there is a good stretch of river, turn out with lighted wisps and hold a burning of the water with a view to kill any otters they can fall in with. In saying this much I am not dealing with what is on hand in the way of sport at the present time, but am harking back " on the charity of memory."

III.

Upon one occasion while passing a few days in the North, I saw what is now not a very common sight, a specimen of the wild cat, which has during late years become a scarce animal in Scotland. The cat in question had just fought with, or rather killed without any fight, a poor little rabbit; it was a beautiful animal that cat, agile and eager, a little larger than the domestic variety, but of a fine grey colour regularly striped with black. These animals, when they were plentiful in the Scottish Highlands thirty or more years ago, committed great depredations among the game, annually killing thousands of the beasts and birds of sport. The wild cat was described to me by a Highland shepherd as a "most devilish being," so that it is somewhat surprising to find that several landlords and lessees of shootings have given orders for their preservation. Doubtless, like

other wild animals, they have had a part assigned them
to play in the economy of nature. The old idea is
being revived that grouse disease is owing to the
balance of nature being disturbed by the over-destruc-
tion of birds and beasts which have been designated
" vermin." Had the enemies of the bird of sport not
been ruthlessly killed off, the crippled and weak grouse,
it is said, might have been seized upon and dealt with,
so that none but strong and healthy animals would
have been left to multiply and replenish the heather;
but it is now pretty well known that " the disease "
has largely prevailed in places where gamekeepers
had proved rather lax in vermin-killing, and it is, moreover, now a pretty general opinion that the good health
of the bird of the heather is more dependent on a
proper supply of fresh food than on any other condition
of the grouse moors.

Returning to the wild cat, I remember being taken
to view "the midden" of a household of these pests.
It was a sight! The bones of a score of different
animals that in literal hundreds had fallen a prey to
these tiger-like beasts lay around, telling an eloquent
tale of daily devastations committed. I cannot give an
account of the origin of these beasts or how they
breed; all I know is that they are, when excited,
perfect fiends incarnate, and can fight with an earnest-
ness which, I have been told, is quite awful to see. I
am writing, of course, of the true wild cat. There are
other cats which also live in the wildest state of
freedom, and breed in plantations and in rocky places;
these, I take leave to suppose, are deserters, or the
descendants of deserters, from the family circle—cats
of evil disposition gone to the bad. All such when

seen by keepers are remorselessly shot, and on some
lowland estates in particular scores are killed in the
course of a year. A lady friend of the writer having
had a favourite cat trapped and destroyed, I interviewed, at her request, a neighbouring keeper to hear
what explanation he would offer on the subject.

"Yes, sir, my men trapped the cat," was the reply
made, "and there is nothing to be said about it—he
acted on my orders. We kill a dozen or two in the
course of a year—they are awful poachers, these brutes;
I have known one to carry off in a couple of days a
whole covey of partridges, and I have seen another one
tear a poor young rabbit almost to rags; there is
nothing in the poaching line that cats are not up to,
and I shoot them down without mercy, and everybody
knows that here about."

Many, I dare say, who peruse these pages will be able
to recall poaching incidents committed by domestic
cats; some persons have in rural districts largely
benefited from the work of such animals. One can read
in some sporting reminiscences of cats that were excellent
caterers and brought in a daily something for the pot.
One cat known to me used to frequent a rookery and
bring home any of the young crows which had fallen
from their nests. A cat I was told about by a friend
was a famous poacher—in one season it brought home
fourteen young hares.

Something may now be said regarding the polecat,
another of our most destructive vermin—a bloodthirsty
animal, as all who know its habits will admit. It is
not often seen, but gamekeepers are occasionally made
to feel its presence; it is active but somewhat repulsive-
looking, and is known to do a great deal of damage in

game preserves. Happily the polecat is much less plentiful than it used to be, although more abundant than the wild cat. The polecat is an exceedingly active animal, and has been known to travel long distances in search of food for itself and young ones—fourteen or sixteen miles at a stretch. Attempts have more than once, I believe, been made to tame this animal, but without success. One reason for the growing scarcity of the polecat is, undoubtedly, the high value which is placed upon its skin, the fur being in request, and as much as 2s. has been netted by gamekeepers for good samples.

It is not my intention to enumerate all the beasts that are obnoxious to game preservers and are fast being exterminated by the more zealous keepers, who in many instances are rewarded by payments in the shape of " head money " for the wild animals trapped or shot, the tails of which may be often seen nailed to doors about the gamekeepers' quarters. The marten, like others of our formerly abundant vermin, is now exceedingly scarce, although many are of opinion that it did as much good as harm in the preserves. The marten used, I think, in the olden time to be accounted a beast of the chase, and was fairly hunted. The weasel is so well known as not to require much description, neither do I require to say much about the stoat.*

* The following graphic extract from the supposed ' Diary of a Stoat ' affords an admirable illustration of the life of a beast of prey. It is from the pen of Major Morrant of the Cape Mounted Riflemen :—" Slept rather heavily, having drunk too much hen-pheasant's blood the evening before, but went for a stroll about 5 A.M. I soon found a yellow-hammer's nest, but, jumping a little too far, just missed the old hen. However, I sucked her eggs. Shortly afterwards I winded something in a low old thorn tree, and,

These beasts, doubtless, have their work to do. The balance which Nature has established and guards so jealously must not be disturbed; if it be, we know well that, in some shape or other, we shall have to pay the bill of costs. When, for instance, grouse become too plentiful on a stretch of heather, their enemies begin to multiply. Whenever vermin are over-abundant, it is a sure sign of there being more birds than there ought to be; and it is the same throughout animated nature. When the French gardeners shot down their small

climbing up, found a nest with four fine young blackbirds in it, and I made a nice light breakfast of their blood and brains. How the old birds did scream, and what a fuss they made about it! Perhaps they will remember to build higher another season. I then made a neat stalk and killed a skylark, and, as the sun was getting high, thought of retiring, when I came on the fresh track of a hare. I knew her form would be close by, so followed it in breathless silence. Sure enough she was sleeping on the side of an old back. Getting well above her, I leaped lightly on her back, and my teeth were fast in her neck before she was fairly awake. Then how the stupid creature screamed and struggled! Just as if it was of any use. I suppose she was thinking of her little ones, for she was giving suck, I afterwards noticed. However, I left her quiet enough in about ten minutes. Being rather tired, I had a long and refreshing sleep under the root of an old tree, but, waking thirsty about three o'clock, went down to a little stream and had a drink. Two ladies were sketching the old bridge, and I played about for a little while and heard them admire my graceful movements, and wonder how any man could be barbarous enough to set a trap for such an interesting creature. Had another long sleep, and a pleasant stroll in the evening, but had not much sport, a nice covey of partridges giving me my supper and a quarter of an hour's amusement. The old birds kept fluttering under my nose, apparently both lame and broken-winged, but I had been served that trick before, so I only laughed at them, and managed to chop eight of the young ones. Then I retired for the night, hoping for as happy a day to-morrow."

birds because they took tribute of the fruit, they were speedily made to encounter a worse plague in the abnormal increase of the insects which used to be preyed upon by the birds which had been so unceremoniously killed.

There is some philosophy in this; we can at least draw an inference or two from it, and teach what seems to be sometimes forgotten in the terrible anxiety which is always expressed for a large number of birds, namely, that it is better to have a hundred birds in fine condition and of heavy weight, than two hundred half-hungered " piners."

IV.

The rat must now be noticed as an animal of evil repute; in some quarters no good qualities have ever been placed to his credit. Not many years since it was brought before a learned society as a subject of debate whether or not the rat ought to be utterly exterminated. This rodent affords another instance of the strength of the old proverb about a dog with a bad name; the poor animal has quite a number of good qualities, and, like a few other animals of evil repute, has, undoubtedly, " a mission " to fulfil; but, for all that, men's hands have been so long as I am able to remember actively turned against it, and the rat is every day in consequence hunted to death by farmers, gamekeepers and others; and in the course of a year countless thousands of them are remorselessly killed.

It is a curious circumstance that the rat with which we are all so familiar—the common brown rat—is an interloper, that has displaced the old original black rat of the country, at one time so plentiful in the United

Kingdom. This animal, like many other rodents, is a breedy creature, and if it were not industriously massacred day by day would speedily multiply its kind to an extent that would prove intolerable. To show the rate of kill, I may mention that I once saw 470 skins of rats that had been trapped on one farm in the course of ten months. I very stupidly neglected to ask what was to be done with them. The rate of rat increase is little short of that ascribed to rabbits; a mature pair will yield thirty in a year, and the young ones will breed as soon as they have attained the age of four months. We are a long way yet from probably seeing "rat-pie" on our dining tables, but, as the man in the burlesque says, " a day will come "—when rats may have to form a portion of our food. And why not? There are nations that eat their rats, and there are those among ourselves who have eaten rats and liked them. Farmyard or granary rats are known to be wholesome enough, and are quite as palatable as rabbits when nicely cooked.

At certain periods of the year rats migrate to the preserves and commit havoc among the nests of the partridge and pheasant; they seem to have a penchant for the eggs of birds and fowls of all kinds. A game-keeper told the writer that the rats accounted for a very considerable portion of the eggs of all game birds : " They are arrant and ingenious poachers," he said, " constantly at work and so numerous that their depredations are soon felt, and so keepers, in duty bound, show them no mercy."

It would be bad policy to exterminate the rat; it performs important duties as a scavenger, and is thus a factor in the promotion of health in our cities, and the good it does in this respect ought to be placed to its credit as a set-off to its evil deeds as a general marauder.

The balance of Nature cannot be disturbed without " something happening," and man is surely intelligent enough to know that. To him has been given dominion over all created things; by the aid of superior intellect, he is enabled to exercise controlling power. Some persons who have thought out the many and varied problems presented to man in connection with all created things are of opinion that, had man not interfered, the balance established by Nature would never have been disturbed; but these opinions may be traversed; it is surely man's duty to take the good of all he sees, and turn it to his own uses. No doubt the wolf has some kind of mission to fulfil, or it would not have been created; man will certainly take care, however, that the business of the wolf shall not be to devour man. Different opinions have been enunciated so far as the balance of Nature affects our sports and pastimes; one thinks there should be no bird on the heather but grouse, and no beast in the deer forest but the stag and its kind; whilst another person thinks that, were hawks allowed to increase and take their share of the small birds, we should get about the right balance. A close time for *all* birds has been more than once advocated; but a close time for *all* means a close time for the sparrow as well as for the sparrow-hawk. " Every man for himself," said the keeper as he told his master that he shot the nightingales because they sang so loud at night as to keep his pheasants awake.

How many of our wild animals, it has often been

asked, die a natural death ? The answer is, Few indeed. Some birds and beasts would, no doubt, but for the cunning devices of man, live to a grand old age. Elephants, we are told, occasionally exist for a period of 400 years. Camels also attain a very old age; many are reputed to live for a century. Eagles are believed to live as long as camels, and swans have been known to live three times as long as any eagle. The pelican, too. is a bird that, when left alone, sees many summers and winters. How long a deer may live has already been discussed. The fox, if left unmolested, would likely see his seventeenth year, whilst the timid hare might die a natural death in half the time were it not hunted to death long before. The lives of wild animals are full of privations—a series of never-ending troubles. When no danger may be apprehended from man, they are fearful of their " natural enemies "—the sweet-singing lark fears the hawk, which in turn may become the prey of the falcon ; saddest of all, thousands of wild animals die annually from absolute starvation, whilst other thousands, nay, tens of thousands, as in the case of grouse and salmon, are carried off by periodical epidemics.

V.

Gamekeepers are not in agreement as to the degree of criminality which attaches to the owl as a destroyer of birds that are more valuable than it is. Many keepers, indeed, continue to kill this picturesque animal as if it were a villain of the deepest dye, and I have more than once seen a long row of their heads displayed on gates and doors as a token of the gamekeeper's

336 Out-door Sports in Scotland.

industry. There are several varieties of this bird, but the barn owl is the one which is best known. From careful inquiries made in several parts of Scotland, I deduce that with the owl, as in the case of the pigeon, it has hitherto been a case of " Jeddart Justice " ; the bird has been killed first and then been tried, by examining his stomach, when what was seen at once testified to his innocence, so far as the gamekeeper had any interest in it. There are usually two sides to all questions, and no doubt these birds have been caught doing mischief in the preserves ; but, if a balance of the good and evil they do be struck, it would, I fancy, be found that the good predominates. From its instinctive love of mice, and the activity which it displays in catching them, this bird has been called a cat in feathers. On one estate on which, for a time, to " protect the game," all the owls seen were ruthlessly shot, rats and mice speedily became so abundant as to show that a blunder had assuredly been made in dooming the birds to destruction—another instance of improper meddling with the balance of Nature.

Among the more destructive of the feathered vermin, may be named the hen harrier, which, I have reason to believe, kills a large number of grouse and partridges. Birds, it must be borne in mind, can make the circuit of an estate in a much shorter period than any four-footed animal can possibly do, and are therefore quite capable of doing four times the mischief. We must not forget, in estimating the evil done by birds of prey, that the very worst of them even do some good in killing off the lame and the halt on grouse moors, pheasantries, and partridge preserves, leaving only the strongest birds to multiply their kind.

I have even to put in a good word for the jay and the raven, although both are severely frowned upon by vermin-hating keepers, who decline to listen to any plea of extenuating circumstances. No doubt these birds are adepts in sucking the eggs of other birds, and unfledged young ones of all kinds afford them a dainty meal, as when impelled by hunger the raven will do wondrous deeds of evil. I have myself found a couple of these feathered fiends busy "murdering" a tender young lamb, which crime they commit in a semi-scientific way, by first of all depriving it of its eyes, after which the poor animal is at their mercy. My father, who was a keen observer of animals of every kind, was on one occasion an eye-witness of a case of poetic justice which befell a couple of ravens, or more likely carrion crows. They were busy preying on the carcass of a ewe, which, being disabled by falling into a ditch, had become an easy prey to the black marauders, and after enjoying a good gorge on the eyes of the animal and a part of its tongue, were indulging in a rest—in fact, they had feasted so sumptuously that they were hardly able to move. A fox, which had been watching their movements from the bank of the ditch, then stealthily crept up, and in a moment had seized one of the crows, and giving it a severe crunch with its teeth, flung it aside, and had made the other bird a prisoner before it had time to realise what had happened to its companion.

The carrion crow—there is a variety of crows, and it would require more space than I can afford to describe them all—is much hated in some parts of the country, and is remorselessly killed when opportunity serves. I have preserved some anonymous verses of a

z

sort of poetic rhapsody uttered on this crow, of which
the following is an example :—

> " I am the dreadful carrion crow, ca ! ca !
> I can choose and devour whatever I may,
> And gouge out the eyes of a sheep, ha ! ha !
> The rook and the raven are keen for prey—
> But I feast as I like by night or day,
>   I am the fiendish carrion crow, ca ! ca ! "

Having had numerous chances of studying them,
nothing in regard to the crow family has ever struck
me so much as the eye power of the raven, which seems
to be really wonderful. I remember some years ago
seeing a sheep killed by an excited dog in a field in
Berwickshire, and of its lying dead on the grass. I
was fishing near at hand, and went on with my work,
being all the time well within sight of the dead animal;
in about fifteen or twenty minutes after the sheep
had been worried to death, I was startled by the
hoarse croak of a raven—where it had come from I
know not, and I could see well around me, but a few
minutes only had elapsed before another, and another,
came on the scene, and soon a score of these birds were
seen coming in a darkening train to enjoy an anticipated feast; curiously enough, the birds all came from
one point of the compass, but the wonder for me was
where they had come from and how they had so quickly
seen the carcass of the dead animal.

CHAPTER XXI.

THE FOX : FOX-HUNTING.

MASTER REYNARD, as all connected with the sports and pastimes of the period know, is an animal of consequence, and was long since acclaimed " King of Vermin." The fox is " protected," and we were told by the late Lord Malmesbury that upon making his appearance at school he received the cold shoulder from his companions, because his father was a fox-killer. Farmers and others who wantonly kill the foxes on their grounds are looked down upon and " cut " by all who delight in fox-hunting. The fox by consensus of sporting opinion has been nominated *the* animal of " the hunt," and yet fox-hunting is the simplest of all sports. Curiously enough, however, no one can give a very good reason for its long-continued popularity, but it affords an excuse for the meeting of many persons at the coverside, previous to which there has probably been provided for the corinthians of the company at the mansion-house of the master an excellent breakfast of many good things.

It is undoubtedly a rather mixed company which assembles, all kinds of persons being permitted to be present, the masses mingling with the classes for the moment. Look at the horses! What magnificent animals some of them are—there may be a dozen on the ground that it would probably cost several thousand pounds to purchase, and along with these cracks of the hunting field there are sure to be two score or more that would be dear at thirty pounds a piece. Again, there are animals on the scene which, while not at first sight looking "up to any hounds," will probably, before the day is done, change hands for not less than a hundred, or probably twenty pounds over that sum; they have been brought there to be sold : faultless at their fences, they beat in the course of the run many of the more showy animals, and are quickly spotted by those gentlemen who know a good hunter when they see one. My old acquaintance, Richard Rayner of Edinburgh, used to make many a deal on the hunting field, and as horse-dealing men go, "Dicky," as he was familiarly called, was perhaps a shade or two better than his compeers.   His brother, John, wrote hunting sketches for the *Courant* newspaper, and was able to pen a pretty graphic account of such runs of the Midlothian hounds as he attended.

In "the memory chambers of my brain-house," to use a Carlylean phrase, I have sundry recollections of these exceedingly fine and much-enjoyed Midlothian meets, ready to come forth at call.   There are, perhaps, few now living who remember the stirring days of "the thirties," and early on in "the forties," when there was such marked individuality of style among the men who followed the hounds, and when of an evening there ensued lots of fun in "The Rainbow," or the "Old Café," or sometimes in "Ramplings," or in the house on the opposite side—it is of Edinburgh I am writing.   Hunting has been, so long as I can remember, a favourite Scottish pastime, but fifty, or even forty years ago, it had a finer flavour about it than during these later times. It is to be regretted that no capable writer has given us a history of the Royal Caledonian Hunt, which would be of great interest, especially if garnished with personal reminiscences and stories of its members, together with memories of " the packs," and also of the persons who took an interest in the fine sport of fox-hunting.

It is of the fox, however, as one of our "Vermin," that I have set myself the task of writing, having collected a considerable amount of information regarding Reynard, having besides analysed the information of others, and selected such portions of it as look most reliable. In reality the fox is an animal about which little that is exact is known; still one finds occasionally men in every hunting field pretty well informed regarding the natural history of the chase and the beasts and birds of sport, and therefore able to follow the fox or the hare with intelligence. I am not much of a fox-hunter, but having witnessed as a youngster many meets, and sometimes " been in at the death," probably know as much about the fox and the hounds as most outsiders. It is not too much, perhaps, to assert that seven-eighths of those who join a meet know little about the animal, in proof of which let me give the opinion of one mighty hunter. " Well, of course you know we hunt it, and, as you also know, it is good sport; but really now, I cannot, upon my word, tell you any more about it. We start it somewhere, and when it breaks cover we hope to kill it after a good run, but it often earths up, and we lose it. It appears to me, do you know, that the fox has originally been a breed between a wolf and a dog, and has then, in course

of time, taken on various characteristics on its own
hook. But I dare say you will find all you want in
some of the natural history books—there are different
kinds of them, you know, away abroad."

The following bits about the fox are a selection from
much matter I have collected bearing on the natural
history of the animal: they are worth repeating as
examples of the old-time knowledge that was current
about most animals of sport, but which is now of course
known to be ridiculous. "It is the cunningest creature
known; it can cheat its enemies by suddenly halting
and lying as still as a clod or a stone, which it becomes
like whenever it pleases, so that it hath often proved
able to cheat both the huntsmen and his dogs by means
of this very wonderful gift, which Providence hath not
bestowed on any other animal. The fox is libidinous
in its habits, and enters into amorous commerce with
any other brute so inclined."

Regarding the smell of the fox, according to one
writer, "if greyhounds course him on a plain, his last
refuge is to wet his tail, and flap it on their faces as
they come near him, sometimes squirting his thicker
excrements on them so as to make them give over the
pursuit." These are curious but certainly not savoury
details. *Pennant* says about the *scent:* "The smell of this
animal, in general, is very strong, but that of the urine
is most remarkably fetid. This seems so offensive even
to itself, that it will take the trouble of digging a hole
in the ground, stretching its body at full length over it,
and there, after depositing its water, cover it with earth
as the cat does its dung. The smell is so offensive that
it often proves the means of the fox's escape from the
dogs, who have so strong an aversion to the filthy

effluvia as to avoid encountering the animal it came from."

Another story which is told of the "filthy fox" is, that when it covets the nice hole of the "cleanly badger," it straightway stinks it out and takes up its quarters in the vacated living place, which it at once proceeds to enlarge and improve, constructing two or three distinct entrances and exits in case of danger.

The cunning of the fox is remarkable. I have myself seen one steal up to a couple of young hares and pretend to be friendly with them, play with them, and make fun to them, if I may use such an expression, then like a flash dash at one of the pair, and seizing it firmly be off, and out of reach in double-quick time. The tricks of the fox to evade its pursuers are numerous, and many stories have been told of its devices for out-witting its enemies. A whipper-in relating some of his experiences told of one that circled several times in lessening ranges from two or three gigantic boulders, and, concentrating its power, effected a leap that cleared the rings, and so, throwing the dogs off the scent, ultimately escaped. Mr. Stables gives currency in one of his works to a curious anecdote of the fox, indicative of its resource upon an emergency. One of these animals escaped from a wood, from which it was likely to be dislodged by the hounds, and proceeded to a piece of furze waste, where it had its hole and its young ones. The main body of the pack took off in another direction; two of the hounds, having scented Reynard, found him out in his hole, but Master Fox was equal to the occasion: he made the hounds welcome, showed them his cubs, and danced about and gambolled around the visitors till they took off, much, no doubt, to the relief of the clever actor, which must have endured a rather bad quarter of an hour of it, but the action taken by the animal was very remarkable.

Those who have seen Reynard dug out have been surprised to find that his home had been constructed with the skill of an engineer. Although cunning and of sneaking habits, the fox is game to the end and dies hard. The animal is in bad repute as a general robber of game preserves and hen roosts, but it ought to count in his favour that he kills and eats a great many rats and mice, as also a large number of the weaker game birds that would die in any case. I have gleaned from various persons, pretty well acquainted with the natural history of the fox, that its period of gestation is two months, when it produces a litter of six or seven young ones. The female enjoys the credit of being dotingly fond of her cubs, which, when danger threatens, she conceals with wonderful cunning, and if their hiding-place be attacked she fights for them till she is killed. The young ones become reproductive in the course of eighteen months, and foxes have been known to live for fifteen years, but it is very questionable, considering the hard conditions of their life—being so regularly and keenly hunted by clever hounds—if these animals will live, on the average, for more than seven years, during which period, if no accidents have befallen, the bitch will have given birth to from fifty to sixty young ones. Young foxes are as playful as young lions, but they become dangerous in time, and the bite of a fox is a thing to be carefully avoided.

Dogs and foxes have never, I believe, in spite of what has been said to the contrary, been known to interbreed ; nor has it been found possible to domesticate the fox, although numerous attempts have been made. The fox often proves a match for its enemies, and has been known to achieve wonderful escapes from imminent death, solely by its cunning, while the animal possesses a happy knack of escaping traps, or rather of avoiding them; for one taken five will escape—the fox can sometimes manage to " spring " a trap and then quietly enjoy the bait, first looking it all over and smelling it very carefully to find out if it be genuine. These notes on the natural history of the fox might be largely extended were it necessary.

There have in my time been regularly instituted hunts in Scotland, and I have been present at several, but cannot say I have ever been able to pen such a record of the runs as some others of the men who seem to write on such subjects with a good galloping pen. One of half-a-dozen men who had been enjoying a good run one day with a Midlothian pack, on being asked to describe it, said, and it was all he could say, " Oh, it was stunning and no mistake." Another good hunting man said, " Capital, capital ! thirty-five minutes without a pause, and killed—a fine kill ! " It is certain that the art of vividly describing a fox-hunt has not been widely bestowed; on a person saying so to Mr. John Rayner, his answer was, " No, it is a gift: some of us see more than others." Happening to see one of the runs which he wrote about in the *Courant* newspaper, I quite agreed with him; on that occasion, at all events, he had seen much more than the writer of these remarks. The recollection of my first run as a boy is still green in my memory. It lasted for forty-five minutes and was tolerably varied; I kept well up with the best of them, thanks to the good advice of a friend of

Mr. Ramsay's (of Barnton); advice which is worth transcribing for the benefit of novices.

"Look here, my boy," said my mentor, "you will see the find and the break away, but never heed the music; hold your tongue and keep a firm bridle, let the rest of the fellows make as much noise as they like, you be quiet. Don't be in a hurry, there is plenty of time; keep near me if you can. I always take a stern position for the first couple of miles; after that, when two-thirds of the field are tailed off, forge your way to the front. Another thing, never put your horse at a fence if there should be a gap or a gate handy; above all, take care to keep behind the hounds. Sit firm on your horse, and then look about you a little; study the old stagers, and do as they do. Keep your eye on the pack, and always try hard to be in the same field with the huntsmen. Now, then, we're off, my boy; come on."

Any description that could be offered of my first run would not much enrich the "literature of the hunt." The affair dwelt long in my recollection, as was natural enough. To those who know the country it may be stated that we started the fox a little way west from Corstorphine, and killed in a field close to Kirkliston Distillery, probably five miles from the start, the bit of country traversed being exceedingly varied, part of it being occupied by the Edinburgh and Glasgow Railway. Like most novices of the hunt, I was not much afraid of the hedges and ditches we had to face; but, seeing my friend making for safe places, I followed his example. We crossed the Union Canal by the bridge, but not so the river Almond, which tried my nerves a little, but in the end I was well to the front when we killed, and was complimented by the Hon. Mr. Sandilands and other gentlemen who were in the run. The laird of Barnton was present. At the period of which I am writing he was about the best-known sportsman in Scotland; "Ramsay of Barnton" was a household word throughout Midlothian and some neighbouring counties, and his name, as I had recently occasion to know, is still green in his own countryside. I have sat behind him now and again on the " Defiance " coach, which he often drove as far as Cramond Brig. His portrait in the well-known " Barnton Hat " is still to be seen in some of the comfortable Scottish country inns.

Needless to say, Mr. Ramsay was hail-fellow-well-met with all sorts of people. No event of a sporting kind was thought a success unless he was present to see it. I have seen him spear an otter in the Almond where it flowed through the grounds of Mr. Hope Vere above Cramond Bridge, and in many of the coursing matches, held on his own and neighbouring estates, he was a keen participator. One of his favourite " howffs " when residing at Barnton was " Jemmy Jack's " smiddy, and he was never more delighted than when he was treating the miscellaneous crowds that of an evening assembled there to bread and cheese and ale, with occasional supplies of hot mutton pies from a neighbouring baker's shop. The "characters" of the community seemed instinctively to know when Mr. Ramsay would be at the " smiddy," and some dozen or so of persons who were connected in some way with the sport of that time would assemble to see him and partake of his hospitality. By the aid of my mind's eye I am yet able to picture some of those " worthies." Jamie Skinners has been already mentioned as one of Jemmy Jack's constant visitors; then there was John Omit from Paddy's

Row at the village of Blackhall, he was nicknamed
" Ferret Jock," and travelled the country as a professional mole-catcher, and, at the same time, did a
little poaching " on the quiet"; there was Robbie, the
tailor, the fleetest runner in all the country-side, and
Tam Clephane, the best shot in the parish of Cramond,
which was famed for good guns; then there was Jemmy
Jack himself, and young Sandy Semple, a sporting
farmer. To these men sport of some kind was as the
breath of life; when they could not enjoy it, they
talked about it; and nothing delighted Mr. Ramsay
more than to hear their varied reminiscences, their tales
of hairbreadth 'scapes by flood and field. I have heard
Tam Clephane relate how he swam across the river
Almond, just where it debouches into the sea, and when
it was in full flood, to visit his sweetheart, then a
servant in Dalmeny House. He carried his clothes on
his back, tied up in a 'mackintosh,' at that time a
newly invented substance. Having paid his respects to
Mary, now his wife, he again crossed the water, and,
after hurrying on his clothes, would get a tumbler of
reeking hot toddy at Mrs. Maccara's inn by the river-
side, and " never feel a bit the waur ot."

CHAPTER XXII.

GOLF.

THERE has within these last few years been something like a boom in golf. Men play now who never played before, and men who played before now play all the more, no one being in the least the worse in consequence of the boom, whilst some feel all the better— the players in their health, the dealers in the upholstery of the game. Some of our literary gentlemen, too, have benefited by the boom ; or, to put the case the other way, the boom has probably benefited by them ; either way, however, it may be set down as an instance of cause and effect. The votaries of golf have increased largely within my remembrance, and, although many good golfers have crossed the bourne, the places they left have been more than occupied. It was on Bruntsfield Links, which has for a long period been famous as a golfing ground, that I first saw the game played, and as a boy took many a longing look at the men in the red coats who so dexterously handled their clubs, and oftener than once it crossed my mind that some day I might be able to don a red coat myself, and strike the ball from hole to hole with the best of those I saw playing of an afternoon ; moreover, the after-dinner mirth proceeding from the club-room strengthened this ambition, and "what fine dinners I shall get" became a factor in my juvenile speculation.

Since those days golf has gathered to the greens fresh crowds of disciples. Not only here in Scotland has the game been growing in favour, but in England likewise. "Golf" is at the present time a standing heading in the *Field* newspaper, and the game now boasts an "annual," in which much is recorded concerning the pastime that is of interest to its votaries. And abroad, all over the world, especially in those places where two or three Scotsmen are to be found (and in what part of the world will not two or three Scotsmen be found?), golf has become a much-loved pastime. Seeing the game is of ancient origin, and has been played by kings and commoners alike, it is well that its history should be summarised, and that some incidents which have signalised its progress should be related, that its social surroundings should be described, and a word or two said about the poetry and song to which it has given birth.

Golf, it may be at once stated, derives its name from the club it is played with, which in German is *kolbe*, and in Dutch *kolf;* as to the name of the inventor of the pastime history, so far as I know, is silent.

The difference in their social aspects between golfing and curling is, that one is the game of the professional and mercantile classes, the other being a pastime common to the masses as well as the classes. There are men who, having only seen golf played on one or two occasions, have called it "a pastime of fools." It has been related of an eminent Scottish lawyer who, when living at St. Andrews during the vacations of the court, used to sneer at and mock "the madmen," as he

called them, who found delight in driving a ball from
hole to hole; " It is a mere exercise of muscular force,"
he used to exclaim, "needing no effort of the brain ";
but that lawyer in time became a player, and afterwards used to tell his friends that "all good golfers
must have intellectual power, judgment of distances, a
fine hand, and possess powers of calculation." In
saying so Mr. MacFees only spoke the truth, as many
find out when they join the band. For men of
sedentary habits golf is "just the very thing they
need." As a literary friend once said to the writer,
" Golf is A1 for a person like myself. I am at my desk,
as you know, full five hours a day, and an hour on the
links in the afternoon sets me up; in fact, I can drive
my ball and consider my articles at the same time."

Golf has a history; it is of great antiquity, and
it is rather remarkable that a book dealing with it
in its antiquarian aspects has not yet been compiled. Probably now, when many of our *littérateurs*
play the game so well—especially on paper—we shall
not be much longer without a complete chronicle of
golf as played, and by whom, in its earliest days.
Mr. Robert Clark's handsome collection of essays and
articles on the pastime has been greatly appreciated by
all who have seen it, and many were hopeful that his
volume would prove the precursor of the kind of work
now indicated. The information contained in it will
certainly be found useful by the future historian; as a
matter of fact, Mr. Clark's book might be taken as
furnishing the foundation stones of such a full history.
In Scotland, in days of old, golf was the sport of kings,
and in modern times many of our eminent men have
deftly handled the cleck and the sand-iron.

Centuries ago, when golf seemed too flourishing, it was frowned upon by the authorities as likely to interfere with military training. As early as the fifteenth century golf had become so popular as to attract the attention of the State to the fact, and straightway it was "cried down," because it interfered with the serious work of learning the use of arms, then thought to be the first duty of all. James I. is reputed to have been a golfer, the first Charles was also a disciple of the game, and, while on a visit to Scotland in 1641, it is said he was golfing on the Links of Leith, when a messenger reached him with the unwelcome news of a rebellion having broken out in Ireland, on hearing which he threw down his club, and at once hurried up to Holyrood House to read the despatches which had been sent to him.

The game of golf is eminently social, although some disciples have been known to nourish hatreds against rival players; but there are many clubs, and many good fellows are members of them, despite the fact of passing fits of jealousy. Eating and drinking together in the name of good fellowship used, perhaps, to be more a feature of golfing some thirty or forty years ago than it is to-day. Much interesting information can yet be picked up about the table practices of former days, and the details of the commissariat, as regards some of the Scottish clubs, "Many of the members being well inclined to the good things of this life," as was said by Dr., then Mr. William, Chambers at a Lord Provost's dinner. By way of illustration, I have selected the following "items." Such entries in the club records, for instance, as the following are plentiful: "The meeting as usual cracked their jokes over a full glass,

and enjoyed the evening harmoniously with a song."
In the club minutes of the "Honourable Company of
Golfers" (1782), it is intimated that port and punch
shall be the ordinary drink of the society, unless upon
the days when the silver club and cups are played for;
at these meetings, claret, or any other more agreeable
liquor, will be permitted. In 1788, it was a rule that
the preses of the club should call for the bill before it
exceeded half-a-crown per member; failing to do this,
the preses might be called upon to pay the overplus.
Port and sherry wines, rum, brandy, gin, and small
beer were allowed at dinner at the discretion of
members, the charges being included in the general
account. How modest those banquets were may be
readily gathered from such an entry as the following:
" Resolved that, as the price of provisions is very high,
Mr. Moir should be allowed 1s. 6d. each for dinner."
The " drink " formed a separate item.

These club dinners were always satisfying and very
enjoyable indeed, despite their cheapness. The cost
of a dinner for fourteen of the " Honourable Company of Golfers " in the year 1801 is set down as being
£10 13s. 4d., including twenty-three bottles of wine
(sixteen of the number being claret). Let the reader
bear in mind, that at the time referred to a quarter of
excellent lamb could be bought for a shilling, a good
fat capon only cost ninepence; vegetables for a large
dinner-party sixpence ! The following is a characteristic
club entry of a later day: " 24th June, 1815. No
particular business occurred at this meeting; but, as
news had arrived that morning of the entry of the
Allies into Paris, it put the whole members into such
spirits, that the glass circulated pretty freely, and the

usual hour of departure was protracted to the detriment
of the stock. Bill, £4 8s. 6d., whereof from stock,
£2 0s. 6d." Not till the year 1830 (24th of April)
was champagne placed on the table of the Bruntsfield
Links (Edinburgh) Club. The introduction of that
wine was an innovation that excited comment, especially
among outsiders. At that period champagne was
seldom drunk in private life, except on the tables of very
wealthy people ; claret, and occasionally hock, being the
chief liquors used, in addition to the universal port and
sherry of the dinner-table, and the Madeira produced at
ceremonious calls. Claret was always a "Scottish
wine ;" centuries ago, barrels of it were hawked through
the streets on sale to all and sundry in "stoups" or in
pints or half-pints.

To-day champagne and other expensive wines are in
use in Edinburgh, and are presented at dinner, or at
evening parties, by many whom one would not expect
to involve themselves in such expenditure as the consumption of that wine implies. As to champagne on
the golfing green, I was not a little surprised three
years ago, at being told by a couple of caddies who
were sitting in a house much frequented by golfers, that
they were waiting to drink a bottle of champagne that
had been promised them by the players of a "foursome." A champagne luncheon or dinner is often
battled for on the golfing links, matches of many kinds
being made. Apropos to the first introduction of
champagne at the club dinner alluded to, Mr. James
Ballantyne of happy memory, the author of several very
fine Scottish lyrics, and himself a keen golfer, used to
tell of an old merchant to whom the wine in question
came as a revelation. " I'm real fond o' that fizzin'

French wine," he used to say, "it gangs a' ower ye; some drinks gangs till yer heid, but lord, sir, the shampane gangs till yer feet as weel. I maun buy a bottle to drink the wife's health at her birthday dinner."

It forms no part of my plan to notice the different golf clubs of Scotland, but an exception may be made in the case of "the Honourable the Edinburgh Company of Golfers," which may presumably be looked upon as the chief institution of golfers in Scotland. No one knows the date of its formation, but it was incorporated by a charter from the magistrates of that city eighty-eight years ago; its origin is, however, lost in the mists of antiquity, but the first of a series of regular minutes signed by Professor Forbes, of Culloden, bears date 1744. The club, or golf-house, of that body used to be situated at Leith, but is now in the ancient burgh of Musselburgh, on the same links where is held the Edinburgh race meeting. Many of the best men of Scotland have in their day and generation been members of this club. The secretary and treasurer of the Company, who died in October 1795, a worthy gentleman and noted *bon vivant*, was much lamented by his friends, his mode of singing many of the classic Scotch songs of the period being long remembered; his humour and style were quite irresistible. He saw out three sets of boon companions, but himself gave way about the age of sixty. It used to be said of Jamie Balfour that he could run well enough at times when he was unable to stand.

At St. Andrews, in "the ancient Scottish kingdom of Fife across the Forth," will be found a colony of keen and constant players. St. Andrews, indeed, may be described as the golfing capital of Scotland. There many people who have little else to do "talk golf" from early morning to bedtime : old matches are over-hauled, new ones made. Players are freely criticised and ancient jokes and stories revived. All classes are more or less interested in the game at St. Andrews : the merchant as well as the retired colonel or major, the tailor, the shoemaker, and the regiment of more or less reputable hangers-on that "get a living out of golf." Coming from church any one with alert ears may be sure of hearing much golf talk ; returning from a dinner-party, the golf talk of the table is sure to be continued. The ancient town is famous in many ways, and is visited at suitable seasons by the celebrities of all places.

There is a golfing club still extant in St. Andrews which was in existence a hundred and thirty-five years ago. It is now housed in the Union Club-house, a commodious and comfortable building, and its members play for its medals. On great days quite a concourse of spectators gather round the players, and an immense degree of interest is taken in the play. St. Andrews is the home of a large number of educated persons, and the seat of two universities. Its society is excellent, and on fitting occasions all the celebrities of the place may be found on its links. The following lines occur in a poetical address :—

" St. Andrews! they say that thy glories are gone,
That thy streets are deserted, thy castles o'erthrown :
If thy glories be gone, they are only, methinks,
As it were by enchantment transferred to thy links ;
Though thy streets be not now, as of yore, full of prelates,
Of abbots and monks, and of hot-headed zealots,

Let none judge us rashly, or blame us as scoffers,
When we say that instead there are links full of golfers,
With more of good heart and good feeding among them ;
We have red coats and bonnets, we've putters and clubs,
The green has its bunkers, its hazards and *rubs*,
At the long hole across we have biscuits and beer,
And the Hebes who sell it give zest to the cheer."

" But what is golf ? " will doubtless be asked by
some who may peruse these remarks on the surroundings and economies of Scottish sport. " You have
told us much about it, but you have not said what
it is."

Well, I am coming to that part of my work, with
which, doubtless, I should properly have begun. I once
heard the same question put to Mr. Robert Chambers
(it was at a little luncheon party in the London Fisheries
Exhibition), and the champion golfer's reply was
characteristic.

" It is," he at once answered, " a medicine or tonic
we take north of Tweed for all sorts of ills ; it cures
many current maladies in the shape of megrims, or
indigestion, and for colds or coughs there is nothing
like golf."

" And how do you play it ? " was further asked.
" Oh, in our kilts, of course," was the reply ; " it is a
national pastime."

Mr. Robert Chambers was exceedingly fond of a
little fun, but, as will be admitted by those who knew
him, he was an excellent authority on all that pertained
to the game, and he has described it in a brief and pithy
way. According to Mr. Chambers, " the object of the
game is, starting from the first hole, to drive the ball
into the next hole with the fewest possible number of

strokes, and so on round the course. The player, or couple of players, whose ball is holed in the fewest strokes has gained that hole, and the match is usually decided by the greatest number of holes gained in one or more rounds; sometimes it is made to depend on the aggregate number of strokes taken to hole one or more rounds."

It may be further stated for the benefit of the ignorant that it is played on links, or downs of considerable area, from hole to hole, with a ball made of gutta-percha, two ounces in weight, and propelled by means of a club. These holes are about four inches across, by three or four inches deep, and are cut in the turf at unequal distances, ranging from perhaps one hundred yards to four hundred yards, and so arranged as to form a circuit of the ground. Some circuits are rather considerable ; if I am not in error, the full round of St. Andrews Links is nearly four miles, there being nine holes to encounter each way. Two persons usually play together, or the match may be a " foursome," a mode of playing now very much in vogue. It is seldom that golfers play in single file, by " themselves alone." When one is seen doing that, it may be taken for granted he has some particular object in view, such as improving his style of play, or he may be practising industriously for a coming match of importance, many good golfers believe in " practice."

Golf is eminently a social game, as Ballantyne's song has it :—

> " We putt, we drive, we laugh, we chat,
> Our strokes and jokes aye clinking,
> We banish all extraneous bat,
> And all extraneous thinking.

" We'll cure you of a summer cold,
    Or of a winter cough, boys,
  We'll make you young even when you're old,
    So come and play at golf, boys.

" Three rounds of Bruntsfield Links will chase
    All murky vapours off, boys,
  And nothing can your sinews brace
    Like the glorious game of golf, boys ! "

The game, it may be said, never changes ; its surroundings may be varied, but the good old round goes on as
before ; what it was fifty years ago, when I first handled
a club, and used to lounge in Gourlay's workshop at
Bruntsfield Links, it is to-day, and has been since the
days of " Old Edinburgh," when merchants were accustomed to shut their places of business for an hour
or two that they might indulge in a game of golf.
" Gone to the links," would be written on the door,
" will be back in two hours."   On the occasion of a fine
old-fashioned High Street shopkeeper not being back
at the specified time, a wag who was passing pencilled
underneath the legend, " Got drunk and can't return."
" An awfu' like thing to say aboot a Baillie," as the
merchant observed when he saw the legend.   Those
were primitive but happy days, business not being
" driven " as it is now.

Recurring for a moment to the " business " of the
game, it is hardly possible to describe it very minutely.
What has already been said under that head cannot
convey any adequate idea of the finesse required when
playing in earnest.   An experienced player, endowed
with the necessary strength, can send his ball any
distance at the first try, but, even if able to propel it
two hundred yards at a stroke, that feat may not gain

him a victory. Much more is required than mere strength. It is not till the ball has arrived near home that the fine play, on which success chiefly depends, commences. Long "driving," to a man possessed of great physical power, is not difficult to achieve; his powers of play are not tested till he reaches the holes; then, being at close quarters, he must bring into use his nerve and dexterity, his fine touch and his "measuring eye," all of which are needed to get the ball home and win the match. It is the man who gets his ball from hole to hole in the least number of strokes that wins the match.

As a general rule golfers look well to the upholstery of the game, which is not very varied. "With what instruments do you play the game?" asked an English gentleman who was recommended to try golf. "Oh, just clubs and cleeks an' a bit baa," was the homely reply of the boots at the hotel who had been asked the question. As a general rule, golfers are very particular about the make and quality of their "clubs and cleeks"; each player usually possesses a complete set of six or eight, or even ten; these instruments of play differ a little from each other; in a few instances considerably, as some positions require a play-off club, others a cleek, others a sand-iron, &c. The clubs are carried by a caddie, who may be, as it may happen, either an old man or a boy. Many of the caddies are adepts at the game, and able occasionally to instruct even good players. Once upon a time, 1836 to 1842, there was a caddie on Bruntsfield Links who was a wonderfully fine player, and who earned a considerable sum of money by showing the game to novices: as a companion said of him after his death, "Jock was a by-ordinar player!"

But " Jock," as he was generally named (that was not, I believe, his real name), was more than a player, he was a shrewd judge of character, and possessed the happy knack of spiriting sixpences and shillings, and, on not a few occasions, half-crowns from the pockets of his patrons. "Weel, sir," he would say to a novice on his *début*, " it's easy wark to prophesy that ye'll soon be a player, ye hit the baa like an auld yin already."

Such words from an authority like Jock were well worth the readily handed-over shilling, and the pint of ale at the far end of the links. To an old visitor, who had been playing for a few months at North Berwick, he was heard to say, " Dear me, sir, ye're no' like the same player ye was when ye went awa' till the sea-side, ye'll bate awbody here except my Lord; I ha'e never before seen such improvement *for the better !*" Jock was a pawky fellow, and there are many left who follow in his path. I have in the course of my conversation with golfers heard many fine stories and anecdotes. Mr. James Ballantyne used to relate one of a man who, having got married at two o'clock, was doing a round on Bruntsfield Links at five, quite oblivious that at that hour he ought to have been dressed for departure on his marriage tour. Many good stories of golfers of the olden time were in circulation throughout the clubs a few years ago, but, as old members died, they gradually became forgotten, and are now seldom related. "Caddies who have risen in the world" might form the heroes of a volume, as many boys who in their day " carried the clubs " ultimately obtained fortune and fame of a kind. Some caddies become " professionals," and earn a good deal of money by playing matches and teaching the game.

This sketch of golf and its surroundings may be drawn to a conclusion by saying that all who play the game are in love with it, and much prefer it to any other, curling excepted; and the two happily never clash; the one is a summer pastime, whilst the other can only be played when John Frost has been proclaimed king. As may have been gathered from the foregoing remarks, "character" is sure to manifest itself on the golfing ground. Temper, good or bad, as the case may be, comes to the front, and persons have been known to worry on the golfing links for days over trifles that at other times and in other places would only excite a smile. Men who take to golf when they have grown old are ill to learn; they don't like to ask a caddie for instructions, and suffer in consequence, the player showing himself to be " a greenhorn, that canna strike his ba'." Beginners should study to get well entered, and not fly into a rage or turn sour when the urchin who is attending them exclaims, " That's no' the way ! " A good beginning is essential, and learners, however venerable, must not be thin-skinned.

Note on Shinty.—Shinty was at one period a wonderfully popular game, especially with boys, but I seldom see them playing it now; it seems, indeed, to have gone altogether out of fashion, cricket and football having no doubt largely taken its place in the neighbourhood of all populous towns. In some parts of the Highlands, however, matches at shinty are still played with great vigour by opposing sides. In playing golf both sides go the same way, each opponent as a rule driving a different ball, and to the player who succeeds in getting through all the holes in the fewest number of strokes is adjudged the victory. In shinty one side fights against another : a ball or small block of wood being laid down at a given place is fought over by the combatants till one or other side succeeds in getting it to the appointed goal or boundary, which may be denoted by a small hole in the ground, or by such a mark as may be agreed upon—it used to be called " hail." The machinery of the game is simple : the ball aforesaid, which may be a barrel-bung or be made of wood, and a long stick with a crooked end, with which to propel the ball to the goal or hail ; these sticks are of a rough-and-ready sort. At most places where the game is played, rules have been devised for its conduct, and these differ in some respects in different localities. Generally the sides are composed of equal numbers, each of the players having but one object in view, that being the driving of the ball to the hail as speedily as possible. As a rule the ball must not be " handled," except on such occasions as it may be caught; it ought to be propelled by the stick only. I have seen a game last for hours, and then be abandoned because of the daylight having passed away. At some matches they fight to time as in football. Play extends over a good length of ground, the line being sometimes as long as three hundred yards. When the writer first visited the Highlands, he was an eye-witness of several most exciting matches at shinty, the Highlanders being enthusiasts at playing the game. At certain seasons of the year bouts of play are arranged between various parties, as, for instance, the married and single men of the same parish or district, or between the bachelors of two neighbouring parishes. The matches on such occasions are fought with a wonderful amount of vigour

and determination ; some of the combatants indeed are
so earnest in pursuit of their pastime, and so determined
their side shall win, that they will be found fighting,
sans all dress but their kilts. Many a sharp tussle
occurs on the occasion of such matches, which have
been known to end sometimes in broken shins and
bloody noses ; when the blood "gets up" among these
Highlanders, they are sure to get angry, and then
begins a quarrel that may not easily be healed. I am
unable to state the origin of the game of shinty, which
may be classed with hockey. The word in use to
denote the game should, some learned persons say, be
"shinny," as that word denotes the penalty exacted
from persons who violate the rules of the game—
namely, a rap on the shin or ankle with the stick.

CHAPTER XXIII.

CURLING.

THE jubilee celebration of the Royal Caledonian Curling
Club was held in Edinburgh in 1888. Appropriately
enough it took the form of a dinner, 350 persons sitting
down to table. As may be supposed, there was much
speech-making and much talk of the " roaring game,"
as curling has been called from the noise made by the
stones as they career over the ice. Dinner always
forms a feature of curling matches. Sometimes the
sides playing make a bet, the one defeated having to
pay for a modest dinner for those taking part. It is a
poor club that cannot on the occasion of the annual
match afford to dine ; the fare, the *pièce de resistance* at
any rate, being of course the usual well-boiled junk of
salt beef with the time-honoured accompaniments of
carrots and greens ; "a noble plat i' faith," as Sir
Walter Scott said—a dish always warmly welcomed, and
promptly done justice to by hungry curlers fresh from
a prolonged bonspiel, even although it has been preceded
by well-filled tureens of hare soup " rich and ruddy,"
made from the formula left as a legacy to her country
by Meg Dods, of the Cleikum Inn, at St. Ronan's :—

> " Let the Englishman boast o' his roast beef and radish,
>   O' his pies and his puddings, and mony things mair,
> Just gi'e me the best o' auld Scotland's ain dishes,
>   The beef and the greens, the true curler's fare."

The dish just named, salt beef and greens, was doubtless selected in early days for the curler's dinner for
the reason that it could be supplied in true " cut-and-
come-again " fashion at moderate price. Many of the
keenest curlers of Scotland were (and are) poor men, not
able to pay a share of a large dinner bill, and so in those
days of curling, when shillings and even sixpences were
scarce, a rule was made by most clubs that the cost
of dinner should not exceed a sum ranging from two to
four shillings, and for the latter sum an excellent dinner
of soup and fish, in addition to the stereotyped salt
beef and greens, with pies and puddings in profusion,
not to speak of a liberal supply of the national beverage
to be converted into toddy, was provided. In some
clubs a stand was made in seasons of depression against
the higher charge for dinner, which bore hard on poor
men, who, despite their poverty, made a point of dining
at the club.

No end of toasts, at any rate a long string of them,
all more or less appropriate to the work of the season
follow, many of the speeches being well worth hearing;
songs well sung, and recitations powerfully given
form a feature of such festive occasions. Some clubs
" keep a poet " to sing in praise of the game, and
his new " lay " is generally looked for with feelings of
pleasure. Sometimes when " the bawbees " become
scarce, one or two of the choice but poorer spirits of the
club will not be present, greatly to their regret. The
following little story under this head is apropos :—A
poor weaver, unknown to his wife, a woman of penurious
disposition, had saved up, throughout the year, a little
sum for his curling dinner, all in sixpences, which coins
were hid away in an untenanted birdcage, but his antici-

pated pleasure was never realised. His wife thought one day that the cage would not be the worse for being well scoured ; taking it from the nail on which it was hung, the hidden sixpences were discovered and at once confiscated, greatly to the horror of the poor weaver, who saw his anticipated feast vanish into thin air. In that weaver's house the grey mare was the better horse.

To begin an essay on curling with an account of the dinner bill of fare is, as Scotch folks say, " putting the cart before the horse ; " properly some historical outline of the game ought first to be given.

At the dinner in question Lord Breadalbane, who occupied the chair, reminded the company that, " though they were assembled for the purpose of celebrating and doing honour to the fiftieth year of the Royal Caledonian Curling Club, it was by no means to be insinuated that the game of curling was only fifty years old. In fact, the exact origin of the game was not known, being lost in the dim ages of the past."

There are writers about this game who maintain that it was introduced into Scotland by Flemish immigrants about the end of the fifteenth century. The pastime was known when Camden published his ' Britannia,' as he tells his readers—or rather one of Camden's translators tells them—that, in the little island of Copinsha, near the Orkneys, " are to be found in great plenty excellent stones for the game called curling." It is not necessary to recapitulate the many discoveries made of old stones, which have been numerous. It may, however, be received as authentic that stones, bearing a pretty ancient date, have at various times been found ; one was recovered from an old curling pond, bearing the date of 1551 ; another, with the date

of 1611, was found near the village of Torphichen;
whilst a third was taken out of a loch at Roslin, having
the year 1613 deeply cut into it. The game was
doubtless in full swing at the dates indicated. Curling
stones belonging to later periods have often been found
in walls of houses, which falling in ruins had been
the means of their being discovered.

When wintry weather sets in and symptoms of a good
black frost begin to make themselves felt, the tongues
of a curling country-side at once begin to wag, and conversation is speedily concentrated, even when going and
coming from the kirk, on what is uppermost in the
minds of all, namely the coming match, or the grand
time of it that they experienced last winter. Atmo-
spheric appearances are keenly scrutinised; keen curlers
know how to " measure the weather," anxiously scanning
the starry firmament at night, wondering, while so
engaged, if the frost will hold. Bold weather prophets
emit their fearless " yes," whilst doubting and timid
spirits shake their wise heads and pronounce their
" not very sure of it, after all." But hope is not to be
extinguished. It is the eve of a great match, and
the country-side expectant; the best curlers of six
different districts are to take part in the contest—men
of many battles who have tried their strength on the
same ice in the fights of successive winters, and, while
sometimes victorious, have been often beaten, but
eagerly come up when called upon, and buckle to their
work as if they were certain that in the end victory
would be the reward of their skill. At such a time " the
stanes " are taken from their summer resting-place and
carefully looked over, their settings cleaned up a bit,
the granite receiving an application of the polishing

cloth which causes it to shine like glass. The struggle for the Derby is not of greater moment to votaries of the Turf than the match of the season is to those around the place where it is to be played.

As regards the formula of the game, it can only at best be described in a somewhat bald manner. The spirit which the players infuse into it, the style of play, and the niceties which are characteristic of individual players—these must be seen, because much of what is enacted beggars description. The diagram of a curling rink on the preceding page is for the benefit of those who have never seen " a match."

The ice is selected with care where a choice can be obtained ; it should be quite smooth and free from cracks. To obtain a stretch that is absolutely level is not always easy ; but, if it prove to be off the straight, any *bias* is speedily discovered, and those playing act accordingly ; such a *contretemps* adds to the zest with which the game is carried on. Every one playing ought to possess a pair of stones ; these are round and rather flat, not more than ten inches in diameter, made in many cases of polished granite ; each stone will weigh with its handle, taking an average, about thirty-six pounds. In order to play sides are made up, usually four against four ; one of each four, a foreman, is known as the " skip." The stones are hurled, or, as may be said, dashed along the ice by means of the handles provided, the stretch of ice being usually some thirty-six yards long, and two or three yards broad. The object of the curler is to place his stone as near to the *tee* as possible. It is in the skill with which this is accomplished that the interest centres. Some attempts do

2 B

not count; unless the stone has been driven a certain length the effort is barren; this position is marked off by what is called the hog score, represented by a line drawn across the ice at a given distance from the tee. Rival sides do everything they know, each, of course, being eager to secure a victory. The game consists of placing so many stones nearest to the tee, around which one or two rings have been placed for easy measurement—tees and rings and hog scores are all *duplicated*, so that players may change ends. (*See diagram.*) One of the four of each side plays alternately, and it is a point of honour with every man to do his best to get his stone to the winning point, or to knock away the stones of his opponents, and to avoid collision with those of his own side. As the game progresses, the players work themselves into a state of great enthusiasm: any one ignorant of what is going on who happened to come suddenly in view of the scene would fancy he had fallen among Bedlamites, such is the noise and racket to which a heartily played bonspiel gives rise. And wonderful are the various phrases and expressions made use of during the continuance of a game. " Yes, wonderful indeed," said a dignitary of the English Church, who had just made his first appearance on a curling rink near Edinburgh. " What does he mean by ' Soop him up ' ? " asked the Archdeacon ; " and what am I to understand by ' Kittle him weel,' and that toast given at luncheon, pray what is. ' gleg ice ' ? " But it would require many pages to provide a glossary of the sayings emitted by curlers in the heat of their work, seeing that the curlers of different localities use peculiar expressions of their

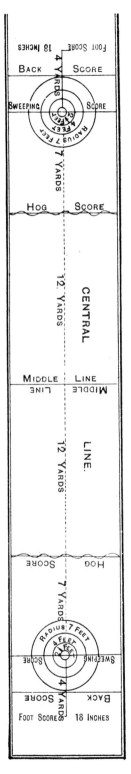

PLAN OF "THE RINK."

own relating to the game, and that each club has toasts
of its own.

> " ' Chip the winner,' ' Pass the guard,'
>   ' Inwick ' a ' draw,'
>   ' Ettle for my broom, lad,'
>   When ye come awa';
>   ' Put the weight o' your hand till't
>   And drive tae the snaw,'
> Hurray for the jolly game o' curling ! "

The stones now used in the game might be called
works of art when compared with those at one time in
use, drawings of which have been preserved. When
given by way of prizes, " stanes " are always made of
fine material (of granite usually), and of elegant shape,
and they are never made so heavy now as they used to
be in " the long ago." The history of curling in its
modern aspects, say as it has been practised during the
present century, is well known, many of the clubs being
in possession of annals which extend over a hundred
years

The history of one of these institutions, that of
Sanquhar, in the county of Dumfries, was published by
its secretary on the occasion of its centenary in 1874.
The following paragraphs give a brief *résumé* of the
work:—

It appears from the records that there has never
been keener curlers in Scotland than those of that good
town—who were so numerous in the year 1774, that
upwards of sixty of them were able to meet upon the
ice. Townspeople who took no part in the game, other
than watching its progress, often acted to the players in
a despotic manner, hooting and hissing them when they
were beaten ; when the players of Sanquhar sustained

2 B 2

defeat, their townsmen told them they had tarnished
the good name of the parish. On one occasion when
the curlers came sadly home from a match in which
they had been worsted, the news having preceded them,
they were received with a storm of groans and hisses,
the state of the game in which they had taken part
being roughly marked in chalk on the door of the town
hall. One man on such an occasion left his rink in
tears, and, so it has been told, returned to his wife
crying like a child, only to be well scolded by his
better half. So anxiously on some occasions was
the news of defeat or victory awaited by the non-
combatants, that a little purse was made up for the
messenger who came first with the decisive news of an
important bonspiel. It is on record that a Sanquhar
woman, whose husband, a keen curler, and, of course,
member of a club, had been one year so long out of
work that he was unable, in his poverty, to attend a
match to be played at a considerable distance, that she
stood in the churchyard on the Sunday previous to the
match, and begged the needed money from all and sundry
so that " her man " might go to the bonspiel !

One day, a large number of the Sanquhar Curlers,
thinking their side had lost the game, retired to a public-
house, to drown their sorrows in a " wee drappie," but,
while lamenting their sad fate, news came that their
side, instead of losing, had won the game, so that the
" wee drappie " indulged in for consolation was speedily
swollen into a " big drappie " in celebration of the
victory.

In addition to parish rinks and district clubs, not a
few Scottish gentlemen have a pond or lake, to which
they invite their curling friends to play a friendly

match, entertaining them to luncheon, and generally
doing their best to make a good day for those present.
At these friendly bonspiels good play is often witnessed,
many taking part having a fine eye for placing their
stones, and being well able to use the besom, in order
to smooth the path to the tee. "It is as good as a
well-played game of billiards!" exclaimed the English
Church dignitary referred to. "I have never seen such
fineness of touch even on the board of green cloth."

Lord Balfour of Burleigh, in his after-dinner speech
at the Jubilee banquet, was quite right when he said
that the curling rink afforded a meeting-place for all
ranks and conditions of men, and that "upon the ice
all ranks and conditions of men were equal with one
exception, and that was that the best curler was the
best man." His lordship, continuing, gave an amusing
illustration of that being so. "One day in a railway
carriage in which a party were travelling the somewhat
tedious journey to Carsbreck (where the great match
between North and South takes place), an individual in
the carriage had bought a morning paper, and while
reading it turned to a friend seated in the other corner of
the compartment and said, 'Eh, Geordie, A' see you are
drawn ag'in a Lord the day." Geordie did not say much
in reply; but, looking round, he quietly remarked,
'Weel, maybe A'll be the Lord afore nicht.'"

Than their winter game no pastime is dearer to the
country-people of Scotland, as is proved in part by the
Scotsman having introduced curling wherever he has
settled down to live. The Scots have been called a
"sour" and "dour" people, but no signs of that being so
ever become apparent on the ice, where all playing seem
bound in the bonds of good fellowship. "There is,"

says a recent writer in praise of the game, " a brother-hood, fraternity amongst curlers ; they seem bound by a sort of invisible tie almost stronger with them than the votaries of any other pastime." Curlers, at any rate while handling their stones, are eminently social ; at a match Jack is as good as his master, and they meet as equals on a common platform. All are interested : the peer who owns the land, the farmers and peasants who till it ; the ministers of the parish, the schoolmaster, and the doctor ; the village blacksmith, the carpenter, the mole catcher ; the " daft man " of the district—everybody in fact, and the wives and children most of all, have their minds occupied with " the match," the morning of which dawns clear and cold as the neighbouring farmers drive into the village with buxom wives and winsome daughters by their side, " the summer of their discontent," if it be permissible to alter a well-known quotation, " made glorious winter by a touch of frost."

About a century and a half ago, the Lord Provost, magistrates, and councillors of the city of Edinburgh, headed by their officers in their state liveries, are reputed to have walked in solemn procession to witness the curling carried on by the citizens in the North Loch (now Princes Street Gardens). Edinburgh curlers since that time have always held their own in the game, many of them being in great repute on the rink. Happily for all concerned in curling, the professional betting man has not yet been permitted to make his appearance on the rink—on the ice there is never heard any shouting of " I'll take odds," or " 6 to 4 on the Paisley man." Some players may risk a tumbler of toddy or " drinks " on the score to be made by their side, and sides may be made up to play for the beef and greens, but, so far as I know the surroundings of the game, the roaring bookmaker has not yet found a place in connection with it, nor is he wanted.

The literature of curling may now be briefly referred to; the pastime has been time and again celebrated in print, in interesting and distinctive works, as well as in a thousand fugitive pieces, scattered throughout the pages of our periodical literature, whilst the encyclopædias give formulas of the game. One or two of the works devoted to the rink may be briefly alluded to.

The earliest attempt to compile a formal history of curling was made in the year 1811; the pamphlet was the work of a Scottish minister, the Rev. John Ramsay, of Gladsmuir; copies of this print have now become very rare, especially those printed on large paper. A work on 'Curling' was printed at Kilmarnock, in 1828, which has gone through several editions, some of them with "additions"; an essay on 'Curling and Artificial Pond-making,' by Dr. John Cairnie, of Largo, was also published in the year 1833. Many local works have from time to time been issued from the provincial press —chiefly reports of dinners and meetings; one of these is of more than ordinary interest, it is the 'History of the Sanquhar Curling Society,' already referred to.

The game has, of course, afforded no end of "matter" to many of the humbler Scottish poets who have written in its praise. An official work on curling is, I am glad to hear, in preparation.

The poetry which has been "made" on curling, if not of a high order of merit, is generally conceived in a hearty and happy spirit. Few of the poems dedicated to the rink are of a sentimental cast, but the verses which follow give a fair idea of the never-failing self-esteem which is a pronounced feature in the character of all curlers, and especially of their poets :—

> " Old England may her cricket boast,
>   Her wickets, bats, and a' that,
> And proudly her eleven toast
>   Wi' right good will, and a' that;
>   For a' that, and a' that,
>   The channel stone on icy plain
>   Is king o' games for a' that.

> " Green Erin's sons at wake and fair,
>   Wi' roar and yell, and a' that,
> May toss shillelahs in the air
>   And crack their crowns, and a' that;
>   For a' that, and a' that,
>   And better far than a' that,
>   Our roaring game aye keeps the flame
>   O' friendship bright, for a' that."

Like the game itself, the poems written in its honour contain a good deal of what may be called the roaring element in them. As a matter of fact, many of them are not a little Bacchanalian, but in consequence are all the better suited for the after-dinner hours of the clubs. A few quotations will serve to show the kind of stuff of which curling songs and poems are composed. Many of them have been written to suit the music of popular tunes, and to celebrate the prowess of well-known local knights of the rink.

One of these local songs begins as follows :—

> " Here's a health to the glorious name,
>   In this company needless to name,
>   The game of all others
>   That must make men brothers,
>   Three good cheers for the glorious game."

The following lines are from a poem, spoken at a provincial club, in honour of a victory :—

> " A hundred hats and besoms wave, 'mid that triumphant yell,
> Old bald heads throw their hat in air, and the loud chorus swell ;
> The nervous fair at distance start, the schoolboy in amaze
> Rests on his skates, and marvels much at father's loud hurras."

A selection of the poetic effusions which appear every year in the 'Annual' would make an interesting volume. Here is a verse or two from the latest of these year books :—

> " They tell o' games in ither lands
>   Where tyrants haud their sway ;
> Gi'e me the manly game in which
>   Baith peer and peasant play,
> For I've nae skill o' games, my lads,
>   That arena' for the free.
>   Auld Scotland's game and Scotland's ain,
>   The channel stane for me," &c.

The following is from another of the curling songs, of which so many are extant—

> " When dolefu' dumps an' carkin' care
> Torment a man an' fash him sair,
> At curlin' let him tak' a share
>   And channel stanes set birlin' O !
> He'll find, I'm sure, in half a crack
> His dumps a' flee, an' spunk come back,
> He'll face the de'il an' a' his pack
>   After a game at curlin' O."

One more sample and I am done with the poetry of curling—

> " Enthroned in snowy splendour,
> Lo ! the winter reigns around,
> And dark blue rolling waters
> Now in icy chains are bound.

> To the rink, then, let's away
> While the sun smiles faint on high,
> For the western wind may blow, boys,
> And old Winter soon must die.

> " Come, swell the glorious scene, boys,
> On the snowy plains so cold—
> Come, swell the roaring game, boys,
> With its social joys untold.
>   To the rink, then, let's away," &c.

By way of concluding these desultory remarks on curling, it may be stated that the game is regulated by the Royal Caledonian Club, which is to the rink what the Jockey Club is to horse-racing. That society was instituted in 1838, the want of such a governing body having long been felt. When the Royal Club was first proposed a committee was appointed for the purpose of considering the mysteries and ceremonies, as also the rules and laws of the curling clubs of Scotland, and to prepare a mode of initiation, and a set of rules and regulations to be observed by the Grand Caledonian Curling Club, and the different curling clubs associated therewith. Under the auspices of the national institution, the laws of curling were collated and revised, and rules laid down for the conduct of the pastime. That the society was required is shown by the fact that at the present time nearly six hundred clubs and about 24,000 curlers obey its laws, and carry on the sport of the rink according to the rules laid down for their guidance. Under the auspices of the Royal Club there have been several grand matches between the societies of the north and south of Scotland, which have all excited keen interest, and attracted large crowds of spectators.

CHAPTER XXIV.

PATRONS AND PARASITES OF SPORT.

HARKING back for fifty years, the grand tournament given at his castle in Ayrshire by *the* Earl of Eglinton, of " Flying Dutchman " celebrity, whose name is associated with the Derby and other sporting events of his day and generation, stands out as the most prominent social function of the year '39. The tournament would have undoubtedly proved a very brilliant spectacle but for the downpour of rain which spoiled the show, at any rate on the first day, when the gallant knights looked sad, and the brilliance of their armour was dimmed by the pitiless fall of water, and her majesty the queen of beauty was compelled to come to the lists not on her cream-coloured palfrey, but, alas ! in a close covered carriage in which no one could see her. I had something to do in connection with the tournament, my particular mission being to bring to Edinburgh an article from the pen of Sir Thomas Dick Lauder, which he wrote on the scene of the chivalric show for one of the popular magazines of the period. I remember having had pointed out to me in Glasgow, while standing on the stairs leading to the " Buck's Head " Hotel, two of the great actors in the Eglinton spectacle ; one of the pair, as an old waiter

said, was the "wicked marquis" (of Waterford), the
other was Prince Louis Napoleon. Those who would
read of the Eglinton tournament as it should have been
can turn to the pages of Lord Beaconsfield's brilliant
novel of 'Endymion,' and read his description of what
took place at Montford Castle.

As the noble baronet, Sir Thomas Dick Lauder, said
of the Eglinton spectacle, "Here on these two days
were found assembled the chivalry of the kingdom,
and all our finest women." The chief patrons of Scotland's manly sports were present at the tournament, as
many of them were afterwards at the Caledonian Hunt
meeting at Cupar, which proved a gay and successful
affair. The race meeting held at Stirling always drew
crowds of sporting men. Mr. Ramsay of Barnton, who,
if I am not mistaken, had at the time an estate in the
county, always came to the front on the Stirling course.
In that year his mare *Sunbeam* landed the Gold Cup,
whilst the genial laird of Ladykirk won the Sauchie
Stakes with *Berwickshire*. Among those present were
Mr. Merry, the Hon. Mr. Sandilands, Wauchope of
Edmonston, Falconer of Carlowrie, and Mr. Mure
Younger, of Caldwell, as also Mr. Binning Munro.
Lord Kelburne, afterwards better known as the Earl of
Glasgow, was in evidence at the Paisley meeting, and
many still living remember the sporting eccentricities
of this generous-hearted nobleman and his dare-devil
friends. In the days to which I am alluding, the
"Western Meeting" which took place at Ayr was undoubtedly the best of all the Scottish race gatherings;
in 1839 the Gold Cup was won by Mr. Ramsay by the
aid of *Lanercost*, amid the cheers of the "noble throng"
present on the occasion, "all our sporting patrons being

on the ground," as was stated by the gentlemen of the
press who then reported Scottish meetings.

The opportunity has been taken throughout the foregoing pages to note in passing brief particulars of a few
of the characters—and they have been numerous—
connected with Scottish out-door sports in the days
when the fourth William was our king, and since. The
work exacted from many of the persons engaged was of
the most humble kind, and some others who hung about
on occasions of sporting functions might be described as
" rogues and vagabonds," which in reality they were.

I shall venture to name a few of my old acquaint-
ances who were " always at it," who hunted the fox,
coursed the hare, fished for trout, or trod the moors in
search of grouse, and most of whom, like Tam Samson,
one of the heroes of Robert Burns, have crossed the
bourne—

> " Now safe the stately salmon sail,
>   And trouts be-dropped wi' crimson hail,
>   And eels weel kenned for souple tail,
>   And geds for greed—
>   Since dark in death's fish creel we wail
>   Tam Samson dead ! "

It would not be difficult to arrange a long procession
of " characters " connected with Scottish sport, leading
off with " Money Bob," as his familiars were wont to
call him, who had his finger during his lifetime in many
a pie. Bob furnished the sinews of war in his day
for more, perhaps, than a hundred sporting events ; he
was in the latter years of his life a money-lender, but
never a Shylock. He began, I am told, as a public
coachman ; from the box he gravitated to the bar of the
Gun Tavern, then he fitted up a house in Shakespeare

Square (a place that is now covered by the General Post Office of Edinburgh), and in which men who *would* gamble in a naked way could shake "the bones" all night long if it pleased them to do so, and many of the young bloods of the modern Athens elected to "keep it up." Afterwards the proprietor of a well-known suite of billiard-rooms, Bob became a bill discounter, but, so far as I could learn, his rates of discount for doing a "bit of stiff," as he called it, were not exorbitant, and so long as the interest was paid he never evinced much desire to have the bill taken up. Many a fine hunter was bought by means of a bill discounted by Bob, and for a few sporting matches he found the money. When after the Edinburgh and Ayr meetings any fellow was short of a hundred or two, Money Bob was seldom appealed to in vain, if the man was at all what he should be or had a friend whose name was good enough for the amount. Bob had a couple of galloping horses of his own that occasionally, when pulled out at the local meetings, won a race. His get-up was a picture; his linen was always irreproachable, his hat glossy in the extreme, and his boots polished to perfection. It used to be said that he dressed himself carefully three times every day. On several occasions Bob played the part of judge at Musselburgh on the occasion of the Edinburgh meeting, and there were owners of horses who raced there who asserted that the judge was on occasion colour-blind. When so accused, he used to smile meaningly, and say in his quiet way, "Ay, ay, we a' do it; at least we get the blame of doing it, whether we do it or not." As an indication of the esteem in which he was held, it may be mentioned that in one week, shortly before his death, Bob received no less than twenty-nine presents of game ! He deserved all he got ; he was really a good fellow.

Many of the sportsmen of Midlothian, and the officers of the regiments in garrison frequented the Edinburgh billiard rooms, Joe Bootland, Moon, and also Taylor being well patronised. Whilst playing an occasional game at pool, I was much struck by one of the *habitués* of Taylor's. I allude to a gentleman known as "the Squire," who according to his own confession was down "on his luck ;" "but, look you," he used to say, "I still have as much left as will insure me bread and cheese for life." What the Squire's "bread and cheese" meant will be understood, when I state that I more than once partook of it, having spent an occasional Saturday and Sunday with him at his house in Portobello. For breakfast we had sheep's kidneys and mutton cutlets beautifully done by his housekeeper—an excellent cook ; then, after a walk to Fisher Row, three miles distant, where the Squire would purchase a cod fish or small turbot, we came back to a luncheon of oat cakes and Stilton cheese washed down with a few glasses of prime Edinburgh ale, then an excellent liquor, "Scottish Burgundy" it was christened by the dethroned French king who once lived in the palace of Holyrood. Luncheon finished, a run up to Edinburgh was the rule, and after a game or two of billiards at one or other of the rooms, and a call at the Rainbow or the Café Royal, we would stroll to Portobello going by way of the King's Park to Jock's Lodge, where we halted, then after a glass of Madeira with two or three of the officers, a leisurely stroll of half-an-hour landed us at dinner. *The menu :* Ox-tail soup, delicious cuts of broiled codfish with oysters stewed in beef gravy. *Note*—Oysters were in those days plentiful and cheap. A very tasty curry would come next in order, followed by some of Mrs. Tait's excellent pancakes, and then the Squire would say, " Now, my good fellow, you have had your dinner."

A few glasses of port to our cheese, and then the host would relate some of his shooting experiences, which had been extensive. I only know of one questionable act of the Squire's. One season he allowed himself to be seduced by a certain " Mr. Peters " to spend a month on his moor and have as much shooting as ever he could stand up to. The Squire was a born sportsman and could not resist an invitation to a moor or to a meet of the hounds, provided he was promised a good mount. The " Mr. Peters " alluded to was a mystery, but he always turned up a fortnight or so before grouse shooting was timed to begin, seeking for some one to spend a month with him at his little place. " Mr. Peters " was an adept in selecting a shooting, and, on the occasion of the Squire's visit, he had got one long coveted, a full mile stretch of which ran like a wedge between two of the best moors in the North. " Mr. Peters " did not mention that fact to his guest, and never hinted that the sheaves of corn thrown down at several places had been knowingly placed there to attract birds from his neighbours' moors. Unfortunately there arose a scandal about the matter, and the poor Squire, although perfectly blameless, was thought to have been " art and part," as we say in Scotland, in the sharp practice of " Mr. Peters," who had contracted for the sale of his birds with a poaching game-dealer, and contrived to make his shooting pay handsomely. No one knew who this man was; he was a good player at pool, and always stood on his dignity ; after one night rebuking a fellow-

player for calling him " Peters," the prefix of " Mr."
was afterwards always ostentatiously added whenever
it became necessary to address him. What became of
this person I could never learn, he disappeared from
the billiard rooms as quietly as he came to frequent
them.

One of the Squire's reputed feats may be here related.
For a wager of twenty pounds he engaged to hit with a
pistol bullet twenty out of twenty-five George the Third
penny-pieces placed in a row, each one distant three
inches from the other, and all placed at the same height !
The peculiarity of the feat was that the Squire under-
took to fire blindfold at the coins, the bandage being
removed by agreement three times in the course of the
performance. I was not an eye-witness of this feat of
the Squire's, but, as it was talked about, have no
doubt it took place. On one occasion twenty-one of the
pennies are said to have been hit, almost in the centre.
Another remarkable feat of the Squire's, which was
greatly talked about at the time, was his having twice
in one night made a ten stroke at billiards !

It is not to be expected that I shall say a word here
regarding the " young bloods " of the period I am writing
about ; some of whom are now very grave gentlemen
indeed ; I do not pun when I say so, as I am speaking
of those who are still alive. Many of the then happy
young fellows are, however, dead. The sons of a great
man of the North, who had a big estate and plenty of
sport, all died in exile and in poverty. The Charles
Edward Stewart who died lately in London, and his
brother John Sobieski, who, in the days I refer to, used
to pose in Edinburgh as descendants of the Pretender,
were fond of having a quiet bout at billiards, and once

or twice I had the pleasure of marking for them.
Charles Edward, if I am not mistaken, was, when he
died, something in the wine trade in the great metropolis. They published, I remember, with Tait of
Edinburgh, a work on Scottish tartans, which they
entitled the 'Vestiarium Scoticum,' and they enjoyed,
if I am not in error, through the kindness of Lord
Lovat, plenty of sport at a charming place in the
county of Inverness, called Eilean Aigas.

Descending now from princes to peasants, I wonder
how many in Edinburgh will recollect "Cuddy Wully";
very few, I fancy, as he was growing old when I knew
him. The first time I was present at a coursing match
on the north end of Corstorphine Hill, I saw a hunch-
back composedly looking on from the back from, I am
sure, the largest ass that was ever seen. "Who is
that?" I said to the slipper. "Oh, that is Cuddy
Wully," he replied; "have you never seen him before?"
I never had, but afterwards beheld him frequently, and
often had a chat with him. He had a mania to be an
onlooker at all kinds of sport, no matter the distance he
required to travel to see it. The last time I saw him
was at a fishing match on the river Almond; there were
half-a-dozen competitors along with a few friends to see
the sport. I was astonished as we approached an old
bridge to see perched upon it "Cuddy Wully" on his
patient ass; the match having been kept as private as
possible, I never knew how he learned it was to take
place. It was a somewhat curious circumstance that,
as "Cuddy Wully" was being carried to his grave on
spokes by eight bearers in the old homely Scottish fashion,
a party of huntsmen and lookers-on at sport came up
to the funeral procession, and on learning whose funeral

it was all of them uncovered and allowed the mourners to pass on to a lonely kirkyard " close by the sands of the sea." A still more curious fact comes to my memory as I recall the burial of Cuddy Wully—it is that the old man who dug his grave, the sexton of the parish, had officiated during the season as earth-stopper to the hunt, taking for a time the place of his son, who was confined to his bed for several months from the effects of a kick given by one of the hunters at a meet near Queensferry.

I shall now take leave to say a few words about a Midlothian family of my acquaintance, the Omits, all of whom, as may be said, were parasites of the trees of sport. Old John, the mole-catcher, was well employed far and near, and was a dexterous hand at his business ; he occasionally officiated as an earth-stopper, and was by " profession " a hedger and ditcher. Young Bob was employed as a trainer of greyhounds, and as occasional slipper at coursing meetings. Tam was learning to be a gardener at Lauriston Castle, when I first knew the family. Old " Mother Omit " and Bell, the eldest daughter, were frequently employed by the neighbouring foresters in " barking " ; all the family worked, and attended church regularly. It was noticed, too, that they had good clothing and looked well fed. In course of time it leaked out that the Omits did a *little* in the poaching way, but the little was ultimately found to be a great deal. Every member of the family poached, " Mother " being the leading spirit in the business—an adept in robbing the nests of the pheasants, but only taking an egg at a time. Old Bob got as many hares as he could carry, and an uncle, who was head carter to the goods delivery contractor of a steamboat company trading from Leith to London and other ports, had great facilities for disposing of the surreptitiously obtained birds and beasts of sport, and so for a time the Omits flourished exceedingly.

I need not weary my readers by stating how they were discovered, or by reciting the story of their flight to America, where I was told they had succeeded in settling themselves in a prosperous manner. These reminiscences might be greatly prolonged, as all Scottish sports have in times past had their hangers-on, just as they have to-day. Well-known faces were to be seen at the hunts, men who would rather earn a sixpence by holding a horse or stopping an earth than a shilling at some more legitimate employment. I have brief chronicles of many such stored away in old note-books, but shall not venture to bring them before the curtain at present.

LONDON : PRINTED BY WM. CLOWES AND SONS, LIMITED,
STAMFORD STREET AND CHARING CROSS.

Printed in the United Kingdom
by Lightning Source UK Ltd.
135925UK00001B/97/A